The Research Game in Academic Life

Lisa Lucas

The Society for Research in Higher Education
& Open University Press

Open University Press
McGraw-Hill Education
McGraw-Hill House
Shoppenhangers Road
Maidenhead
Berkshire
England
SL6 2QL

email: enquiries@openup.co.uk
world wide web: www.openup.co.uk

and Two Penn Plaza, New York, NY 10121–2289, USA

First published 2006

A catalogue record of this book is available from the British Library

ISBN – 10: 0 335 21191 7 (pb) 0 335 21192 5 (hb)
ISBN – 13: 978 0 335 21191 3 (pb) 978 0 335 21192 0 (hb)

Library of Congress Cataloging-in-Publication Data
CIP data applied for

Typeset by YHT Ltd, London
Printed in Poland by OZ Graf. S.A.
www.polskabook.pl

The Research Game in
Academic Life

SRHE and Open University Press Imprint

Current titles include:

Catherine Bargh *et al.*: *University Leadership*
Ronald Barnett: *Beyond all Reason*
Ronald Barnett & Kelly Coate: *Engaging the Curriculum in Higher Education*
Ronald Barnett: *Reshaping the University*
Tony Becher and Paul R. Trowler: *Academic Tribes and Territories (2nd edn)*
John Biggs: *Teaching for Quality Learning at University (2nd edn)*
Richard Blackwell & Paul Blackmore (eds): *Towards Strategic Staff Development in Higher Education*
David Boud and Nicky Solomon (eds): *Work-based Learning*
Tom Bourner *et al.* (eds): *New Directions in Professional Higher Education*
John Brennan & Tarla Shah: *Managing Quality Higher Education*
Anne Brockbank and Ian McGill: *Facilitating Reflective Learning in Higher Education*
Ann Brooks and Alison Mackinnon (eds): *Gender and the Restructured University*
Burton R.Clark: *Sustaining Change in Universities*
James Cornford & Neil Pollock: *Putting the University Online*
John Cowan: *On Becoming an Innovative University Teacher 2/e*
Vaneeta D'Andrea & David Gosling: *Improving Teaching and Learning in Higher Education*
Sara Delamont, Paul Atkinson and Odette Parry: *Supervising the Doctorate 2/e*
Sara Delamont & Paul Atkinson: *Successful Research Careers*
Gerard Delanty: *Challenging Knowledge*
Chris Duke: *Managing the Learning University*
Heather Eggins (ed): *Globalization and Reform in Higher Education*
Heather Eggins & Ranald Macdonald (eds): *The Scholarship of Academic Development*
Howard Green and Stuart Powell: *Doctoral Study in Contemporary Higher Education*
Merle Jacob and Tomas Hellström (eds): *The Future of Knowledge Production in the Academy*
Peter Knight: *Being a Teacher in Higher Education*
Peter Knight and Paul Trowler: *Departmental Leadership in Higher Education*
Peter Knight and Mantz Yorke: *Assessment, Learning and Employability*
Ray Land: *Educational Development*
Dina Lewis and Barbara Allan: *Virtual Learning Communities*
David McConnell: *E-Learning Groups and Communities*
Ian McNay (ed.): *Beyond Mass Higher Education*
Louise Morley: *Quality and Power in Higher Education*
Lynne Pearce: *How to Examine a Thesis*
Moira Peelo and Terry Wareham (eds): *Failing Students in Higher Education*
Craig Prichard: *Making Managers in Universities and Colleges*
Stephen Rowland: *The Enquiring University Teacher*
Maggi Savin-Baden: *Problem-based Learning in Higher Education*
Maggi Savin-Baden: *Facilitating Problem-based Learning*
Maggi Savin-Baden & Claire Howell Major: *Foundations of Problem-based Learning*
Maggi Savin-Baden and Kay Wilkie: *Challenging Research in Problem-based Learning*
David Scott *et al.*: *Professional Doctorates*
Michael L Shattock: *Managing Successful Universities*
Maria Slowey and David Watson: *Higher Education and the Lifecourse*
Colin Symes and John McIntyre (eds): *Working Knowledge*
Richard Taylor, Jean Barr and Tom Steele: *For a Radical Higher Education*
Malcolm Tight: *Researching Higher Education*
Penny Tinkler and Carolyn Jackson: *The Doctoral Examination Process*
Melanie Walker: *Higher Education Pedagogies*
Melanie Walker (ed.): *Reconstructing Professionalism in University Teaching*
Melanie Walker and Jon Nixon (eds): *Reclaiming Universities from a Runaway World*
Diana Woodward and Karen Ross: *Managing Equal Opportunities in Higher Education*
Mantz Yorke and Bernard Longden: *Retention and Student Success in Higher Education*

Contents

List of tables and figures   ix

Preface and acknowledgements   xi

1   Introduction   1
All universities are equal but some are more equal than others   3
Critical social science, reflexivity and higher education   4
Institutional case studies and methodology   4
Organization of the book   6

**2   Globalization, International Competition and the International
      Research Game**   7
Globalization and international competitiveness of universities
     and university research   7
Academic capitalism, entrepreneurialism and marketization:
     changing university values and practice?   13
Institutional organization and collegial practices with academia:
     a nostalgic ideal?   17
Managerial practice and managerial power within universities   20
Universities as political organizations: power and decision making   22
The 'core values' or ideals of (Western) universities: the legacy
     of Humboldt, Newman and Kerr   25

**3   Research Funding and Evaluation Policies: setting the agenda
      of the national research game**   29
The national 'game' of research rankings: universities and
     measures of 'research intensity'   29
Funding and evaluating research: the development of the
     UK RAE   31
Problems with the RAE process: costs, bias and validity?   35

The Research Assessment Exercise: distortions, deceptions and
   degradations?   38
Funding and evaluating research: a comparative perspective   46

4   Researching the Academy: the game of reflexivity   53
An introduction to Bourdieu's sociology: a relational analysis   54
Bourdieu's conceptual 'thinking tools': field, symbolic capital
   and habitus   56
What can Bourdieu's thinking tools bring to the study of higher
   education?   59
The need for a reflexive study of universities and academic life   65
Limitations and possibilities for applying Bourdieu's thinking
   tools   68

**5   Institutional Management of Research: the game of reputation
and resources**   73
Institutional management of research at Golden County
   University   76
Institutional management of research at Royal County University   79
Management of research activities in the biology departments   84
Management of research activities in the sociology departments   87
Management of research activities in the English departments   90
Collegial or corporate: managing research within universities   93

**6   University Departments: the game of research struggles,
strategies and stakes**   95
Research strategies within the biology departments   97
Struggles and stakes in capital accumulation in biology   102
Research strategies within the sociology departments   109
Struggles and stakes in capital accumulation in sociology   114
Research strategies within the English departments   121
Struggles and stakes in capital accumulation in English   126
Research struggles, strategies and stakes: comparing across
   different disciplines   130

**7   Academic Struggles for Recognition: the game of publications
and priorities**   133
Structural positioning and the construction of an academic
   'habitus': changing dispositions and practices   134
A biological habitus: changing dispositions and practices   135
Biology staff classified as research active   136
Biology staff classified as non-research active   143
A sociological habitus: changing dispositions and practices   148
Sociology staff classified as research active   149
Sociology staff classified as non-research active   153
An English habitus: changing dispositions and practices   157

English staff classified as research active   159
English staff classified as non-research active   160
Struggles over researcher identity with academic life:
   academic habitus and principles of differentiation   163

8   The Future of the Academic Research Game   165
Funding and evaluating university research: global convergence? 165
Differentiation of universities: divisions between research and
   teaching   168
A competitive or collaborative future for university research 170

Bibliography   172

Index   179

List of tables and figures

Table 2.1   Ranking of nations based on top 1% of highly cited publications, 1997–2001

Table 2.2   Ranking of G8 nations within different subjects, on number of journals and impact factor of publications

Figure 2.1   Research income to English higher education institutions (HEIs) in 2003–4 (£ millions)

Table 2.3   Components of the ideal model of collegiality

Table 2.4   Summary of characteristics of possible university models (McNay 1995)

Table 3.1   A comparison of core teaching and QR research funding awarded to universities in 2005–6

Table 3.2   The RAE rating scale and criteria for evaluation

Table 3.3   Information provided by the RAE on each unit of assessment submitted

Table 5.1   Details of interviews with senior management and research committee meetings attended at each university

Table 5.2   Overall change in institutional RAE grades from 1996 to 2001 at Golden County University

Table 5.3   Overall change in institutional RAE grades from 1996 to 2001 at Royal County University

Table 6.1   Numbers of biology departments with 1–5* grades in RAE 1992, 1996 and 2001

Table 6.2   Selection of research strategies and plans in biology at Golden County University

Table 6.3   Selection of research strategies and plans in biology at Royal County University

Table 6.4   RAE submission 2001 for biology UOA, by type of publication

Table 6.5   Total research funds for all biology departments submitted in the 2001 RAE, separated by grades

Table 6.6   Numbers of sociology departments with 1–5* grades in RAE 1992, 1996 and 2001

Table 6.7   Selection of research strategies and plans in sociology at Golden County University

Table 6.8   Selection of research strategies and Plans in Sociology at Royal County University

Table 6.9   RAE submission 2001 for sociology UOA, by type of publication

Table 6.10   Total research funds for all sociology departments submitted in the 2001 RAE, separated by grades

Table 6.11   English departments with 1–5* grades in RAE 1992, 1996 and 2001

Table 6.12   Selection of research strategies and plans in English at Golden County University

Table 6.13   Selection of research strategies and Plans in English at Royal County University

Table 6.14   RAE submission 2001 for English UOA, by type of publication

Table 6.15   Total research funds for all English departments submitted in the 2001 RAE, separated by grades

Table 7.1   Biology departments interviewees

Table 7.2   Sociology departments interviewees

Table 7.3   English departments interviewees

Preface

I would firstly like to thank Professor Bob Burgess who was a great support and mentor throughout much of this research. A note of thanks is also given to Professor Frank Webster, who gave me a lot of help and encouragement in the early stages of the study, and also to Professor Jim Beckford who gave much support towards the end of the study. Thanks are also due to my colleagues at UCL, Professor Stephen Rowland, who was the person to first suggest I write this book and to Professor Lewis Elton for always encouraging me to keep writing and thinking. I would like also to give a huge thank you to Professor Rosemary Deem and Professor Ian McNay who patiently spent time reading the draft manuscript and giving me extremely helpful and insightful feedback. I would also like to give a big heartfelt thanks to all my colleagues in the Department for Education and Professional Development at University College London (many of whom are now in other institutions) and the Graduate School of Education at Bristol, and in particular Gerardo Moenne, whose ingenuity and skill helped to produce the tables and charts throughout the book. You all make academic life fun and exciting and provided much motivation for writing this book. Finally, I would like to thank all the biologists, sociologists and 'English people' who made this book possible. One head of department asked me why he should allow me to take up the precious time of academics in his department. I had no real answer for him despite the possibility of invoking many arguments around the necessity of gaining a greater understanding of the academic world. There is no reason why anyone should give up their time, or indeed, 'give up themselves' as subjects to any research project. But I am grateful to the inspirational academics who did give up their time and I hope that this book reflects in part the worth of that generosity.

This research was supported by the ESRC, award number R0042962495 which allowed the initial study to be conducted, a Society for Research in Higher Education (SRHE) Newer Researcher Award in 2003, which allowed some data collection in Hong Kong and the Netherlands and also a grant from the Graduate School of Education at Bristol University, which allowed for research to be conducted in Australia.

1

Introduction

There will be no laughter, except the laugh of triumph over a defeated enemy. There will be no art, no literature, no science. When we are omnipotent we shall have no more need of science. There will be no distinction between beauty and ugliness. There will be no curiosity, no enjoyment of the process of life. All competing pleasures will be destroyed. But always – do not forget this, Winston – always there will be the intoxication of power, constantly increasing and constantly growing subtler. Always, at every moment, there will be the thrill of victory...

(George Orwell, *Nineteen Eighty-Four*)

It seemed appropriate to begin a book that deals ostensibly with the issue of research funding and evaluation within UK universities, the Research Assessment Exercise (RAE), with an inflammatory statement and the one from George Orwell's *Nineteen Eighty-Four* captures something of the derision held by some people of this now pernicious feature of academic life. I held back from including the devastating line to come with the boot smashing into the human face forever, not wanting to open a book on universities with the sentiment that the future of academic life is its potential devastation. However, there are many who perceive the RAE to have had a particularly damaging influence on the values and ideals of academic life and to be at least partly responsible for a 'changing structure of feeling' (Sidaway 1997) that has eroded the strong community lives of universities. This book is not positioned to recall the return of some never-existing 'golden age' of academia but it is intended to raise critical questions about the direction that UK higher education is currently taking.

There is certainly more to the story of the intense upheaval in the UK academy over the last 20 years than the RAE but this policy above all has tended to dominate discussions in the academic press and to permeate the consciousness of every academic working in a UK university. The interest in the research which underpins this book began when I was involved in a research project in the early 1990s investigating the impacts of a move to a mass system of higher education, with large increases in student numbers and the resultant large class sizes (Gibbs et al. 1996). However, when asking academics about this issue the interview invariably turned to the RAE; no matter where the interview began, it often ended up with them talking about the RAE and in the main voicing concerns and reservation about this policy. I was intrigued by how this was a dominating issue for almost everyone that I interviewed and the fascination and obsession that it seemed to invoke.

The introduction of new funding and evaluation regimes for university research is not unique to the United Kingdom but in fact is commonplace across many countries, although the precise form that this takes is substantially different in each case depending on the degree of direct involvement by the government in funding university research, the extent to which funding is linked to evaluation and the difference of belief in either quantitative or qualitative measurements of research quality. The will by national governments to manage, monitor and to some degree influence the direction of university research, however, is common to all.

In their book *The Enterprise University*, Marginson and Considine (2000), writing within an Australian context, talk about 'research power' and they argue that the 'meaning' of research has changed. Status in research terms has come to mean financial power and the ability to attract vast amounts of research funding. The content of the research has been somewhat sidelined in the desire for demonstrations of greater research prowess. As the Orwell quotation suggests, the intoxication of power and the thrill of victory have become perhaps the greatest prizes. Can this be true for modern academic life in the United Kingdom or at least for the managers who run the institutions? Has research success within universities been turned into a competitive sport (Tight 2000)? There is no shortage of sporting metaphors when the RAE is discussed but what are the consequences for the winners and more importantly the losers in this game?

Using the concepts of 'research capital' and 'academic capital' (Bourdieu 1988), this book analyses the changing rules of the 'research game' and attempts by universities, departments and individual academics to maximize their 'research capital' and thus reap the rewards of status and positioning afforded by success in the 'game'. The implication of this work, however, is not simply that greater strategying and game playing has been encouraged for RAE purposes, but that it has served to infiltrate the cultures and values of academic life such that these ends and means become the raison d'être, or the 'symbolic capital' in Bourdieu's terms, which govern the meaning and value of research work and activities within universities more generally.

All universities are equal but some are more equal than others

In the United Kingdom as elsewhere there are clear hierarchies of universities. This is not new but has been a perennial feature of academic life. What is more clear is the extent to which success, particularly as measured in the RAE, has come to influence the status and hierarchical positioning of UK universities. Research studies from many different countries have demonstrated the significance of research success in determining the status of a university. The concern of this book is to explore this phenomenon by looking in more detail at the, perhaps, unintended consequences (Elton 2000) that funding and evaluation policies have had on institutions, university departments and the individual academics who work within them. This is not to suggest that the RAE or indeed research funding and evaluation policies established in any higher education system are influential in some simple cause and effect relationship. As discussed in Chapter 2, the impacts of globalization, marketization and managerialism are highly significant on the current development of higher education. Indeed, the concern here is to explore where possible the means by which neo-liberal management and monitoring policies within public sector organizations interact with these other developments (Clarke and Newman 1997). What is important is the way that these processes impact on systems of higher education and the organization, management and culture of universities on the ground rather than at the purely abstract or theoretical level. The intention of this book, therefore, is to provide an in-depth study of university life that serves to illustrate the impact of research evaluation and funding policies, as they are mediated through global, national and institutional structures and processes. In particular this book aims to provide

- a theoretical exploration of the processes impacting on universities in the twenty-first century, including globalization, marketization and managerialism;
- a brief international comparison of research funding and evaluation policies across a number of countries including Australia, the Netherlands and Hong Kong;
- an in-depth study of the impact of UK funding and evaluation policies on university departmental research work, using the theoretical framework of Bourdieu;
- an insider view of university research management and organization during a period of rapid change;
- an analysis of the importance of research within university life for determining the success and status of institutions and the careers of academics.

Critical social science, reflexivity and higher education

It can be argued, that there is a need for greater sociological understanding and investigation of higher education, although it is already becoming a growing research terrain. It would seem from the choice of opening quotation that this book may be positioned as taking a critical stance in relation to the current developments in higher education. Following Bourdieu, I would argue that there is a need to be more reflexive about the social processes within higher education and to better understand the positioning of universities and their role in reproducing as well as critiquing the social order (Bourdieu 1988).

This reflexivity is also important within the research process and most significantly in the role of the researcher. It is important to be clear about this at the outset and to maintain a critical vigilance of how assumptions, values and ideals may influence the research process. My own academic positioning can be gleaned from my experiences of working and studying in a number of pre-1992 and post-1992 universities in the United Kingdom and of researching UK higher education over the last ten years. Also, my background in sociology and the positioning of my approach as primarily within a 'perspectively enriched' critical theory (more on this in Chapter 4) has influenced the conduct of this study. This positioning has also been influenced by my move from a working-class background into higher education and of wanting to ensure that the privileges and wealth of experience that have been awarded to me, continue to be available for all, irrespective of their social background. This means not just allowing more students from all social class backgrounds into higher education but of ensuring that they are not entering a socially differentiated system, where privileges of experience and knowledge are differentially available at elite and non-elite institutions.

Institutional case studies and methodology

The research evidence presented in this book comes from a variety of sources and uses an eclectic methodology. The primary data comes from an initial study of two universities in the UK and three departments within each; biology, sociology and English during the academic years 1997–1999, just after the 1996 RAE and prior to the 2001 RAE. The study was primarily qualitative and semi-structured interviews were conducted with over 70 members of academic staff and senior administrators across these three departments and two universities. The two universities were Golden County University, an averaged size pre-1992 institution with a successful research mission, and Royal County University, a post-1992 institution, with a predominant teaching mission but also moderate success in research. Interviews were also conducted with senior officials at the Higher Education Funding Council for England (HEFCE).

The majority of the interview and ethnographic evidence presented comes from members of staff in these universities reflecting on the 1996 RAE submission and looking forward to strategies and plans for the 2001 submission. This is an appropriate period to study universities and their responses to the RAE primarily because it was a time when many universities dramatically increased their RAE scores. So it is important to uncover whether institutions were simply more astute at 'playing the game'. In order to preserve confidentiality and to better protect the staff involved in the research, it was also appropriate to leave a significant time between data collection and publication.

Evidence was also drawn from the RAE submissions for 2001 and other relevant documentary sources in order to make comparisons with the outcome in the 1996 RAE of those departments and across the sector as a whole. Extensive quantitative data was drawn from the 2001 RAE submissions for the Units of Assessment (UOA) of biology, sociology and English and this is examined in the light of qualitative evidence presented from the case studies. The study was small in scale and no claims for generalizations to other institutions can be made. Indeed, it is part of the argument of this book that institutional and individual responses, position-taking and practices can only be understood within the context of specific historical and cultural locations and so for this reason a mainly qualitative, in-depth approach was taken.

The issues of ethics and confidentiality were very important within this study. I have done everything that I can to protect the identity of the institutions and the individuals that have taken part in this study. As I have stated, the gap between data collection and publication helps to ensure that it is more difficult to trace any details that might compromise confidentiality. All names of departments, universities and individuals are pseudonyms and where necessary 'correct' information is not given for organization units such as departments, schools, or faculty in order to ensure that the institutions cannot be traced. I have taken further steps such as aggregating data responses to hide individuals and, where necessary, disguising some responses in order to protect confidentiality in a way that does not detract from the analysis. In some instances, the need to protect confidentiality has had implications for the analysis of the data as certain kinds of information have had to be withheld. For example, exact details on RAE grades for departments and disciplinary specialisms within departments had to be disguised or omitted. It is vitally important to protect the confidentiality of institutions and individuals and I hope that the significant time lag as well as the measures to protect individual identity has served to do this.

There is some presentation of data and analysis from interviews and document analysis that I conducted on small-scale studies in Hong Kong and the Netherlands in the summer of 2003, and Australia in the summer of

2005. Interviews were held with academics and key administrators in both Hong Kong and the Netherlands. In Australia, interviews were conducted with a small sample of education academics from one institution. Data from these interviews will serve to illustrates some differences as well as similarities of policies and perceptions and experiences in different national contexts.

Organization of the book

It is not intended that this book should be concerned only with the level of national funding policies for research in the United Kingdom, without putting this into the changing international context, and particularly debates around globalization and debates on marketization and increased managerialism within higher education. Chapter 2, therefore, sets out this context and engages in the debates on globalization, marketization and managerialism and the intersection with national research policies and the drive for international competitiveness in university research. The historical antecedents to the RAE are then set out in Chapter 3, and comparisons are made with other national systems of funding and evaluating research in Hong Kong, the Netherlands and Australia. A critical review is also given on the research literature exploring the impacts of the RAE on UK universities. In Chapter 4, the work of Bourdieu is discussed and his set of 'thinking tools' are explored for their relevance and use in understanding contemporary higher education systems. In Chapter 5, the institutional management of research is explored in the case study universities. The roles of senior managers and research committees in determining research policy and enacting research strategies are investigated. In Chapter 6, the research strategies and policies of the university departments are compared and explored, both in relation to the RAE submissions and in the management and organization of research more generally. In Chapter 7, the positioning and perspectives of the individual academics within these departments are given a voice and the myriad positionings of academics in response to institutional policy pressures are analysed. Finally, in Chapter 8, an attempt is made to think beyond the current possibilities of research funding and evaluation and the potential creation of more collaborative rather than competitive institutional frameworks for the future.

2

Globalization, International Competition and the International Research Game

> ...we have to make better progress in harnessing knowledge to wealth creation. And that depends on giving universities the freedoms and resources to compete on the world stage. To back our world class researchers with financial stability.
>
> (Charles Clarke, foreword to 'The Future of Higher Education', White Paper, DFES 2003)

National higher education policy does not happen in a vacuum but must be understood within the context of the complex global political, social and economic forces that shape national priorities and policies. This chapter attempts to unravel some of the multiple and complex economic processes conceptualized in terms such as globalization, neo-liberal ideology, marketization and new managerialism and the ways in which they have been applied to better understand higher education policies and processes. The RAE, and other forms of state monitoring of public sector institutions, can be seen as but one link in a chain of a political ideology that sets out to redefine state and public sector relations.

Globalization and international competitiveness of universities and university research

Universities and the business of higher education is no longer simply the concern of nation states but is interconnected within a global space. Nowhere is this more apparent that in the league tables of world-class universities, the most pernicious of which is that produced by the Shanghai Jiao Tong University, which lists the top-ranking universities in the world, the top twenty of which are American except for the universities of Oxford and Cambridge in the United Kingdom and the University of Tokyo in Japan. The rankings are based on information primarily in relation to research (such as publications in prestigious journals, citations indices, Nobel prize winners), although the team members who collate this data are quick to point to the methodological problems that are endemic to the process (Lui, N.C. and Cheng, Y. 2005). This database provides, as Marginson (2005) has argued, a 'neat, accessible summation of a world hierarchy' and 'completes the evolution to a single world-wide (network) of universities' (Marginson 2005: 5). The methods and the basis for judgement may perhaps be flawed but there is no doubting the power and symbolic fascination held by these tables. They ensure that universities are evaluated not just nationally but globally and to understand this, therefore, we need to appreciate the multifaceted processes of globalization. However, we may firstly ask the question, what exactly is meant by globalization and how does it differ from internationalization and what are the implications for higher education policy across national systems of higher education? It may be necessary to attempt a definition of some of these terms.

Globalization refers to the transnational interconnectedness of economic and social processes and in particular the success of neo-liberal capitalist economics as the governing ideology across different countries (R. King 2004). Marginson (1999) provides a useful explanation of the differences between internationalization and globalization, arguing that globalization consists of a 'supra-national dynamic of perpetual transition' to world affairs, particularly economic ones providing a whirlwind process that leaves no stone unturned in its ability to influence national economic and social policies across the globe. Internationalization assumes a unified nation state that allows bilateral or multilateral connections between states but the idea of globalized economic and social processes transcends nations and localities. Marginson (1999) argues that globalization is about 'world systems' as opposed to the interconnections of national systems. These 'world systems' can operate efficiently and effectively primarily because of the instantaneous flow of exchanges and information that can cross national borders electronically and effortlessly (R. King 2004). The process of unfettered information flow leads some theorists to argue for a 'networked society' (Castells 1996) and the deterritorialization of space such that a new space of flows is created that is almost virtual, again transcending the national borders (Urry 1998). In many ways, the extent of these transformations has yet to be realized but it seems clear that increased knowledge flows will have differential benefits to richer and poorer nations.

However, the extent of 'globalization' can be overstated and indeed the role of nation states may be more significant. The processes of 'globalization' are more complex and the sphere of influence can be multi-directional such that there can be 'globalised localism', where local phenomenon have a global impact and 'localised globalism', where global forces impact on local areas (Santos 1999). It seems likely that the goods, services and ideologies of the dominant richer nations will be exported to poorer localities and equally the influence of global directions will be more forcefully felt by the poorer nations less able to defend themselves and more vulnerable to the economic power of the West.

It is also possible to differentiate globalization between that which refers to the increasing interconnection between nation states in relation to increased knowledge flows and easier transfer across borders and that which refers to the links between economic policies, including deregulation of government policy and privatization and marketization that impact across nations (Olssen 2004). The latter, Olssen (2004) argues, is dependent on the power of the nation state to drive it.

There is a need, therefore, to understand the complexities of globalization but more significantly here to understand what impact it has had on the organization, funding and reforms to public services, particularly higher education. The main issue can be seen as a case of globalized localism where the neo-liberal ideology of the need for markets to be generated within public services as a means of improving their efficiency and of utilizing them as a means to create wealth has increasing influence. In the case of higher education, the perceived role of universities as the front line within the knowledge-creating society ensures that they have a highly significant role. Governments are keen to expand and capitalize on the economic potential of universities both in terms of educating and training future generations of professionals and in their capacity to generate new knowledge through research. This relates to the notion of 'convergence' across different nation states in relation to social policies, whereby neo-liberal policies are adopted by different nations. One of the main components of globalization is that of homogenization of economic and social processes. In the same way that fast food outlets and chain stores can be found in identical format in city centres in different countries across the globe, so too can government education and social policies take on a similar appearance.

This process of 'convergence' of higher education policy across different countries has been theorized by Slaughter and Leslie (1999) and forms the basis of their arguments that universities across different countries are engaged in a system of 'academic capitalism' and the drive to better serve the needs of industry in terms of science and technology innovation. In addition, the intention is to produce highly trained graduates and precipitate the shift toward a more competitive and market-driven university system. Central to this process is resource dependency theory, whereby governments reduce the amount of funding available to universities and in so doing encourage universities to seek those same funds elsewhere, most likely from the private sector. Policy makers are interested in expanding their share of global markets and so are likely to reduce or eliminate funding to 'programs thought likely not to contribute in a direct way to technological innovation and economic competitiveness' (Slaughter and Leslie 1999).

In their in-depth study of four countries, Australia, Canada the United Kingdom and the United States, examples are given which demonstrate the convergent policy decisions within higher education, influenced by the effects of global competition. These include policies concerned with

> economic competitiveness: product and process innovation, channelling students and resources into curricula that meet the needs of a global marketplace, preparing more students for the postindustrial workplace at lower costs, and managing faculty and institutional work more effectively and efficiently.
>
> (Slaughter and Leslie 1999)

There is considerable variety across the four countries in terms of how these higher education policies were implemented and the particular areas of emphasis, mainly due to the political agendas and differences in central state funding structures in Australia and the United Kingdom versus more diversified province and federal state funding structures in the United States and Canada. However, commonalities are apparent and detailed examples of these are given across the different nations.

> Tertiary education policies in all countries moved toward science and technology policies that emphasized academic capitalism at the expense of basic or fundamental research, toward curricula policy that concentrated moneys in science and technology and fields close to the market (business and intellectual property law, for example), toward increased access at lower government cost per student, and toward organizational policies that undercut the autonomy of academic institutions and of faculty.
>
> (Slaughter and Leslie 1999)

Slaughter and Leslie (1999) provide some interesting evidence for the commonalities across countries in the policies described but they perhaps exaggerate these convergences a little and provide a rather simplistic adherence to the notion of a global dimension that can exceed national and local specificities (Deem 2001). There are also criticisms of the methodology utilized, where only one country was studied and generalizations made from this (Deem 2001). Comparative work on this scale, however, is complex and there is little substantial research so more is needed to provide a much more qualified analysis of these processes.

Other researchers have looked more at the local, national, global dimensions and the complexity of the interlinking of these processes (Mok 2003; Cai 2004; Vidovich 2004). Mok (2003) in his study of higher education policy in Asia, predominantly, China, including Hong Kong SAR (Special Administrative Region of the People's Republic of China), Taiwan and Singapore, argues that these processes cannot be seen as an 'undifferentiated universal trend' (Mok 2003). In his study of these different systems, he argues that there are common themes occurring in the decisions around education policy, including, in particular, comprehensive reviews of education systems and fundamental reforms and marketization and privatization of higher education.

But all of these have to be understood in the light of national and local political and cultural historical situations. Like Slaughter and Leslie, Mok recognizes the significance and importance of what seems like an almost global move towards neo-liberal economics and in particular the way that the public sector is managed and controlled by governments and policies introduced to make them more efficient, better managed and more in service to economic ends. The term 'glocalization' is used to emphasize how the economic demands of global competitiveness can only be understood in relation to the specific local conditions that also continue to make nation states unique (Mok and Lee 2003). A similar point is made with the concept of 'hybridization', whereby it is more useful to understand the complex range of organizational forms, practices and cultures within different national and local contexts rather than concentrating on convergence and commonalities (Deem 2001). However, the lack of 'a totalising convergence theory', and the recognition that convergence at one level does not imply convergence at all levels of instances' (Dale 2005) does not mean that the impact of globalization on the knowledge economy of nation states is negligible. Indeed, the global competitive element, which is endemic with globalization can be seen to exert power by its ability to activate and exert influence across a new domain that becomes 'supranational' (Dale 2005).

The important driver behind globalization is that of international competitiveness. Economically, socially and culturally the role of the university in terms of education and knowledge creation is central, particularly in western states, where knowledge rather than production runs the economy (Dale 2005), hence the idea of the 'knowledge economy'. As R. King (2004) argues, the reduced role of the state within a globalized economy means that its role serves to become one of 'accommodating the structure of the domestic economy to the imperatives of international competitiveness' (R. King 2004). Universities are seen as a significant force in boosting the economic competitiveness of a nation and governments are keen to support the competitiveness of universities nationally and internationally. Indeed, this can be seen as a key driving force behind the policies to fund and evaluate university research.

Across all nations but particularly the economic superpowers, the significance of international standing on research excellence is vital and needs to be protected. In the United Kingdom, as elsewhere, this is a central driver of government policy on higher education. What is demonstrable, at least by quantitative measures, is the competitive advantage of the United Kingdom in relation to other countries and the government's concern to maintain and increase its competitive lead where possible.

The United Kingdom holds a strong position on the number of publications and associated impact factors. D.A. King (2004) confirms that the UK has a high share of science and engineering citations, second only to the United States in terms of 'citation intensity' (see Table 2.1).

A report by Universities UK looks at the ranking of different academic disciplines in the United Kingdom with other G8 nations (Universities UK 2003), as shown in Table 2.2.

Table 2.1   Ranking of nations based on top 1% of highly cited publications, 1997–2001

Rank	Country	Top 1% of highly cited publications 1997–2001
1	United States	23,723
2	EU15	14,099
3	United Kingdom	4,831
4	Germany	3,932
5	Japan	2,609
6	France	2,591
7	Canada	2,195
8	Italy	1,630
9	Switzerland	1,557
10	Netherlands	1,435
11	Australia	1,049
17	Russia	501
20	China	375
23	India	205
24	Brazil	188
31	Iran	14

Source: King, D.A. (2004) The scientific impact of nations. *Nature,* **430.**

Citation indices and quantitative measures of scientific excellence must be interpreted with care (Johnes and Taylor 1990), not least because the United States dominates the tables largely by scale and in particular 'preferential US citing of US papers may distort the analyses, given the sheer size of the contribution' (King D.A. 2004).

Table 2.2   Ranking of G8 nations within different subjects, on number of journals and impact factor of publications

Disciplinary grouping	Ranking of UK within G8 countries	
	Number of journals	**Impact factor**
Clinical	2	3
Pre-clinical and health	2	3
Biological	2	2
Environment	2	2
Mathematics	4	2
Physical	5	2
Engineering	4	3 (joint with France)
Social	2	4
Business	2	2
Language and Culture	2	Difficult to measure
Humanities	2	1
Visual and Performing Arts	2	2

Source: Universities UK, 2003 Report

A key feature of UK government policy has been how to improve on international rankings of research excellence, together with a commitment to increase spending on the science budget in order to augment the spending on R&D to 2.5 per cent of GDP by 2014 (Treasury 2004). This more recent commitment to increase spending, however, comes after many years of reduced resources for supporting university research. The extended period of government cuts on spending were accompanied by the neoliberal ideology for improving public services, namely to create and sustain a system of marketization that can improve efficiency and bolster declining public funds with private money. This neo-liberal agenda, it has been argued, has driven universities towards more entrepreneurial and market driven activities, as discussed in the next section.

Academic capitalism, entrepreneurialism and marketization: changing university values and practice?

The argument about global 'convergence' for Slaughter and Leslie (1997), is that universities across different nations are becoming more engaged in 'academic capitalism'. Despite reservations about the concept of globalization, Mok (2003), in his identification of common themes affecting higher education systems across the globe highlights major education reform and the increased marketization of higher education. These ideas are further substantiated by the notion of universities becoming more entrepreneurial (Clark 1998; Marginson and Considine 2000).

Indeed, in theorizing globalization, it is argued that nation state governments effectively become facilitators of 'market-building' in the public sector and to a certain extent this is seen to be the case for state–university relations in some countries. Slaughter and Leslie (1997) present a convincing case on the increased marketization and capital accumulation activity of universities in the countries they studied, the USA, Canada, Australia and the United Kingdom. There is plenty of evidence across a number of countries that governments are keen to support this increased competitive and commercial activity of universities but some care needs to be taken in unpacking exactly what is meant by the myriad terms used to describe this process and, moreover, in providing a more substantial evidential basis to back up the rhetorical claims being made.

There is a variety of literature that argues for the increased importance of market and commercial funding of university activities, particularly in the United States where the market has been vital even for public institutions, but also increasingly in other countries where the universities have been traditionally more reliant on government funds (Slaughter and Leslie 1997; Bok 2003). There are notions of the 'enterprise university' (Clark 1998; Marginson and Considine 2000). Across, different countries like Australia, the United States, the United Kingdom, and Canada, similar processes are occurring to increase the competitiveness and market potential of university teaching and research activities. Significant research has been done in Australia detailing the shift towards commercialization and marketization of university activities, notably in research (Marginson and Considine 2000; Harman 2005).

There seem to be at least three central issues here. Firstly, to what extent are government funds for research, including research council grants made more competitive? In some sense, a pseudo-market system of funding is created. There seems to be abundant evidence that this is the case both in the United Kingdom and elsewhere (Mok and Lee 2003). Secondly, the proportion of research funding coming from commercial sources, from industry and elsewhere to universities is shown in Figure 2.1 to be approximately 6 per cent. In terms of research funding from commercial sources, the figures for the United Kingdom are still relatively small, although D.A. King (2004) argues it has the highest level in investment of commercial funds in public R&D (approximately 11 per cent) compared to

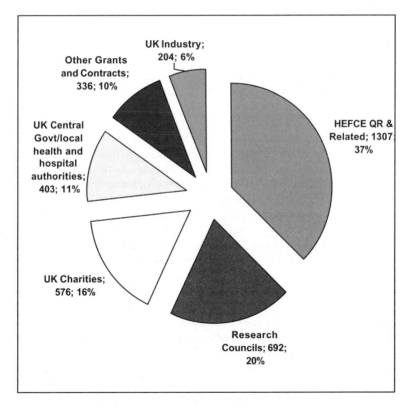

Figure 2.1 Research income to English Higher Education Institutions (HEIs) in 2003–4 (£ millions)

all other G8 countries. There is obviously some disagreement therefore on the extent of involvement of private funding in public R&D.

The impact of both of these developments on 'traditional academic values' and research cultures within universities has been explored in a number of research studies. Harman (2005) argues that this process is corrupting academic values and there are many that agree with him (Willmott 2003). Others maintain that market values and traditional values can coexist (Clark 1998). There is no doubt that increased competition has occurred and that universities are being increasingly forced to seek funds elsewhere (Deem 2001), but there is very little evidence for how this is actually impacting on the cultures and values of universities.

One research study carried out in Finland argues that engaging in 'academic capitalism is no mechanical process' and provides more empirical evidence to demonstrate the complexities of this process across different disciplines (Ylijoki 2003). This study looks at differences between a history department, a centre for work research and a laboratory of surface science and semiconductor technology, all at the University of Tampere. The responses to these pressures to increase research funding ranges from the close to market behaviour and values of the research work centre, the tension between the two sets of values in the semi-conductor lab, to the safeguarding of academic values in the history department. In the laboratory, the tensions are between being able to carry out pure research and commercial product development. Emphasis on the latter to increase financial gain has led to the former being compromised. In the case of the history department, there is pressure to apply for more funding with the consequence that this becomes 'one of the most time-consuming duties of senior academics' providing a sort of 'business politics', that researchers have to engage in rather than 'reading and writing in peace and quiet and also communicating with the public at large', seen as more 'traditional duties' (Ylijoki 2003). This research supports that of Slaughter and Leslie (1997) in providing more empirical demonstration.

> Engaging in academic capitalism is thus no straightforward or uni-dimensional phenomenon but takes a variety of forms in different disciplines and organisational settings. Furthermore, the cognitive nature of knowledge sets limits to the extent and the quality of market responses, for which reason the opportunities for involvement in academic capitalism vary drastically across disciplines.
>
> (Ylijoki 2003)

Much has been written on the possible impact of involvement of universities in 'academic capitalism', on academic organization and work within university departments. Indeed, it is argued by Harvie (2000) that academia itself reproduces and reflects back the inequalities of power found within capitalism such that it produces a microcosm of capitalist activity.

Extending the theoretical and conceptual notion of 'capitalism from a Marxist perspective', Harvie (2000) argues that a distinction can be drawn between research workers and research capitalists. Research capitalists, in having accumulated research capital in the form of high ranking publications and research grants, are able to employ the labour of research workers (or proletarians) who in return for their creative labour power receive little recognition (although this may vary between different situations), and substantially decreased levels of job security and may remain trapped in a 'research-proletarian' position through their inability to accumulate sufficient research capital while the research capitalist substantially increases research capital and thus research power.

Harvie's main thesis is that the academics from the old system of 'intellectual commons' (akin to collegiality), as he terms it, where research facilities and well-endowed libraries were available to all alongside the freedom from too much teaching or administration, are being replaced or usurped by the 'research capitalists'. There is, however, little supporting empirical evidence within Harvie's work and, although he recognizes that this process may be uneven, he provides no analysis of differences across the sector, within institutions and departments. He also gives an inadvertently 'golden age' picture of the 'intellectual commons' as the context of working conditions for academics in the past. Harvie (2000) may be right in highlighting the changing conditions of capital accumulation among academics but this must be addressed by analysing the complexity of this situation across different institutions and within different disciplines. The issues of 'research capital' and the notions of 'research capitalists' are taken up in Chapter 4, where the work of Bourdieu is discussed.

The work of Reay (2004) further substantiates the idea that increasing differentials of status and power are accrued to academic researchers. One of the central arguments in her case was the lack of recognition given to the work of the 'research team' rather than solely the 'lead' researcher on the project. Reay (2004) argues that '. . . processes of corporatisation, casualisation, commodification, contractualism and compliance work against and undermine, collegiality and cooperation' and that 'an upper echelon of elite, predominantly male, academics serviced by an army of casualised teaching, research and administrative staff' now exists within higher education (Reay 2004).

Drawing on the work of Bourdieu, she argues that there is a class of 'cultural capitalists' within academia who succeed in accumulating research capital by harnessing the labour power of an increasingly casualized base of contract researchers (Reay 2004). More specifically, she argues, the low status role of contract researcher is both classed and gender based with women often being positioned as the domestics within academia servicing the more important abstracted work of the predominantly male cultural capitalists who lead the research 'teams'. She highlights Bourdieu's argument that academics, in order to succeed must be liberated into abstraction, into the world of ideas and a servicing community of researchers is necessary in order to allow for this privileged space to be taken up.

The arguments put forward by Harvie and Reay are important in beginning to look at the impact of increased commercialization and market-ization of research on the organization of research work within university departments. However, more systematic study is needed, particularly in relation to differences across the university sector and across different disciplines. Both agree, however that this fundamental change in academic values has served to undermine the collegial ideal. Much has been written about the increase in managerialism, often discussed alongside the move towards 'academic capitalism' and the need to better manage and control university activities. The extent to which there is any possibility of the continuance of the collegial ideal or indeed whether it ever existed in the first place is worth exploring.

Institutional organization and collegial practices within academia: a nostalgic ideal?

> one international group, studying 'the entrepreneurial and adaptive university' at Anglia Polytechnic University's Centre for Higher Education Management, visited Cambridge (University) in 1994. They asked about the research committee – 'we haven't got one'; research policy – 'it's a good thing'; control of quality? – 'we appoint top class staff and let them get on with it'; allocation of funds? – 'there is little held centrally for distribution'. As one Cambridge Don summed up: 'Cambridge works in practice but not in theory.
>
> (McNay 1995: 108)

Despite the ubiquitous use of the term 'collegial' to describe university organization, there is remarkably little written on the subject. Like the self-confidence or 'effortless superiority' exuded in the quote above, this form of organization is possibly perceived to be beyond classification. In this section I review a number of attempts to characterize the 'collegial' model by moving beyond the purely anecdotal anarchic characterization that is given in the quotation from McNay at the beginning of this section. The collegial model, which may or may not represent a version of the 'reality' of university organization as it exists in the modern university, is certainly seen as a powerful normative vision of how universities should be run (Becher and Kogan 1992). Bargh, Bocock et al. (2000) argue that it is not just a normative ideal but does continue to have some genuine influence on the actual decision-making processes of universities.

> Collegiality is a problematic notion in the modern university. It retains a powerful symbolic role in the internal governance of the institution and a powerfully symbolic brake on the actions of the vice chancellor. Academic boards and senates in new and old universities represent in essence the collective will of the academics. Although they are

nominally chief executives, vice-chancellors pay great attention to the hearts and minds of these academic collectivities.

(Bargh, Bocock *et al.* 2000)

Not all academics may agree that their 'hearts and minds' are listened to and it may also be the case that only the top ranking 10–20 institutions have significant collegiality to allow the 'academic heartland' a voice (Shattock 1994). The college system of university organization exhibited by Oxford and Cambridge is the starting place for an understanding of the meaning of the 'collegial' model. These universities represent a particular system of

1   university governance,
2   the organisation of buildings, space and functions, and
3   relationships between academic colleagues (Tapper and Palfreyman 1998).

These two universities have a 'confederal' model of governance with a sovereign body, such as the Congregation at Oxford (Tapper and Palfreyman 1998). The power of sovereignty lies however in the collectivity of the dons. Administrative powers are rotated, and all members are required to take on these responsibilities and to take part in all committees. Decision making must be conducted in committees and must involve all participants.

Bush (1998) defines this as 'pure' collegiality as distinct from 'restricted' collegiality that would involve power being shared by only a few representative senior colleagues. He maintains that 'informal consultations with staff do not constitute collegiality. Where heads seek the advice of colleagues before making a decision the process is one of consultation whereas the essence of collegiality is participation in decision-making' (Bush 1998: 69). Within a 'pure' collegial model in the Oxbridge tradition there would be no seniority but all participants would share equal status. The normative ideal states that, 'all Dons were college fellows and no more or less' (Tapper and Palfreyman 1998: 152). This is illustrated in Table 2.3.

Table 2.3 Components of the ideal model of collegiality

Component	
1	Normative democratic principles
2	Involves professional staff with an authority of expertise
3	Assumption of a common set of values
4	Size of decision-making groups (if numbers are too large then there is a possibility of *formal representation* for all members).
5	Assumption that decisions are reached by consensus rather than division or conflict

Source: Bush (1998) Collegial models

It could be argued that the normative imperative of the 'collegial' model continues to have a great influence on the organization of universities, whether this is in terms of the social or organizational structure. The extent to which a common set of values can ever be assumed or that decision making within institutions is relatively conflict free, however, is questionable. If the collegial model is a reality within the modern university, or indeed ever has been, then it may be in the more 'restricted' form or it may be one model among many which can be used to describe a complex organization. Despite the idea that in some places at least the limitations of 'god-professordom' and 'amateur organization' that collegialism implied was waning since the 1950s however 'the collegial ideal and some of its practical manifestations outlasted its pure institutional form' (Marginson and Considine 2000).

The collegial ideal is not necessarily regarded in such high esteem or perceived by everyone to be the defining model of university decision making and organization, given the history of elitism and gender-biased practices that it is also associated with (Blackmore and Sachs 2001; Morley 2003; Clegg and McAuley 2005). But in a search for something more open and transparent and less 'old boys' network' or 'white, middle class, male' collegiality (Hearn 2001), the new managerial models are not necessarily panaceas or indeed preferred options, although they may perhaps raise new ideas for possible futures that do not look back to the more elitist collegial models (Clegg and McAuley 2005). But the collegial ideal continues to influence the normative values of universities for perhaps two main reasons. Firstly, because it stands as a more 'humane' alternative to managerialism (depending on your perspective), with an emphasis on collectivism rather than individualism and competition. Secondly, I would argue, it serves as a marker of elite distinctiveness for universities both in terms of separating them from the practices of the commercial world and more importantly, from each other, particularly the 'old' (pre-1992) universities and the 'new' (post-1992), where management structures are historically more common in the latter. In Chapter 5, I argue that the continued existence of the collegial ideal within universities can be understood more as a 'negotiated order' (Hallett 2003).

However, where collegial ideals remain these are forcefully restricted such that collegiality perhaps exists in principle rather than in practice. In an example given from the research of Bargh, Bocock et al. (2000) a vice-chancellor, who appreciates and supports the culture of collegiality and may allow for open discussion on an issue prior to decision making, ultimately demands that discord be abandoned once the decision is taken, a reinterpretation, therefore. of the traditional collegial model (Bargh, Bocock et al. 2000). For many, however, collegialism has already been eclipsed by the onslaught of management practices or 'new managerialism' (Deem, Fulton et al. 2001).

Managerial practice and managerial power within universities

There is much debate on this in the UK and elsewhere and substantial research has been conducted to investigate the issue of management in higher education (Miller 1995; Prichard 2000; Deem, Fulton et al. 2001), as well as the process of leadership of universities and university departments (Middlehurst 1993; Bargh, Bocock et al. 2000; Knight and Trowler 2001). At the time of writing a significant struggle is being waged within the University of Oxford amid attempts by the new Vice-Chancellor to radically change the governing structures of the university in the light of the Lambert Review of Business – University Collaboration (2003). One of the birthplaces of the original conception of the collegial ideal, therefore, is coming under increased strain and pressure to restructure the internal governance and management of the institution.

This picture is, of course, complicated by the different forms of administration within 'new' universities (more managerial and hierarchical structures) and the 'old' universities with a not universal but extended 'collegial' informed practice. The CVCP Report (1985) and its focus on university efficiency was influential in paving the way to managerialism, although ostensibly it was more concerned with financial management than management structures of universities per se (Deem 2004). However, the streamlining of committee systems and budget devolution to cost centres as well as the extended use of performance indicators set the tone for radical change (Deem 2004).

The point is also made that the idea of managerialism is one that has 'been in training' in the last 20–30 years within UK higher education both in the 'old' universities as well as the 'new' universities. So it is perhaps not the new phenomenon that many perceive it to be. But perhaps what can be ascertained is the increasing predominance of managerialist principles by university Vice-Chancellors and heads of department or faculties. Indeed, one key indicator of this is the substantial growth in the 'How to ...' literature on managing universities, a good example of which is the *Managing Universities and Colleges; guides to good practice* series published by the Open University Press (Tight 2003). When I went to interview the Vice-Chancellor of one of my case study universities, Royal County University, he was in the midst of reading *Creating Entrepreneurial Universities* (Clark 1998), and was quoting at length from it, quite enthused by the concepts. These texts it would seem, are being read and utilized.

But what exactly is meant by management within UK higher education or 'new' managerialism as it has been termed (Deem, Fulton et al. 2001), and what models are produced to attempt to capture the complexity of university structures? Deem, Fulton et al. (2001) characterize the major components of 'new' managerialism as,

1 changing cultures in public sector workers,
2 new means of ensuring accountability through external audit of short-term easily-measured outcomes,
3 internal regulation of performance.

This implies that the pressures and demands for external sources, primarily from the government have driven the managerial agenda within higher education as they have done in other areas of the public sector. It is argued that the complex ideology of 'new managerialism' involves public sectors adhering to the principles of the for-profit sector and the constant search for 'efficiency, excellence and continuous improvement' (Deem, in Morley 2003). It is argued to be a set of 'management techniques', which rely mainly on measurements of productivity and output.

> New managerialist hallmarks include: the pursuit of continuous improvement defined economically in terms of productivity and outputs; imposition of tighter financial accountability and quantitative measures of performance; the marketization of structural relationships, for example, purchaser–provider models and the creation of a governmentable and flexible workforce.
>
> (Morley 2003)

However, commentators are critical of what may be seen as an industrial or bureaucratic form of management that imposes hierarchical structures and rigid input–output demands on a university system not suited to this model. Indeed, Morley (2003) argues that 'new' is in many cases a misnomer since in fact the managerial techniques often used are more suited to the early part of the twentieth century and 'Taylorism', where crude methods are being used to control academic workers. Similarly, in his in-depth study of a sample of UK universities and colleges, Prichard (2000) argues that academics 'won't buy' the industrial model of management, which one of his respondents refers to as 'hierarchical management, hard management'. This sits uneasily with the desire for a more collegial, egalitarian and interpersonal approach preferred by many academics (Prichard 2000).

But is this dichotomy quite so rigid and does it adequately explain and account for changing practices within universities? Deem (2004) has argued that managerial practices have long been established in UK universities and so perhaps the question is to look more closely at how this can be characterized. Clegg and McAuley (2005) present a schemata of four 'periods' in their investigation of university middle managers but argue that these are overlapping rather than distinct. Despite a recognition, however, of different potential roles of the middle manager, all represent a form of downward influence rather than an upward representational approach.

1 Middle manager is seen as representing core organizational values – and is also agent of control (up to the early 1980s but persists).
2 Middle manager is seen as conservative, self-directed agent of control (1980s but persists).

3   Middle manager is reinvented as managerialist 'corporate bureaucrat' – as agent of control (1980s but still persists).
4   Middle manager is seen as transmitter of core strategic values and organisational capability (late 1990s).

The continued insertion of the 'but still persists' indicates the complexity of the multi-layered forms of management and organizational structures within modern universities. And this seems to be the consensus of research done in this area where attempts are made to capture the complexities and dualities of this situation with terms such as manager-academic (Deem, Fulton et al. 2001). This conclusion is also reached by McNay (1995) who charts the possible change or development of university organization from 1989 to 1999, based on four possible models (see Table 2.4).

Based on the perceptions of senior staff at one post-1992 institution, from 1989 to 1999, there was a shift away from the collegium and the bureaucratic model from 3.7 to 1.3 and 3.4 to 2.3, respectively, and a shift towards a corporation and enterprise model from 2.2 to 4.0 and 0.7 to 2.5, respectively. The results of such a small study may be tentative but they clearly raise two important issues: firstly, the idea that a number of complex models and forms of organization continue to coexist within universities and, secondly, that there is a quite emphatic shift towards a corporation model. This model most closely fits the new managerialist analysis (Deem et al. 2001), with its emphasis on the power of the directive and senior management teams and perhaps most importantly, the key role of performance indicators.

These dichotomies and dualities, in so far as they capture some sense of the multiple realities, also point to a further dimension of university decision making and organization that is perhaps implicit within but never fully discussed in either the collegial or the managerial model, and that is the 'political model' (Baldridge 1971), although elements of this clearly exist in the corporation model with its emphasis on crisis and political or tactical responses.

Universities as political organizations: power and decision making

The political model of university organization dispels any idea of consensual and common aims and the possibility of a rational and regulated system. Baldridge (1971) in his study of New York University at a time of institutional crisis, argues that the university is like a political system whereby everyone is divided along specific lines of interest and that people take part in decision making only in so far as it directly affects their particular concerns. In contrast to the collegial and bureaucratic models, conflict is seen as normal within an institution; the social structure is perceived as plural rather than unitary; and decision making is by negotiation and

Table 2.4 Summary of characteristics of possible university models (McNay 1995)

Factor	Collegium	Bureaucracy	Corporation	Enterprise
Dominant value (Clark 1983)	Freedom	Equity	Loyalty	Competence
Role of central authorities	Permissive	Regulatory	Directive	Supportive
Handy's organization culture	Person	Role	Power	Task
Dominant unit	Department/ individual	Faculty/ committees	Institution/ senior management	Sub-unit/ project teams
Decision arenas	Informal group networks	Committees and administrative briefings	Working parties and senior management	Project teams
Management style	Consensual	Formal/ 'rational'	Political/tactical	Devolved leadership
Timeframe	Long	Cyclic	Short/mid-term	Instant
Environmental 'fit'	Evolution	Stability	Crisis	Turbulence
Nature of change	Organic innovation	Reactive adaptation	Proactive transformation	Tactical flexibility
External referents	Invisible college	Regulatory bodies	Policy makers as opinion leaders	Clients/sponsors
Internal referents	The discipline	The rules	The plans	Market strength/ students
Bias for evaluation	Peer assessment	Audit of procedures	Performance indicators	Repeat business
Student status	Apprentice academic	Statistic	Unit of resource	Customer
Administrator roles. Servant of...	The community	The committee	The chief executive	The client, internal and external

bargaining (Baldridge 1971). Despite criticisms that this particular model was developed during a specific time of crisis within one university (Walford 1987) and may not, therefore, reflect university organization at other times, I would argue that this conflict model is a useful tool for analysing the current university system in the United Kingdom and elsewhere. Furthermore, it links with a Bourdieuian analysis of the struggles and strategies engaged in by staff, managerial or otherwise, and the power they wield at all levels within the institution.

Bourdieu's analysis of power within social fields, which is presented more fully in Chapter 4, is concerned with the accumulation of forms of symbolic capital, social, cultural and economic. The determination of these forms of capital which are 'symbolic' or apportion symbolic value to the beholders is not fixed but is a constant site of struggle. Bourdieu argues, therefore, that traditional studies of power as focused on individual decision makers miss the point of the diversity of ways and means by which (symbolic) power is actualized within a field.

> In fact, nobody knows any longer who the subject of the final decision is. This is true when you study business firms, which function as fields, so that the place of decision is everywhere and nowhere (this as opposed to the illusion of the 'decision-maker' who is at the basis of numerous case studies on power).
>
> (Bourdieu 1994b: 92)

This analysis fits more closely with that presented by Prichard (2000), working more within a political/conflict model where a 'state of hostilities' exists in his case study institutions between what he terms the 'management station' and the 'locale'. These positions (and the individuals who inhabit them) are not fixed but instead are fluid, and the strategies and struggles utilized to effect an outcome can vary across different circumstances and contexts.

Rather than attempting to characterize university organization using one model, Becher and Kogan (1992) provide an analysis of British university organization as a plurality of decision-making frameworks and organizational processes. Furthermore, they separate both the normative and operational processes within the university into different levels: the individual, the basic unit (department or school), the institution and the central authority (governance). At each of these levels, therefore, they analyse the organizational practices and decision-making processes and they find a mixture of hierarchical and collegial forms of organization.

Clegg and McAuley (2005) in their schemata, present managers within higher education in a potentially more positive light as transmitting and/or representing the 'core values' of the university. But aside from the ideals of collegiality, what are the core values of modern universities, and to what extent can it be argued that the higher education sector and individual universities are perhaps better viewed as a site of struggle over what these 'core values' are and how they are best actualized within university practice?

The 'core values' or ideals of (Western) universities: the legacy of Humboldt, Newman and Kerr

The modern idea of the research university began with Wilhelm Von Humboldt's struggles against Napoleon and the movement within France to separate teaching and research into different institutions within the French higher education system. In charge of the newly-founded University of Berlin, Humboldt wrote a memorandum in 1810 to plead for a different course to that taken by Napoleon in fashioning the French system (Fuller 2000). Napoleon's intention was to create research institutes, what became known as the 'Grande Ecoles', which allowed for teaching activities only to take place in the universities, instituting a process of teaching as a vocation separate from professional research (Fuller 2000).

In opposition to Napoleon's plans to modernize/revolutionize the ancient universities, Humboldt was concerned to protect the universities from the strong arm of the state and to substantiate further the important link between research and teaching as central functions of the university. His idea of a modern university rested on four main conditions:

1 the integration of teaching and research, including the obligation to foster the creation of knowledge as well as its preservation and transmission;
2 the complementary principles of Lehrfreiheit (freedom to teach) and Lehrnfreiheit (freedom to study);
3 the demand for Einsamkeit (solitude) and Freiheit (freedom) in the autonomous pursuit of truth; and
4 the introduction of the seminar system as the backbone of a community of teachers and students ('Gemeinschaft der Lehrenden und Lernenden').

(Krull 2005)

Despite the little written by Humboldt – only the 10-page memorandum – and the lack of explanatory clarification of these central principles, his ideas have continued to be extremely influential in the ideals afforded to a university, if not in actually being evident in practice in systems of higher education around the world. These are, the important link between research and teaching, the centrality of Freiheit in research and Lehrfreiheit for teaching and the notion of a 'community of scholars' forming the relationship between academics and students in the joint endeavour of investigation and the process of discussion institutionalized in the seminar. These ideas did not have universal appeal but they did inform the ideals of many universities across Europe, including the United Kingdom and the formation of the research universities in the United States.

The central idea of the link between research and teaching is very important to the Humboldtian vision of a university, and he saw the university professor and the student as embarking on a journey of discovery where, despite their unequal positions, they were jointly engaged in a process of enquiry. This idea applied not just to graduate but also to undergraduate students. Humboldt insisted that research is an important part of a university and that there is a synergistic relation between research and teaching that must be defended (D.A. King 2004).

An alternative vision of the university was put forward by Cardinal Newman, who argued for a liberal education with strong pastoral bond between tutor and student and the aim of 'cultivating the intellect' of the young student (Newman 1931). His primary emphasis was on teaching, with less concern for research, so in that sense he was very far from Humboldt. However, they did share a common concern with knowledge as an end in itself and in maintaining a liberal humanist vision for the university (Fuller 2000). Newman's vision became known as the 'Oxford model' and was influential in the English system of higher education.

In terms of influence, however, Humboldt set more of a precedent for the ideal of university system across many university systems in Europe, including Scotland and in the research universities of the United States, Australia and Canada. It is important to talk of influence since it could be argued that Humboldt's ideal vision was never fully realized even in Germany (Schimank and Winnes 2000; Krull 2005). Schimank and Winnes (2000) argue that modern higher education systems can be separated into pre-Humboldtian, Humboldtian and post-Humboldtian, although their central argument is that all are moving towards a post-Humboldtian future in one way or another. Their central measure is the institutionalization of the separation or integration of research and teaching.

France, they argue, despite beginning at a pre-Humboldtian stage has moved towards being post-Humboldtian as links between the Grandes Ecoles and the universities are strengthened. In particular, those in the universities involved in graduate programmes are assigned a research team. In Germany, they argue that despite the continued guiding principle of the unity of research and teaching, pressures from the increased numbers of students have in turn encouraged universities to move towards a post-Humboldtian model. This includes driving out some research work to extra-university research institutes, and there has been some 'epistemic drift' within the Fachhochschulen (Professional Training Institutes) as they attempt to be more involved in research. This pushes universities towards having a close research teaching link only for graduate schools.

The United Kingdom provides the exemplary post-Humboldtian example, where pressures from increased massification of student numbers and decreased funding for universities have forced 'a differentiation of research and teaching along financial lines ... leading to a corresponding differentiation at the level of organisation and roles' (Schimank and Winnes 2000). As discussed later in Chapters 5 and 6, my research supports this assertion to some degree with the influence of funding mechanisms on the organizations of university departments and the differentiation of research and teaching roles.

The overall conclusion of Schimank and Winnes (2000) is that throughout these different systems of higher education, one commonality remains: financial scarcity (a conclusion similar to that of Slaughter and Leslie's resource dependency model). Coupled with the pressures of a mass higher education system, they argue that this has pressed policy makers to say 'farewell to Humboldt' for all but the most wealthy graduate universities or departments. They argue that self-interested professors who want to cling to the Humboldtian ideal will continue to struggle (and probably lose) with policy makers.

Another model of the university, one which is less concerned with an idealization of the university as an institution and more concerned with the 'uses', the 'relevance' and the 'purpose' of universities within society is that by Clark Kerr (1963) and his claims for the 'multiversity'. This vision sits more easily with the idea of the new 'mode 2' production of knowledge (Gibbons, Limoges et al. 1994), where research is perceived not as a controlled domain of the university but as a 'trans-disciplinary' enterprise, which is socially distributed though global interconnections of exchange based on multiple sites. Research takes place within and beyond the university and the aim is for knowledge, as 'produced in the context of application', to be determined and steered by the competition from the plurality of knowledge producers, serving societal (and perhaps more importantly for these theorists) commercial and industrial demands.

A common theme in all of these arguments is the emphasis on the scarcity of funding to universities. Schimank and Winnes (2000) talk of 'financial scarcity' and the impact of this on the drive towards greater differentiation of teaching and research across universities. Slaughter and Leslie (1997) argue that 'resource dependency' of universities has resulted in a greater search for commercial funding to fill the gap left by a reduction in government funds.

Universities as a result are struggling to prove their worth and prestige to their potential funders, government or others. The status and value of a university is dependent to a large degree on its 'research power' (Marginson and Considine 2000) and successive government funding policies in the United Kingdom and elsewhere have served to enhance this further. Competition over research funds and the 'symbolic capital' accrued from research ratings serves to dominate the national system of higher education in the United Kingdom both nationally and internationally.

In summary, this chapter has discussed the arguments around the globally competitive imperative on universities in the United Kingdom. This is most easily evidenced by the desire for UK universities to be 'world class', with a cursory search on the world wide web producing numerous references to Cardiff, Manchester, Leicester, Glasgow and Southampton as 'world class universities'. The precise meaning of a world class has yet to be researched and understood but the ranking and league tables produced by the Shanghai Jaio Tong team have done much to raise the starting gun. Pressures to meet the research targets and other demands have arguably led universities from a collegial/bureaucratic form of organization to a corporative one, driven by principles of new managerialism. Despite these cultural turns, however, the argument remains that not all universities can be 'world class' or indeed aim to be 'research intensive' or 'research-led' and that government policies must aim to direct research funds selectively to institutions, an intended aim of the UK RAE.

3

Research Funding and Evaluation Policies: setting the agenda of the national research game

> It is argued that the significance of the Research Assessment Exercises (RAEs) does not reside primarily in their rationalisation of resources for research or in securing improvements in accountability for their expenditure, but rather, in their contribution to legitimising the restructuring of higher education, which has included the withdrawal of research funding from an increasing proportion of academics and departments.
>
> (Willmott 2003: 129)

This chapter gives a brief analysis of the historical background to the introduction of the RAE in the United Kingdom and explores the literature that has investigated the impact on universities and departments, the production of disciplinary knowledge and academic identity. A brief comparative analysis of different systems of funding and evaluating research in Hong Kong, the Netherlands and Australia is also discussed to determine the key terms of debate within this process and to demonstrate their relevance outside of the UK context.

The national 'game' of research rankings: universities and measures of 'research intensity'

As discussed in Chapter 2, league tables dominate the higher education landscape nationally and globally (Tight 2000). One of the main aims of national governments in relation to higher education is to create universities that are of international standing and excellence or 'world class'. It is perceived that the best means to achieve this is primarily through selective funding of university research.

A huge and varied number of indicators are utilized to evaluate the standing and status of individual universities. But research is the primary, dominating, indicator. Table 3.1 highlights the significance of research funding for universities and demonstrates quite clearly the widening divide among universities in terms of the amount of research funding they gain from the RAE (quality-related/QR research) and how this compares to the core funding for teaching. The table also lists universities in terms of the proportion of funding they gain from QR and core funding for teaching.

Table 3.1 gives just a sample of the total number of universities in England. The full list shows that 32 institutions (almost 42 per cent) have 5 per cent or less of their funding from QR. At the other end of the scale only five institutions (less than 1 per cent) have 50 per cent or more of their funding from QR. There is clear differentiation, therefore, on the research capacity of individual institutions and the extent to which they have any chance of increasing their participation in research and share of research funding. League tables which focus on other measures of excellence can produce different hierarchies of institutions. However, the significance of research

Table 3.1 A comparison of core teaching and QR research funding awarded to universities in 2005–6

University	Core funding teaching	Quality-related research	Difference (research-teaching)	Ratio (% research)
University of Cambridge	57,369,801	92,377,770	35,007,969	62%
University College London	58,057,383	92,989,937	34,932,554	62%
Imperial College of Science, Technology and Medicine	49,841,070	82,441,897	32,600,827	62%
University of Oxford	57,723,724	90,164,963	32,441,239	61%
University of York	20,730,787	20,752,050	21,263	50%
University of Southampton	44,487,137	41,714,404	−2,772,733	48%
University of Surrey	19,209,576	16,532,051	−2,677,525	46%
University of Warwick	34,566,965	27,702,148	−6,864,817	44%
University of Sheffield	54,284,118	40,169,172	−14,114,946	43%
University of Bristol	53,228,193	37,864,321	−15,363,872	42%
University of Leeds	76,933,289	42,147,321	−34,785,968	35%
Keele University	16,569,252	6,218,659	−10,350,593	27%
University of Kent	29,460,272	7,197,881	−22,262,391	20%
University of Salford	38,182,892	7,272,683	−30,910,209	16%
University of Portsmouth	43,632,842	4,044,175	−39,588,667	8%
University of Plymouth	61,352,986	3,041,316	−58,311,670	5%
University of Northumbria at Newcastle	46,505,598	1,006,935	−45,498,663	2%
Bournemouth University	26,564,300	409,567	−26,154,733	2%
Staffordshire University	37,147,467	545,565	−36,601,902	1%
University of Wolverhampton	41,775,755	237,493	−41,538,262	1%
London Metropolitan University	56,922,096	118,225	−56,803,871	0%
University of Derby	26,309,873	33,552	−26,276,321	0%

Source: HEFCE: Recurrent Resources for Academic Year 2005–6

funding and evaluation is critical to university status and so the measure and means used to evaluate research activity is crucial.

Funding and evaluating research: the development of the UK RAE

The historical development of the RAE process has undergone a number of changes since the early 1980s, when demands for university accountability first began under the Conservative government of Margaret Thatcher. Cuts to university funding were being made alongside demands for accountability and increased efficiency for university resources. The New Labour government of the late 1990s and early 2000s has continued many of the same policies. The emphasis on harnessing higher education more tightly to economic concerns and demanding greater efficiency with fewer resources continues (DFES 2003).

The early introduction of a general 'assessment exercise' happened in 1981 under the then University Grants Committee (UGC), which carried out a survey exercise of all subject areas in universities, looking at student numbers, resources, the balance of subjects and the quality of individual institutions. The results of this survey formed the basis of a published report in September 1984 entitled *A Strategy for Higher Education into the 1990s*. This report laid out the prospects for an effective university sector based on strong empirical evidence collected on institutions. The government response to this report was published in a Green Paper (DES 1995) which reiterated the Thatcherite mantra for market forces to prevail and indeed, that higher education was 'a consumption good ... something that was inessential from an economic point of view and should be linked with quantity to the rise and fall of the economy' (Moore 1996).

The government's resources plans for universities predicted a fall of 1.5 per cent in each of the years 1985/6, 1986/7 and 1987/8. The UGC's response to this was to instigate a more formal assessment exercise than the review of 1981. This would involve all institutions putting forward a number of statements on their overall objectives for the planning period, research plans, student numbers and financial forecasts. This information was used by the UGC to determine the amount of funding given to each institution. It amounted to a form of selectivity based on these elements although there was no detailed information given as to how the final funding decisions were taken. The process was 'shrouded in mystery at a micro level' (Moore 1996).

The UGC was therefore, struggling, to distribute diminishing funds while trying to protect the unit of resource for universities and chose the option of selectivity in order to protect the unit of resource for at least some institutions/cost centres. Arguably, the UGC was failing in its task of protecting the university sector; it was simply becoming an arm of government

(Scott 1995). The major antecedent to the introduction of the RAE was the Jarratt report (CVCP 1985). The main significance of this report was that it argued for 'an improved system of monitoring what universities do and how they do it so that their performance can be assessed' (Johnes and Taylor 1990). In response to this recommendation the government set up the Croham committee to examine the activities of the UGC. The result of the findings was the abolition of the UGC in 1989 and its replacement by the Universities Funding Council (UFC), decreed by the 1988 Education Reform Act.

In a retrospective summary of the work of the UGC, it is described as a conservative body which blocked any form of innovation and change within the university sector, protecting it where possible with the block grant system and ensuring that universities remain, as far as possible, autonomous and free from government direction (Shattock 1994). It is also maintained, however, that the UGC fought and conserved to a significant degree a strongly held academic culture.

> But the UGC left a lasting impression on the university system. It can be criticised for not encouraging more diversity and more innovation, but the consequence of managing a system on the basis of academic judgement ... is that it created an environment that had an internal consistency of standards and values, which were secure and instinctive.
>
> (Shattock 1994: 152)

In many ways it can be argued that the legacy of the UGC created the bedrock that enabled the peer review system to form the basis for the 1992 and 1996 RAE.

The New Labour government that came to power in 1997 continued, in many ways, the precedents set by the previous Conservative administrations. In respect of the arguments for more effective management of university activities, using performance indicators, increased marketization and involvement in 'partnerships' between the public and private sector, New Labour has steadfastly carried the Conservative mantle (Cutler and Waine 2000). The use of performance indicators (PIs) is central to the process of performance management. Within higher education, the significant indicators for teaching and research activities first set out in the Jarratt report remain important for establishing the popular university league tables. The most significant indicator for universities in establishing themselves as 'world leaders' is their performance in the RAE as an indicator of their research power.

There have been five RAEs in the UK in 1986, 1989, 1992, 1996 and 2001, with the next exercise due in 2008. Its purpose is to assess the quality of university research based on the judgement of academic peers. This then informs the levels of funding for research to be distributed to each university as part of its Quality Research (QR) budget. The RAE as it is currently conceived began to take shape in the 1989 RAE when the Universities Funding Council (UFC) replaced the UGC as the body responsible for allocating funds to universities. The principle of a selective allocation of funds and the procedure for doing so remained similar to that of the 1986 exercise. Information supplied by the universities, which was then assessed by subject sub-committees, included details of numbers of undergraduates and postgraduates, research students and doctoral submission rates, research contracts and a summary of the research priorities and objectives of each subject unit. Details of research staff and their publications were also included. A rating scale was devised which allowed subject units to be assessed along a 5-point scale from 1 (low) to 5 (high).

The 1992 RAE further substantiated this principle of selective allocation of funds, although there were two major contextual policy changes. Firstly, the ending of the binary divide meant that all 'new' universities were included in the exercise which substantially increased the number of units of assessment (UOAs). Secondly, the block grant principle of the old UGC was undermined by the designation of funding as 'for research' and 'for teaching'. Also the UFC was replaced by the Higher Education Funding Council for England (HEFCE), which would be responsible for the funding across the sector ('new' and 'old' universities). There were corresponding councils for Scotland (SHEFC) and for Wales (HEFCW).

The conduct of the RAE was an extension of the principles set out in the 1989 selectivity exercise. The process of peer review was upheld and assessment panels were set up to judge the 'quality' of the Units of Assessment (UOAs) within each subject area. Panel members were selected from nominations made by academic subject associations, professional bodies, learned societies and other organizations. The names of the panel members were made public. The panel judged each UOA along the 5-point rating scale, developed in the 1989 selectivity exercise. A member of staff from the council would be in attendance at all meetings within each panel in order to ensure that the correct procedures were followed as set out by the council. Submissions for UOAs were to include only those members of staff who were research active and each of these individuals listed their publications and other forms of output to be judged by the panel. The research profile, including priorities and plans of the whole unit was also taken into consideration.

The 1992 RAE introduced the principle of formula funding and also set out the types of funding that would be available. The majority of funds (90 per cent) would be distributed under Quality Research (QR) and would be allocated on a formula funding basis, which would take into account the rating given by the assessment panel, number of research active staff, number of research assistants and research students and money obtained from charities. A smaller proportion of funds would also be made available to enable UOAs with research potential to develop their research activity (DevR) and to encourage research activity relating to basic research (GR). This money was won on the basis of successful bidding.

The main principles set out in the 1992 RAE remained in place for the 1996 RAE. However, a number of significant changes were made. Firstly, only the best four publications for each research active member of staff were asked to be cited (with a summary of other publications). This amendment was made in the hope that the 'quality' of research publications would be judged rather than the 'quantity'. Secondly, the rating scale was extended from a 5-point to a 7-point scale (1, 2, 3b, 3a, 4, 5, 5*). Only those units rated above 2 were allocated funds. This served to increase the amount of funding given to the top-rated UOAs and reduce that given to lower-rated UOAs, thereby increasing the selectivity principle. DevR was replaced by non-formula funding (NFF), which served the same purpose and was allocated the same amount of funding.

Another significant change to the 1996 RAE was the publication of criteria set out by each assessment panel prior to the submissions. This measure was introduced in response to complaints that the council was not making clear the criteria upon which UOAs would be assessed. However, there was still significant debate on the interpretation of these criteria.

In 2001, the RAE operated in a very similar way to the 1996 exercise. There were 68 UOAs. Subject panels were made up of experts in the field of study and a number of non-academic users and a range of international experts were included to contribute to and validate the judgements made by the panels. The measure of quality as previously was related to the demonstration of international and national excellence of the research work being done within UOAs in each university, as shown in Table 3.2.

Each UOA from each university provided a submission for the RAE, to the information as detailed in Table 3.3. It has not been a requirement of

Table 3.2 The RAE rating scale and criteria for evaluation

Rating	Description
5*	Quality that equates to attainable levels of international excellence in more than half of the research activity submitted and attainable levels of national excellence in the remainder
5	Quality that equates to attainable levels of international excellence in up to half of the research activity submitted and to attainable levels of national excellence in virtually all of the remainder
4	Quality that equates to attainable levels of national excellence in virtually all of the research activity submitted, showing some evidence of international excellence
3a	Quality that equates to attainable levels of national excellence in over two-thirds of the research activity submitted, possibly showing evidence of international excellence
3b	Quality that equates to attainable levels of national excellence in more than half of the research activity submitted
2	Quality that equates to attainable levels of national excellence in up to half of the research activity submitted
1	Quality that equates to attainable levels of national excellence in none, or virtually none, of the research activity submitted

Source: HEFCE, *A Guide to the 2001 Research Assessment Exercise*, Bristol.

Table 3.3 Information provided by the RAE on each unit of assessment submitted

Category	Description
Staff information	Summaries of all academic staff Details of research-active staff Research support staff and research assistants
Research output	Up to four items of research output for each researcher
Textual	Information about the research environment, structure and policies
Description	Strategies for research development Qualitative information on research performance and measures of esteem
Related Data	Amounts and sources of research funding Numbers of research students Number and sources of research studentships Numbers of research degrees awarded Indicators of peer esteem

Source: HEFCE, *A Guide to the 2001 Research Assessment Exercise*, Bristol.

universities to submit all staff, so they have been free to choose who to submit as being 'research active'.

With each successive RAE, there were increased levels of transparency and attempts to refine the evaluation process, but there were still many critics of the way in which the RAE was conducted. The critiques of the RAE have been voluminous and have resulted in the funding councils making moderations to each successive RAE. These critiques can be separated into those that relate to the difficulties of ensuring reliability and equity in the process of the RAE, and those more concerned with the negative impacts that the RAE has had on the development and functioning of university departments and academic work, and the development of disciplinary knowledge production.

Problems with the RAE process: costs, bias and validity?

Critics of the RAE process have been expressing their discontent since its inception. Many of those voices have come from within the universities, and not only from those that have been unsuccessful in the RAE. Many from the elite universities have expressed dissatisfaction with the time and effort taken up by the RAE (Fazacherley 2004; Thomson 2004) and the *Times Higher Education Supplement* and other members of the education press contain almost weekly references to and debates about the RAE (Barnard 2004; McLeod 2004). Some critics focus on the difficulties of ensuring a comparable and standard procedure across all the different panels, of defining what it means to be international (McNay 2003), of the potential for bias of panels. The potential difficulty was illustrated well by the confusion caused by the involvement of an international expert in the social work panel during the 2001 RAE (Gambrill 2002). She claimed that despite constantly asking for the 'criteria' being used to make judgements was continually frustrated and concluded that judgements appeared to be being made based more on the prestige of a journal rather than the quality of the research work contained within them, although this was strongly denied in a reply to her article by the chair of the social work panel (MacGregor 2003).

It has also been claimed that the current process does not adequately assess applied work (Fisher and Marsh 2003; McNay 2003) and is too concerned with traditional disciplinary criteria and, therefore, unable to deal consistently with interdisciplinary work (House of Commons Science and Technology Committee 2004). Those involved in applied work and also in pedagogical research (McNay 2003), it is claimed, are disadvantaged in the RAE. As well as potential difficulties and biases that may arise in relation to the type of research work being assessed, there are also claims that the panels are not representative and as a result tend to favour 'old' universities.

A number of reviews and projects have been commissioned by the HEFCE to look at ways of modifying and improving the RAE but perhaps the Roberts report (2003) has been most influential in effecting change to the structure as well as the process of the RAE. The key ideas put forward by Roberts can be summarized as follows:

- separate funding streams to take into account the likelihood of success in the RAE (UOAs destined not to do well could opt out and enter another funding stream),
- a different panel structure with super panels to allow more comparability across panels,
- a measure of institutional competences to be evaluated in terms of their research strategy, development of research, equal opportunities and dissemination of research, and finally,
- replacing a final summative grade to submissions with a 'quality profile' of all the individual researchers submitted to the exercise.

The final construction of the forthcoming 2008 RAE has incorporated only some of Roberts' key suggestions. These are, the introduction of 'main' panels that would be able to oversee procedures across a number of units of assessment and the ending of summative grades in preference to a 'quality profile', which shows the range of staff within a department in terms of their allocation to a 1* to 4* status, evaluated once again along the range of national and international excellence. The change to the panel structure signals a move towards greater comparability across UOAs in terms of standards of research excellence and the use of criteria. It is argued that it will make possible the easier evaluation of inter-disciplinary research. With regard to quality profiles, it is argued that changing from a 7-point scale to a 4-point scale will improve 'the degree of discrimination needed for a continuing policy of selective funding' (HEFCE 2004), and help to 'reduce the tactical element in preparing submissions' by encouraging 'institutions to include all their good researchers rather than aiming for a particular grade' (HEFCE 2004).

The main panel/sub-panel structure is, in part, welcomed for the reasons mentioned but there is some scepticism about its perceived ability to allow for better evaluation of inter-disciplinary research and greater comparability across different panels (House of Commons Science and Technology Committee 2004). The Roberts Review recommended 'moderators' to work across panels and this idea has been further supported in order to ensure greater consistency of practice (House of Commons Science and Technology Committee 2004). The membership of the main panels for the 2008 RAE include a much greater representation of international experts and sub-panels have more representation from potential user groups. However, the representation of panel members from post-1992 universities remains limited, an issue, which is crucial in ensuring parity of results (Sharp 2005).

The well-intentioned moderations to the 2008 RAE may change, to some extent, the structure and process of the exercise which, particularly in the case of the main panel/sub-panel structure, may help to address some of the more restrictive aspects in terms of the valuing of interdisciplinary research as sub-panel judgements can be overseen by the inter-disciplinary main panels. However, the impact might be minimal. Moreover, the proposed changes deal only with some tweaking of the structure and process of the RAE and the opportunity was missed to engage with more fundamental questions, which recognize that the RAE has never been simply a means of identifying and rewarding excellent research but has served to influence the structure of the UK higher education system.

The House of Commons Select Committee on Science and Technology engaged further with more radical ideas for changing the RAE structure and process, primarily the possibility of relying more on a metric formula for funding in science subjects, where such quantitative indicators are more meaningful and for those high performing departments where, likewise, information on funding and citation counts may be good indicators of quality. They argue that, 'a range of measures could be used to replace the peer review process in some subject areas such as the physical sciences. There are strong reasons to believe that they could be as reliable as the current system while being more cost effective and imposing less of a burden on institutions and panel members' (House of Commons Science and Technology Committee 2004). This raises the question of whether all subject areas need to be treated in the same way and also whether more fundamental changes need to be made to the RAE process than have been considered so far. There are many who would like to see the RAE abolished but there are also fears about any possible replacement.

The merits of a purely quantitative measure of research have been debated and it has been argued that at least for the sciences, it would be more prudent and less time-consuming to have a purely quantitative system of research evaluation (House of Commons Science and Technology Committee 2004). One study looking at the Social Policy UOA submission for 2001, concluded that much of the variance in grades could be explained by the number of doctorates awarded, amount of research funding, publications in a particular range of journals and books by major publishers and being a fairly large department (McKay 2003). It is further argued, that lower rated new universities in social policy performed less well than their 'metric' data would suggest they should. Perhaps this leaves some room for the judgement of 'quality' not captured by quantitative measures, or perhaps it indicates a measure of bias. McKay argues that it might then be fairer to give up the intent to measure 'quality' with the all the subjective bias this might entail to a system based on metrics where 'the rules could be known in advance rather than being guessed at' (McKay 2003).

Many critics of the RAE have been less concerned with the possible bias and distortions within the process itself and more worried about the impact that the RAE has had on changing the management structures, organizations and cultures within universities and within disciplinary communities. Furthermore, it is argued that the RAE has had enormous detrimental impacts on the work of academics and the disproportionate value placed on research over teaching. It is to these arguments that we now turn.

The Research Assessment Exercise: distortions, deceptions and degradations?

> because our argument is that (the RAE) merely measures quality. I mean you know that it is just a device and it is done by the communities themselves so it shouldn't actually distort, it should really reflect. But the problem is that if you are not involved in the community you then get into a situation where you play to the rules rather than play to the quality ... making everyone publish does not make people do better research. But I don't think it is an unreasonable requirement that they should both do better research and publish occasionally. So I don't think it is distorting behaviour, the question is, does it not accurately effect real improvements in quality ... But I tend to be optimistic in the sense that you have got to believe that all those people didn't put all that effort into it and it got worse.
>
> (Senior HEFCE official, pre-2001 RAE)

The RAE cannot be separated from other policy changes that have been made to higher education since the early 1980s and indeed, must be understood in relation to the changes associated with wider processes of globalization, marketization and managerialism in higher education. It is impossible to attribute any changes in institutional or individual behaviour directly to this assessment process and that is not the intention of this book, which focuses much more on the perceptions and experiences of higher education institutions and their staff in relation to the exercise. However, the contention of this book is that the RAE does intersect quite directly with these macro-level processes in the ways outlined in Chapter 2. Many of the studies that have examined this issue have tended to conclude that the RAE has been very significant in shaping micro-level activities within universities. The extent to which this effect has been a negative or positive one is central to the debate on how the RAE should best be conducted. HEFCE maintain that the RAE is simply a ranking exercise, a measurement of research activity as it exists within institutions.

There are many assumptions in the opening quote above, given by the senior HEFCE official. The first is that the academic 'communities' are in control of this process, this measurement activity. Secondly, that within this community there may be insiders and outsiders who do not play the research game instinctively but play openly to the stated rules of the RAE. Thirdly, that it is not an unreasonable requirement that academics should do better research and publish. This is stated despite an earlier claim made in the same interview that there are now insufficient funds available for all universities to sustain a research mission. The academic communities may determine the criteria on which judgements are based and carry out the assessment but they in no way direct the purpose of the RAE which is to grade UOAs on a 7-point scale and fund selectively according to merit. It is argued that the peer review process has been co-opted for this purpose. 'Informal peer review within a collegiate system of control is very different from institutionalized peer review linked to a ranking system designed for funding purposes' (Harley and Lee 1997).

Despite the claim made above, that the RAE does not distort behaviour within universities, it is acknowledged that the requirements of the RAE can aid institutional management. The former director of the HEFCE has openly discussed the negative impacts of the RAE and, in particular, that there have been distortions to research practice, damage to non-research activities and stress caused to academic staff (Newby 2001). For this reason, the HEFCE has commissioned many studies to explore possibilities for adapting the RAE to limit any negative impacts or unintended consequences (Elton 2000). Before moving on to the ways in which the RAE has been perceived to be negative, however, I will outline some of the main arguments in favour of the exercise and its positive impacts on universities.

The success of the RAE

Many commentators would point to the achievements of the RAE in raising research activity within UK universities, in providing the impetus for university leaders to improve the organization and management of research activity. It also established a funding mechanism that is emulated by other national systems, most notably Hong Kong.

The evidence, say the proponents, speaks for itself, as with each successive RAE gradings continue to rise; in 2001 almost 40 per cent of all submissions earning the top grade of 5 or 5* and 55 per cent of all research-active staff working in these top-rated departments (McNay 2003). Research studies have given evidence of the power of the RAE to effect substantial changes to the organization of research activities within institutions (McNay 1997; Lucas 2001; Harley 2002; Hare 2003), and the imperative public demonstration of research activity has succeeded in ensuring that academics are keen to have the results of their research efforts in the public domain through publication in research journals, books and other outlets. The evidence presented in Chapter 2 shows that research in the United Kingdom in many science subject areas is second only to the United States, and, it could be argued, this is in no small measure due to the influence of the RAE (House of Commons Science and Technology Committee 2004; King 2004). Evidence indicates that the United Kingdom 'has continued to perform comparatively strongly among the G8 nations, where the greatest concentration of research funding and output is found' (Universities UK 2003). The report emphasizes that indices of research performance for the humanities and social sciences are more complex to compile but in the sciences where it is accepted that they are more reliable there is substantial evidence that, taking some inconsistencies into account, the United Kingdom tends to 'perform above world average and has shown substantial improvement since 1992' (Universities UK 2003). The RAE has been credited with aiding the improvement of the UK science base and competitiveness. It concurs with the current UK government wishes to adopt a neo-liberal model of an efficient higher education sector servicing the economy and increasing its competitive edge world-wide.

But can the RAE really be seen as the prime mover of this research success and if so, how? One of the main answers to this question is the increase in management and organization of research activities within universities. The RAE is seen to have had a positive influence on the improvement of research work. At the very least this would include the organization and visibility of research.

The RAE and institutional management of research

Institutional responses to the imperative of the RAE have made the management of research activities a significant feature in all universities and university departments. This has been shown most clearly in a project carried out by Ian McNay on behalf of the HEFCE (McNay 1997). McNay's report is based on a questionnaire survey of fifteen universities, focus group meetings and institutional visits, all conducted after the 1992 RAE. Questionnaires were sent to members of staff at each of these universities and

393 responses were returned and analysed. A separate questionnaire was sent to heads of department asking more general questions on the research activities within the department as a whole. McNay (1997) acknowledges that it is impossible to separate the RAE from other features of funding and accountability within higher education. However, his survey attempts to throw light on the perceptions of members of staff within universities on the particular significance of the RAE. McNay's report deals with the management and organization of research activities within these universities and includes 33 'institutional strategy vignettes'. These vignettes demonstrate the extent to which organization and monitoring of research activities have increased considerably within all universities.

At the institutional level, the impact of the RAE has been considerable. An audit of

central service support, of protocols, of funding accountability, of monitoring and reporting processes, of decision-making and leadership, of criteria of judgements, of systematic strategic planning against staged targets and performance indicators would find considerable change in 1996 from, say, 1991, according to submissions from senior managers.

(McNay 1997: 31)

The vignettes provided by McNay give a very brief overview of the strategies outlined above and provide only a sketch of the possible multiple changes which have occurred. This makes it difficult to compare universities (although McNay does draw a distinction between post-1992 and pre-1992 universities) and to allow any in-depth understanding of how these strategies interrelate with university processes. Given the methodology, it is also difficult to ascertain the significance and meaning of particular perceptions and attitudes within specific contexts. Furthermore, the methodology does not allow institutional strategies and differences between disciplines to be linked with individual staff members' perceptions, practices and attitudes within specific institutions. However, McNay's work provides a good overview of the specific concerns and responses of individuals across a variety of university contexts and some fascinating summaries of institutional research policy across different universities.

Three-quarters of the heads of department surveyed claimed that the RAE had stimulated major strategic review across the institution. An example from the vignette of university X demonstrates the kind of strategic review that might take place. A research committee was established in 1985 at this university and a policy was set in place to develop research and recruit staff with a research record or substantial potential. Research performance indicators were identified and used to make internal assessments. After the 1989 exercise, the departments who had performed well in the RAE were used as models of good practice. Research strategies were now required from devolved units and a publications database was also established (McNay 1997).

The effects of these research policies and strategies are reported in great detail from the responses given to the open-ended focus group questions and the questionnaire to both department heads and members of staff. There is too much to discuss here, but a few important findings are mentioned in relation to the perceived impact of the RAE on policy and management, staffing issues, teaching and publication and the process and content of research (McNay 1997).

Much has been written and discussed within academia on the 'transfer market' of individuals between institutions. This involves universities 'buying in research stars' from institutions in order to boost their research profile and ensure a higher grade in the RAE. McNay's report argues that this claim has been greatly exaggerated, although it is shown that some institutions did set aside funds for this purpose. The movement of staff, where it did occur, was mainly in the pre-1992 universities, and the greatest loss of staff happened in the departments which had been rated 3 or 4 in the RAE. This implies that the best up-and-coming researchers may be gravitating to more highly-rated institutions, thus increasing the level of concentration of resources and personnel. In terms of appointments and promotions within universities, McNay's report found evidence that the significance of research activity had become a dominant factor both in the recruitment of staff and the internal rewards system. In the pre-1992 institutions especially there was a concern that only 'proven researchers' or researchers with 'potential' should be considered for appointment.

Heads of department believed that the RAE had had a positive effect on research with 71 per cent expressing this view, 67 per cent and 80 per cent from the pre-1992 and post-1992 institutions, respectively. The heads believed that the RAE had reinvigorated staff who had been under-producing and had encouraged researchers to be more 'competitive, proactive and would start to sell themselves and increase productivity' (McNay 1997). The belief that research is now better managed within institutions was held by 63 per cent of heads of department.

Despite the volume of work done on the management of universities and university departments, relatively little has been written on the management of research and in particular the management of the RAE organization and submission. The intention of this book is more fully to address this and update some of the findings of McNay's earlier study.

Impacts on the process of research and disciplinary research

In McNay's (1997) study the views expressed by academic staff on the impact of the RAE on the process and content of research work were mixed and demonstrated the complexity of trying to capture these relations using survey methods. However, there was strong support for the claim that rather than posing a threat to collaboration and cooperation on research, the RAE had increased contact and collaboration within and between universities. A trend was also reported towards team research and away from the model of the lone researcher. In terms of the content of research work, 40 per cent of departmental heads said that the preferences of panel members affected their decisions on which aspects of work to invest in, although the perceptions of staff were that this had less of an impact. Forty-six per cent of heads believed that more conservative approaches to research were encouraged by the RAE believing, for example, that interdisciplinary work was not encouraged. Only 12 per cent perceived a shift towards 'pure' (more highly regarded) research (McNay 1997).

The question of whether the RAE has had an impact on the type of research carried out within university departments has also been posed. Harley and Lee (1997) researching the discipline of economics argue that within this discipline at least there is perceived pressure to move towards the mainstream. They maintain that the narrow definition of excellence put forward within the RAE and 'the continued dominance of a central analytic core' of mainstream, neo-classical economics resulting from the control over the reputational system by the leadership, has resulted in an increase in mainstream economics to the detriment of non-mainstream economics, including Marxian and Post-Keynesian. Those academics surveyed in the study also expressed concern that the list of 'key journals', mostly within mainstream economics, which are highly valued for the RAE will serve to dominate and direct research towards the mainstream and away from non-mainstream economics (Harley and Lee 1997). The study shows, however, that this tendency is uneven across different institutions and different disciplines, so it cannot be taken as a general one across the sector. Economics departments which were rated as a 2 or 3a/3b 'were those where academics, both main and non mainstream felt under most pressure to conform to its perceived demands' (Harley and Lee 1997). Similarly, they argue that other social science disciplines such as sociology have a low degree of academic control over the reputational system and, therefore, have a broader set of approaches and competing aims. In this discipline, therefore, there might be less pressure towards the 'mainstream'.

Further studies within specific disciplines such as geography also found a perception among academics that there has been an overall intensification of work and reinforcement of a division of labour within their departments. This was seen, however, as an uneven process across geography departments. Similarly, a case is made that the uneven intensification of hierarchies and authority structures within a discipline, although maintained, is to some degree made more dynamic since the hierarchies are now overt (Sidaway 1997).

Across the social sciences more generally, there is a concern that the impact of the RAE on knowledge production may severely hamper the need for good quality applied, evidenced-based research (Lewis 2000). This has been discussed in particular in relation to education and social work/social policy (Fisher and Marsh 2003; McNay 2003). Despite the intention to address this issue more fully in the 2008 RAE, there are still concerns that the RAE will continue to put value on pure and basic rather than applied research.

Division of academic labour and the valuing of academic work

According to McNay's (1997) findings, there was also a separation between teaching and research within university departments with individuals increasingly being designated as either research active or non-research active or 'teaching only'. Of the heads surveyed, 44 per cent thought that the RAE had had a negative effect on teaching. They reported an increase in the amount of time spent on research by academics. However, there was also a corresponding rise in reported time spent on teaching, presumably as a result of the large increase in student numbers. According to Halsey (1995) the proportion of time spent on undergraduate teaching remained the same in the universities (26 per cent) between 1976 and 1989 but increased substantially in the polytechnics from 27 per cent to 43 per cent. The amount of time reportedly spent on research activities decreased both in the universities and the polytechnics over the same time period from 40 per cent to 28 per cent in the universities and 18 per cent to 15 per cent in the polytechnics. The output from research activities, however, substantially increased over this time period (Halsey 1995). This conflicting evidence raises issues concerning the methodology of collecting data on how academics spend their time, mainly by self-reporting in surveys. Other research studies have used time diaries which might be more accurate (Court 1996). Questions also arise concerning how research is defined, especially in different institutional and disciplinary contexts.

More detailed research work has been done on the impacts of the RAE on university teaching (Jenkins 1995). From the results of a questionnaire survey of geography departments, Jenkins (1995) argues that the scholarship of discovery has been pushed up the university agenda to the detriment of the three other forms of scholarship, including the scholarship of integration, the scholarship of service and the scholarship of teaching (Boyer 1990). The scholarship of integration would include the writing of textbooks and the interpretation of the discipline for the wider community. The scholarship of service would include the practical application of knowledge.

The extent to which these different forms of scholarship can and should be identified as distinct and separable activities is open to question. However, where Boyer argues that the US faculty reward system has served to devalue the integration, service and teaching forms of scholarship, Jenkins (1995) similarly argues that the funding arrangements in the UK have resulted in a devaluing of academic work which is not defined as an 'original contribution to knowledge'. This is shown, he argues, by the fact that the RAE does not reward teaching-related materials such as textbooks and that more and more teaching is being done by part-time teachers and postgraduate students, though he acknowledges that there are variations between institutions on this practice. According to McNay's report, 62 per cent of heads of department believed that the RAE had had negative effects on teaching, and this belief was more pronounced in the pre-1992 university sector where 72 per cent of heads expressed this view compared to 44 per cent in the post-1992 universities.

There was substantial support for the view that the RAE had increased stress and instituted a sense of 'anomie' among academics who feel that the process of research has become more 'mechanistic and inhumane' and that managerial direction of research activities evidenced as a result of the RAE, has weakened their autonomy (McNay 1997).

The alienation of academics from their research work is expressed more forcefully by Harvie (2000) who argues that the intrinsic creative value of research for academics has been replaced by a pressure to maximize the RAE value of their research so that 'the researcher exchanges their product for RAE-value and through this mechanism of exchange becomes alienated from the product' (Harvie 2000: 112). Harvie (2000) expresses the concern that academics, in seeking to maximize the RAE value of their products, will have as their main goal publishing in the 'highest ranking journals'.

Evidence of younger members or staff being given more teaching and administration and a reinforcement of the academic–practitioner divide was cited. There also seemed to be an interesting tension between the concept of competition and cooperation within academia. Although the RAE may serve as one among many initiatives that serve to increase competition and division between academics, both within and between institutions, there seems to be a sense that the identification of individuals with their department and institutions has become stronger. This identification with one's institution, however, may be encouraged more by fear of negative reprisals than by genuine community spirit.

> through the periodic research assessment exercise, academics have been made individually responsible not only for their own fate but also that of their colleagues and their performance has been monitored in a brutally public way. The objective need to ensure a high rating could lead to long periods of subjective uncertainty and angst for those whose personal identity as a researcher was in doubt.
>
> (Harley and Lowe 1998: 20)

The RAE, therefore, is perceived to have a direct link with career prospects and is seen to challenge the autonomy and identity of academics by forcing them to submit to managerial aims within the institution and direct their research labour to meeting the ends dictated by the RAE. The pressures and demands on academic work and the necessity for research outputs had significant implications for academic identity (Henkel 2000) and this is explored more fully in Chapter 7.

The empirical work done on the impacts of the RAE is on the whole atheoretical, and its intention is primarily to raise awareness of the significant impacts of this policy change on university departments and perhaps advocate modifications to the RAE or its abolition. Exceptions to this are Harvie (2000), writing from a Marxist perspective, and Harley and Lee (1997) who work within labour process theory. It is important that further research on universities be more clearly embedded within a theoretical approach and show more concern for wider social and economic forces serving to influence higher education. Similarly, there should be a more integrated and diverse use of methodology with this research since the work to date has concentrated primarily on questionnaire surveys. These surveys are of undoubted value but there are gaps in terms of the extent to which they illuminate institutional processes and their relationship to the practices of academics. Perceptions are gleaned, for example, that universities have become more managerial and that academics are spending more time on research. Despite the recognition by researchers that the relationship between these two things (institution and individual) is not a simple one of cause and effect, but is mediated through differences between institutions and differences between disciplines, more research is need to demonstrate the complexities and interconnectedness of these processes. These challenges for theoretical development of research work on higher education will be taken up in Chapter 4. However, it is imperative to look more widely beyond the United Kingdom and draw some comparisons with other countries in terms of research funding and evaluation policies.

Funding and evaluating research: a comparative perspective

Chapter 2 discussed the possible convergences around higher education policies across different countries, particularly those in the West. There are indeed common convergences around the driving force of a neo-liberal ideology governing the development of state–university relations. However, looking in closer detail, it is clear that there is substantial diversity in how, in particular, evaluation and funding policies for research are conducted. We can do little more than sketch some of the key themes and issues raised by some comparative work, given the constraints of a topic which merits at least a book in itself, but the intention is to engage with some of the points that are important for research policies across all countries, not only the United Kingdom. The major themes include

- the extent to which the funding of research is directly related to the evaluation of the research work being done within universities;
- the process of evaluation; who conducts the process, the definitions of

research used and how these are evaluated and whether grades are attached to evaluations;

- whether primarily quantitative or qualitative information is used to inform the evaluations and the implications of this both for the cost of conducting evaluations and also for them to be able to adequately reflect the value and worth as well as quality of research work.

We now look at policies of research funding and evaluation in the Netherlands, Hong Kong and Australia in relation to these issues.

The Netherlands

In relation to the first issue, the system in the Netherlands is instructive since despite a complex process of evaluating research activity within the 13 universities, they maintain a historical based funding model. Funding is distributed as a block grant based primarily on historical circumstances, although more recently a small proportion of targeted money has been given to boost the development of 'research schools', trans-disciplinary, trans-institutional research centres (Bartelse 1999). The retention of a historical model partly reflects the continuing strength of the university sector in the Netherlands and the ability of the VSNU (Association of the Universities in the Netherlands) to represent and protect the interests of the universities. The Dutch higher education system also continues to be a binary one with 13 universities and 50 Hogescholen (similar to polytechnics), so there is already a structured systemic selection of distinctive research-based institutions.

One of the most interesting features of the Dutch system of evaluating research activity is the emphasis on self-evaluation, whereby institutions can, to some degree, set the goals and expectations in keeping with their own particular priorities and missions. However, despite the guarantee of continued research funding, these evaluations have had a significant impact at least on the organization and management of research work within universities.

> Through legitimising differentiated degrees of quality of research groups, the VSNU research evaluations for the first time give university administrators the actual possibility to make decisions that differentiate between research groups – this is the most important consequence of the legitimisation function. As a result of the VSNU evaluation report and the talks between the Faculty Board and the university's Governing Board, the faculty is in all cases expected to draw up an action plan. Here we enter the realm of active use.
>
> (Westerheijden 1997)

VSNU reports, therefore, become more integrated within the discourse of institutions and all faculties are looking for ways to improve the quality of the research activity. Westerheidjen (1997) also argues that what was once a fairly fragmented organization of faculties and departments has become a much more 'administratively integrated organization' in terms of management and decision making. Having these evaluation exercises alone can ensure more strategic organization within institutions, without perhaps the sting of potentially losing critical funding and by allowing institutions more self-determination in setting their aims and priorities.

The system of research funding and evaluation in the Netherlands has undergone some changes in 2003. A 'Standard Evaluation Protocol for Public Research Organisations' has been produced by the three main organizations involved in the public funding of research. These organizations are the VSNU, the Nederlandse Organisatie voor Wetenschappelijk Onderzoek (NOW) and the Koninklijke Nederlandse Akademie van Wetenschappen (KNAW).

> In this evaluation system all publicly funded research is evaluated once every six years. Once every three years research units will produce a self-evaluation, alternating between preparations for the external evaluation and serving as an internal mid-term evaluation.
>   (Standard Evaluation Protocol 2003–2009)

However, the system of evaluations, despite having some impacts on the internal organization and management of research within institutions, still remain separate from funding mechanisms. However, recent criticism from the VSNU of the steady reduction in funding to universities from 1999 to 2004 has also been accompanied by worries over the prime minister arguing in favour of 'more dynamic research funding that clearly rewards results' and negotiations over 'performance agreements' (VSNU Annual Report 2004). Despite the arguments of the VSNU that the government would have to increase funding in order to ensure that there was no under-investment to parts of the sector, it would appear that evaluation and funding of university research in the Netherlands might yet become more closely intertwined and this might have important implications for the development of the higher education sector.

Hong Kong

The higher education system in Hong Kong is relatively small with a total of eight institutions, all of which have university status. The Hong Kong RAE uses many of the principles of the UK system, whereby peer review and evaluation is linked directly to funding. The first RAE took place in 1993 with subsequent exercises in 1996, 1999 and the forthcoming one in 2006. There are a number of key differences from the UK RAE, however. Firstly, all staff are required to be submitted to the exercise and secondly, since the Hong Kong RAE 1999, a much broader definition of 'research' has been used, encompassing Boyer's four scholarships of discovery, applied, integration and teaching (Boyer 1990). In the forthcoming 2006 RAE in Hong Kong, the principles behind the use of these categories have been strengthened. It is argued that 'research is not an isolated activity; rather it should support and illuminate teaching and learning' and so for this reason, this broader definition of scholarship will be utilized in order to 'help address the perceived bias in favour of basic/traditional research' (RAE 2006 Guidance Notes, UGC: 6).

However, the process of defining and valuing these different forms of scholarship proved highly problematic in the RAE of 1999.

> Some panel members remarked that even with the definition of research to include scholarship of teaching, it still did not appear to be the case that documented contributions to the scholarship of teaching could be evaluated fairly.
>
> (French, Massy et al. 2001)

There is also the idea that the scholarship of discovery or the traditional notion of basic research is not only more apparent in terms of how it can be evaluated but that ultimately it carries more prestige than other forms of scholarship. This can be taken a step further so that the scholarship of discovery may be seen as more prestigious and may potentially attract greater funding, given the perception of higher cost factors for this kind of research. As French, Massy et al. (2001) argue: 'Can a case be made that the unit cost of research (the scholarship of discovery) tends to be greater than other kinds of scholarship?' To what extent, therefore, can the scholarship of discovery be perceived to be awarded greater prestige as well as potentially greater levels of funding? The UGC, however, seems convinced that all forms of scholarship should be equally valued and in preparation for the RAE in 2006 has run workshops for academics and institutional administrators in order that they should have a better understanding of these different scholarships.

Further to this, a senior academic involved in the 1999 Hong Kong RAE process argued that valuing of different forms of scholarship may lead to institutions being more involved in research in particular areas in relation to discovery, applied, integration and teaching.

> For example, if one were to rate CityU and PolyU (both 'new' universities), I would require 80 per cent of the submissions to be applied research ... and I want to see links with Hong Kong industry and if you are publishing in top-tier journals then that will saturate at 20 per cent of your score, something along those lines. They can still, by doing well in that category get as much funding as Hong Kong and Chinese University (both 'old' universities) but they would have to win in a different race. And that does not necessarily imply a pecking order and I think that would be better for the community as a whole.
>
> (Senior Hong Kong academic involved in the 1999 RAE process)

Despite his claims that this would not lead to a hierarchy of institutions but perhaps a group of institutions with strengths in different areas of research, it is hard to imagine a total parity of esteem between the different institutions and their different missions. One particularly convincing argument in developing the system in this way rests upon the idea that not all universities can win in the traditional discovery research race and that, 'In the long run, the system should provide incentives for people to produce high quality work in one area or another rather than work of mediocre quality in the "discovery" area' (Senior Hong Kong academic involved in the 1999 RAE process).

As a result of the 2002 Higher Education Review, this development has now happened in Hong Kong and universities are charged with particular missions in response to a policy of role differentiation. This includes research missions (or priorities), which relate to either discovery or basic research and applied research or work related to the scholarship of integration and/or teaching. For example the City University of Hong Kong (City U) 'emphasises application-oriented teaching, professional education and applied research compared with The University of Hong Kong (HKU), which 'supports a knowledge based society and economy through its engagement in cutting-edge research, pedagogical developments and life-long learning' (UGC 2004: 12).

What is particularly interesting, however, is that for the mission of HKU there is also an imperative to pursue deep research collaboration not just with institutions outside Hong Kong but also within Hong Kong in order to 'enhance the Hong Kong higher education system' (UGC 2004: 12). The key focus of the 2002 Higher Education review, therefore, was to instigate the policy of role differentiation (by negotiation with institutions) and to ensure international competitiveness within those institutional missions but also to ensure collaboration across institutions. Further to the collaborative imperative, there is also speculation about possible mergers between institutions.

The Hong Kong RAE has clearly been an instrumental process in forging the process of differentiation of institutions. However, the suggestion was made above that this differentiation should not be perceived as hierarchical, a point perhaps reinforced by the imperative for institutions to be collaborating with a perspective of a more integrated rather than competitive and divisive system. These policies are as yet embryonic, however, and further research is needed to explore their impact on institutional management and organization and on academic research work.

Australia

The Australian higher education system comprises 37 public universities and three private universities. The binary system of institutions ended in 1987 when all were awarded university titles. In 1994, a selective distribution of research funding was introduced in order to reward research performance. This was based purely on the quantitative measurement of 'research productivity' and was known as the 'research quantum' (RQ).

> a quantity known as the composite index was calculated, based on the weighted sum of a combination of factors (inputs in the form of competitive grants; and outputs in the form of audited publications and research higher degree completions).
>
> (Ramsden 1999: 341)

This use of quantitative measures was perceived to be a cheap and effective way of distributing research funds. However, the Department of Education, Science and Training commissioned an advisory group chaired by Sir Gareth Roberts (who also carried out the review of the UK RAE) to assess the quality and impact of research in Australia and explore the possibility of a research quality framework (RQF) to replace the research quantum mechanism (Group 2005). Part of the rationale for this move may be reflected in a study which shows that although Australia's share of the Institute for Scientific Information (ISI) publications has been increasing in terms of impact measures, Australia's performance is declining (Butler 2003).

It is proposed that the research quantum mechanism which measures quantity rather than quality research outputs, is encouraging Australian researchers to publish more but not necessarily targeted in the journals with the highest impact factor (Butler 2003). As discussed earlier in this chapter, an overreliance on quantitative measures and impact factors can be problematic when attempting to evaluate the quality of research. There are, however, some significant differences that are likely to inform the RQF, which separate it from some of the priorities of the RAE. One important indictor that will be used is that of the 'research impact' to include such things as 'reports to government and industry, patents; commercial licenses, spin off companies; contribution to social, economic and environmental change; expert advice to government inquiries and influence on national policies; and media presence' (Roberts 2003). The measure of research impact will be given a rating scale of high, moderate and limited. Although, the UK RAE includes submissions of 'applied' research outputs, it is not given the same emphasis as is being demonstrated in the Australian RQF. This approach may answer some of the critiques of the UK RAE as being too discipline focused. However, equal concern may be expressed over the Australian RQF model as placing too much emphasis on applied research to the possible detriment of more 'blue skies' or discovery-based research.

Australian universities are currently bracing themselves for the change to the system of research funding and evaluation and many are worried about the possible impact on institutions. Although, the more elite institutions are supporting the new policy, there may be some concern regarding a possible move towards increased differentiation of institutions and more competition as they compete for hierarchical positioning (Marginson 2005).

One reason for choosing to study the Australian RQ system of funding was to compare a system using quantitative measures of research productivity with a system such as the UK RAE, using more qualitative indicators. However, the Australian RQF system is now moving closer to the UK RAE. Likewise, the Hong Kong RAE, despite its significant differences, has obvious parallels with the UK RAE. Perhaps the Netherlands may yet go down a similar path? Although it is important to recognize the differences in these systems of research funding and evaluation and the particular priorities determined in large part by political and cultural differences, it is also important to recognize the commonalities, the convergences that seem to support some part of the globalization thesis discussed earlier in this chapter. Uniting all the policy discourse within each country is the desire to succeed in creating a world-class or internationally competitive higher education system and being world players within the knowledge economy. There are copious references to these ideas in all the policy literature on higher education. The systems of funding and evaluating university research clearly have a central role to play in this and the debate in particular over the degree of selectivity of research funding is a crucial one. This has implications for the degree of hierarchy and division within systems of higher education. In all national systems, it could be argued that systems of research funding and evaluation are serving to increase institutional differentiation and division.

Further large-scale research is needed to explore the impact of research funding and evaluation policies on the development of national higher education systems but, equally, more research is needed to look at the impact on institutions, on their organization and management of research; on knowledge production; and on academic research work and academic identity. The remainder of this book focuses on these latter questions by looking at the impact of the UK RAE on two universities. Before embarking on this, however, it is first necessary to set out the conceptual framework, which will inform an understanding of the socio-cultural arena of higher education.

4

Researching the Academy: the game of reflexivity

By sketching out this sort of intellectual autobiography, I do not believe I am surrendering to some form of narcissism: on the contrary, by trying to act as an *informant* on the social conditions of the formation of my thought, I would like to serve as an example of and an encouragement to self-socioanalysis...

If I was able, in a way which seems to me to be rather 'exact', to collectivise the field that I had just entered, it was undoubtedly because the highly improbable social trajectory that had led me from a remote village in a remote region of southwestern France to what was then the apex of the French educational system predisposed me to a particularly sharpened and critical intuition of the intellectual field. More precisely, the anti-intellectualism inscribed in my dispositions as 'class defector' (transfuge) disappointed by the reality of an intellectual universe idealised from afar, contributed to my breaking with the intellectual doxa.

(Bourdieu 1995: 269)

Research in the area of higher education has utilized an eclectic body of theories and conceptual frameworks from the disciplines of sociology, psychology, education, economics and philosophy, among others. As a result of a relative lack of established and structured organization of research in the area of higher education, it is remarkably fragmented and difficult to characterize. Like the parent discipline of education, it is interdisciplinary drawing on a variety of disciplinary epistemologies and methodologies (Tight 2003).

To some extent, however, the location of higher education research is changing and becoming strengthened, with a greater number of academics in education departments and sociology departments taking an interest in the area, coupled with the increasing number of specialist research centres. A substantial body of work is building up in the United Kingdom, and also globally including work across Europe, the US and Australia and South-east Asia (Tight 2003).

In particular, a significant body of work is now being established within the area of the 'sociology of higher education' and a case is being made for this link to increase further (Deem 2004). The sociologist Pierre Bourdieu (as well as working in the areas of political sociology, the sociology of culture and education) conducted substantial research in the area of higher education (Bourdieu 1988, 1989, 1994, 1996). His key texts, 'Homo Academicus', 'Academic Discourse: linguistic misunderstanding and professorial power' and 'La Noblesse d'Etat' (*The State Nobility: elite schools in the field of power*), are concerned with the elitism of higher education and its role as a reproducer of privilege within society.

He was concerned also with the divisions within higher education systems, between institutions, departments, disciplines and within academic work, their status and identity. These themes and questions, which were pertinent in the French system of the 1960s, remain so today across all national university systems. His influence in the area of the sociology of higher education has been limited, however, it has grown exponentially in recent years. A special edition of the *British Journal of Sociology of Education* focused on the work of Bourdieu and a significant number of the articles featured looked at systems of higher education (Deer 2003; Grenfell and James 2003; Kenway and McLeod 2004; Naidoo 2004). Bourdieu's framework of theoretical 'thinking tools' is applied in the current study as it provides a useful lens through which we can better understand the modern university system, organization and cultures within universities and the construction of academic status and identity.

In this chapter, I begin by introducing some of Bourdieu's key concepts and theoretical ideas, and then demonstrate how these have been applied in his own work and more recently by others, particularly researchers in the United Kingdom, illustrating the importance of Bourdieu's insistence on the reflexive study of higher education. I then detail how these ideas have been utilized in the current study at the same time as exploring both the possibilities and the limitations of the central theories and concepts.

An introduction to Bourdieu's sociology: a relational analysis

Bourdieu's work defies any simple classification, although many commentators have tried to label him in a variety of ways. These labels are often contradictory such as structural functionalist and/or Marxist, postmodernist and/or modernist. Bourdieu himself takes these differing interpretations of his work as a sign that he is on the right road, if he is able to be challenging to proponents of all sides of the argument. He delights in the idea of being 'suggestive and worrying' to 'the guardians of orthodoxy' (Bourdieu 1993). Fowler (1996) argues that Bourdieu is predominantly a 'realist' or can be categorized under the title of 'new realism' (Sayer 1990), or more appropriately a 'perspectivally enriched realism' (Bourdieu 1990). Realist theory is 'premised on the social equivalent of "intransitive objects" in the natural world, such as forces of gravity ... the generative social relations which possess more causal power than others' (Fowler 1996: 7). Realist social science is also concerned with generating and testing hypotheses but these are constructed merely as claims to truth which must be tested 'through the intersubjective judgement of the scientific community' (Fowler 1996: 7). For Bourdieu, as suggested by the adherence to a 'perspectivally enriched' realism, this would also be a concern with the social position of the researcher which is always a perspective, or point of view on a point of view.

A subjective understanding of social agents is critical to a realist social science, although an exploration solely of subjective understanding can never give the whole picture as other 'semi- or unconscious forces (may be) operating which also have causal force and which sociology must elucidate' (Fowler 1996). The significance of these issues is central to Bourdieu's work and realist social theory is perhaps closest to his sociological project. In this book, I look primarily at the 'subjective' accounts of academics. However, the 'objective' structures governing their accounts, both within the academic and the disciplinary *field*, will also be a corresponding site of analysis as both are implicated together.

Scientific theory, according to Bourdieu, is only possible through the practice of empirical research as a means of actualizing theory (Bourdieu and Wacquant 1992); each is enabled and constructed by the other. Bourdieu's principal concepts of 'field', 'habitus' and 'symbolic capital' were constructed during the process of empirical research and should continue to be evaluated in relation to the practicalities of research projects (Bourdieu and Wacqaunt 1992) rather than be treated as simple 'theories' on the organization of the social world. They are intended to be used as 'thinking tools' (Grenfell and James 1998) rather than as rigid concepts. It is within this spirit of investigation that these concepts are used in this study.

Bourdieu's work is firmly engaged with issues of methodology, although he resists any classification as a methodologist. His research studies engage with debates between structure and agency, and subjective and objective modes of enquiry, but he dismisses any classification of himself as a social theorist. He claims to do 'scientific work that mobilises all the theoretical resources for the purposes of empirical analysis' (Bourdieu 1993). He also describes his research as 'fieldwork in philosophy' (Bourdieu 1994a). He is resistant to the kind of 'distanciation' that occurs when academics think only in abstraction from empirical reality.

This chapter outlines some of the key themes of his work, beginning with his notions of 'field', 'habitus' and forms of 'symbolic capital' and the way in which he uses these to transcend the structure/agency dichotomy and construct his theories on what motivates and organizes the practice and experience of agents in the social world. These concepts, referred to illustriously as 'highly charged epistemological energy matrices' (Grenfell and

James 2003: 518) must first be explained in detail in order to try and capture a sense of what Bourdieu is trying to communicate in his use of them. I then discuss his use of these concepts in studying the examples of the 'academic field' and the 'scientific field'.

Bourdieu's conceptual 'thinking tools': field, symbolic capital and habitus

The intellectual influences on Bourdieu's work have sprung mainly from a desire to rethink classic philosophical and sociological traditions and the dichotomies which divide them. In terms of his treatment of the structure/agency and subjective/objective debates, 'a central role must be granted to the opposition between Sartrean phenomenology and Levi-Straussian structuralism, which Bourdieu regarded very early on as the embodiment of the fundamental option between objectivist structuralism and subjectivist social phenomena' (Wacquant 1993: 246). In contrast to the structuralist emphasis on social structure as determining social action or the phenomonological insistence on the primacy of human experience and perception for understanding social action, Bourdieu's development of the concepts of 'field' and 'habitus' stem from his argument that agents and the social world (structure and agency) are 'two dimensions of the social' (Calhoun, LiPuma et al. 1993) – they are simultaneously constructed. 'Social agents are incorporated bodies who possess, indeed, are possessed by structural, generative schemes which operate by orientating social practice' (Grenfell and James 1998: 12).

'Habitus', a term first used by Plato (Grenfell and James 1998) is understood as the incorporation or internalization of social structures, as lived experience. These structures determine the conditions of possibility of social action, but these processes are intertwined such that 'agents are socially determined to the extent that they determine themselves' (Bourdieu 1989). The knowing subject is a precondition to the structuring of social action. Agents are not automatons responding to the laws of social structure, neither do they exist in a state of voluntarism or rationally make calculated choices and decisions according to rational action theory (RAT). They are instead following a social logic, which propels them towards possible social destinies already inscribed in their historical and cultural background and which they insert themselves into. This is explained as Bourdieu's theory of practice.

> In fact, 'subjects' are active and knowing agents endowed with a *practical sense*, that is, an acquired system of preferences, of principles of vision and division (what is usually called taste), and also a system of durable cognitive structures (which are essentially the product of the internalisation of objective structures) and of schemes of action which orient the perception of the situation and the appropriate response.

The habitus is this kind of practical sense for what is to be done in a given situation – what is called in sport a '*feel*' for the game, that is, the art of *anticipating* the future of the game, which is inscribed in the present state of play.

(Bourdieu 1998: 25)

Bourdieu is concerned that this process is not interpreted as subjects following social rules or their action being determined by a fixed social mechanism. The process is more dynamic and there are multiple configurations of possible social action. The social background of an individual implies a particular social trajectory of possible futures. However, these are in no way inscribed. There is everything to play for. Bourdieu's idea of the 'game' in social life is central to the current work and is outlined in more detail in the following sections.

The structural features of the social world are organized by 'fields'. Bourdieu defines the idea of a 'field' as follows:

Fields present themselves synchronically as structured spaces of positions (or posts) whose properties depend on their position within these spaces and which can be analysed independently of the characteristics of their occupants (which are partly determined by them). There are general laws of fields: fields as different as the field of politics, the field of philosophy or the field of religion have invariant laws of functioning ... But in every field we know that we will find a struggle, the specific forms of which have to be looked for each time, between the newcomer who tries to break through the entry barrier and the dominant agent who will try to defend the monopoly and keep out competition.

(Bourdieu 1993: 72)

A central feature of the understanding of a field is that it must be analysed 'relationally'. For Bourdieu, therefore, the 'real is relational' but this does not refer to relations between agents, as in inter-subjectivity but as 'objective relations' between positions in a field (Bourdieu and Wacqaunt 1992: 97).

In analytic terms, a field may be defined as a network, or a configuration, of objective relations between positions. These positions are objectively defined, in their existence and in the determinations they impose upon their occupants, agents or institutions, by their present and potential situation (situs) in the structure of the distribution of species of power (or capital) whose possession commands access to the specific profits that are at stake in the field.

(Bourdieu and Wacqaunt 1992: 97)

The key to the functioning of a particular field or the main 'invariant' feature, is that it is a site of struggle. The struggle is over the boundaries and who is legitimated to enter. The precise terms of the struggle, however, must be determined by an empirical study of each particular field. The invariants can be summarized as struggles and strategies to be used and interests and profits which are yielded. Bourdieu wishes to distance his form of analysis of fields and interests from the traditional, neo-classical interpretation of interest as economic interest and investment and profit as monetary or material profit. Bourdieu uses these terms to signify the particular 'social' profits obtained by engaging in the struggles within particular fields. He argues that 'the specifically social magic of institution can constitute almost anything as an interest' (Bourdieu 1993). Bourdieu summarizes the interrelationship between field and habitus as follows:

> Investment is the disposition to act that is generated in the relationship between a space defined by a game offering certain prizes or stakes (what I call a field) and a system of dispositions attuned to that game (what I call a habitus) – the 'feel' for the game and the stakes, which implies both the inclination and the capacity to play that game, to take an interest in the game, to be taken up, taken in by the game.
>
> (Bourdieu 1993: 18)

The relationship between habitus and field is not one of a 'cynical calculation' to gain the maximum social profit from any field but more of an unconscious following of the 'natural bent' of the habitus. The process, or game, is not one of conscious rationalization but more one of unconscious involvement and psychological and emotional investment of energy or 'libido'. Misunderstanding of the terminology used by Bourdieu has caused the idea of investment and interest to be interpreted as a 'conscious project' or rational calculation. He argues, however, that it 'is not true to say that everything that people do or say is aimed at maximizing their social profit; but one may say that they do it to perpetuate or to augment their social being' (Bourdieu 1995).

The struggle to augment one's social being, for Bourdieu is a struggle for symbolic life and death. In each social field, agents struggle to accumulate forms of 'symbolic capital'. The maximizing of social profit, therefore, is a maximizing of the symbolic capital, which is operable within any given social field. Symbolic capital is the social product of the field. Symbolic capital, therefore, determines what is deemed important in any given social field and this has implications for the embodied identity and practice of individuals, they breathe life into and sustain it. The identity, motivations and passions of individuals are subsumed within the social 'game(s)' that they are involved in and they exist in symbiotically creating and reproducing the symbolic capital operative within the particular social field.

The different forms of capital identified are symbolic capital, which encompasses 'social', 'cultural' and 'economic' capital. A crude distinction of each would be that 'social' capital refers primarily to the network of social relations one has, or of 'more or less institutionalized relationships of mutual acquaintance and recognition' (Bourdieu 1986). 'Economic' capital refers to the material wealth. 'Cultural' capital is identified as a complex array of educational qualifications and forms of cultural differentiation in terms of language and general proximity to and knowledge of cultural institutions. However, cultural capital cannot simply be thought of as cultural 'objects' to be acquired or possessed.

> Cultural capital can exist in three forms: in the embodied state, i.e. in the form of long-lasting dispositions of the mind and body; in the objectified state, in the form of cultural goods (pictures, books, dictionaries, instruments, machines, etc.) ... and in the institutionalized state, a form of objectification which must be set apart because, as will be seen in the case of educational qualifications, it confers entirely original properties on the cultural capital which it is presumed to guarantee.
>
> (Bourdieu 1986: 243)

Agents are positioned within a social field by virtue of their total accumulation of symbolic capital, which can be gained from any combination of economic, cultural and social capital. Power within a field is ultimately gained by the possession of symbolic capital. The site of struggle within fields, however, is not just over possession of capital but over the very definition of what capital is at stake and what is valued. In this sense, therefore, capital is arbitrary and the determination of what capital is valued is constantly being defined and redefined. As discussed earlier, the invariant of a field is that it is a site of struggle; the variants of a field are what need to be analysed in order to understand its operation. Thus, the variants of forms of capital are different across and within fields, at different times. Analysis of social fields is a process of understanding the different forms of capital and how they are valued within it. Social fields are structured by the differential possession of forms of capital but individuals are also motivated to increase their possession of this capital. There is, therefore, a dynamic process of a reproduction of social fields but also a motivational force either to increase one's capital or struggle to redetermine the conditions of value placed on certain forms of capital. It is these processes which analysis of social fields seeks to understand. Forms of capital are also interchangeable with, for example, economic capital enabling accumulation of cultural capital and vice versa. In order to illuminate these ideas further, I examine them in more detail in relation to Bourdieu's analysis of the 'academic field'.

What can Bourdieu's thinking tools bring to the study of higher education?

The research on the French university field in 'Homo Academicus' was undertaken by Bourdieu in the 1960s, prior to the events of May 1968 in Paris. The research is presented as an analysis of the university system at that time and the structure and functioning of the academic field. The research details the structural and morphological changes which were happening within the system, including the rapid increase in the number of university students and the growth in the numbers of academic staff, especially low-status academic staff. Bourdieu argues that these changes to the structure of the system instituted a form of disillusionment with the academic system, because of the declining value of degrees conferred and the restricted career opportunities for the newly recruited academic staff. These events partly instigated the anti-institutional feeling and forms of rebellion which characterized the events of May 1968. The position which an academic occupied within the university space, argued Bourdieu, determined the likelihood of their involvement in the protests and their political attitudes more generally. In order to understand an agent's attitudes or involvement in the site of struggle which is the university space, therefore, it is necessary to analyse their position within that social space.

> In fact, like the social field taken as a whole, the university field is the locus of a classification struggle which, by working to preserve or transform the state of the power relations between the different criteria and between the different powers which they designate, helps create the classification, such as it may be objectively grasped at any given moment in time; but the representation which the agents have of the classification, and the force and the orientation of the strategies they deploy to maintain or subvert it, depend on their position in the objective classification.
>
> (Bourdieu 1988: 18)

In order to analyse positions within the university field, it is necessary to map out the structures of power within that field, that is, the *symbolic capital.* This involves determining the variants that operate within the field and the possible strategies for accumulating social, cultural and material capital. These forms of symbolic capital are not fixed but are a constant site of negotiation and struggle over the principles of hierarchization upon which value is produced and agents are more or less endowed. There are rival principles of hierarchization within the academic field such that there is a 'multiplicity of scales of evaluation, for example, scientific or administrative, academic or intellectual', offering a 'multiplicity of paths to salvation and forms of excellence' (Bourdieu 1988). Different hierarchies exist, there-fore, across faculties and across disciplines such that agents are able to mobilize their resources to yield the greatest amount of symbolic capital and maximize the value of their activities within the academic field. He maintains, for example, that the division of the academic field into dis-ciplines and further sub-specialisms, although themselves structured hier-archically, are autonomous and, therefore, allow the possibility of maximizing symbolic capital within the specialism. Recognition granted for the work of a scientist within a sub-specialism in biology, for example, may have little value within the academic field as a whole but it serves to legit-imate and recognize the activities within that smaller area.

The different forms of capital which Bourdieu identifies for the university field as a whole, including examples of indicators of possession of these forms of capital, are as follows:

1 determinants of the habitus and of academic success, the economic capital and above all the inherited cultural and social capital: the social origins, father's profession, geographical origins, religion of the family;
2 educational determinants: educational capital, school attended, educational success, establishment attended for higher education;
3 capital of academic power: membership of the Institute of the Universities Consultative Committee (CCU), tenure of positions such as Dean or Director of the UER (Unit of Education and Research = university institute), director of institute etc. (membership of the board of examiners for the national competitive examinations, or entrance to the ENS, for the agregation, etc;
4 capital of scientific power: direction of a research unit, of a scientific review, teaching in an institution of training for research, membership of the directorate of the CNRS, of committees of the CNRS, of the Higher Council for Scientific Research;
5 the capital of scientific prestige: membership of the institute, scientific distinctions, translations into foreign languages, participation in international congresses (the number of mentions in the Citations Index, too variable from faculty to faculty, was not usable, nor was the editorship of scientific reviews or collections);
6 the capital of intellectual renown: membership of the Academie Française and mention in Larousse, appearances on television, writing for newspapers, weeklies or intellectual reviews, publication in paperback, membership of editorial committees of intellectual reviews;
7 the capital of political or economic power: mention in *Who's Who*, membership of ministerial cabinets, of planning committees ... decorations of various kinds;
8 'political' dispositions in the widest sense.

The two main forms of hierarchical structure within this field are those of academic and scientific power, academic capital being the primary involvement of reproduction within the system and scientific capital relating to research activities and the production of knowledge. Indicators for these forms of capital are given above. There is a hierarchical ordering of these activities, according to Bourdieu, with academic power less valued than the research power of scientists.

It is understandable that academic power is so often independent of specifically scientific capital and the recognition it attracts. As a temporal power in a world which is neither actually nor statutorily destined for that sort of power, it always tends to appear, perhaps even in the eyes of its most confident possessors, as a substitute, or a consolation prize. We can understand too the profound ambivalence of the academics who devote themselves to administration towards those who

devote themselves, successfully to research – especially in a system
where institutional loyalty is weak and largely unrewarded.

(Bourdieu 1988: 99)

A similar hierarchical ordering exists for the division between teaching and
research, with the researchers' working life being akin to the 'freedom and
audacity of the artists' life', and teachers' activities being more 'strict and
circumscribed'. The key to the positioning of academics within these
hierarchical divisions of academic labour is the amount of time invested in
the particular activities and means of production, which afford an accumulation of the specific capital operative within each division. Bourdieu's
explanation of this (in full) is as follows:

> Thus nothing could better sum up the set of oppositions established
> between those situated at the two poles of the university field than the
> structure of their time–economy (because of the fact that the kind of
> capital possessed influences the way in which agents allocate their
> time): on the one side those who invest above all in the work of
> accumulation and management of academic capital – including their
> 'personal' work, devoted to a considerable extent to the production of
> intellectual instruments which are instruments of specifically academic
> power, lectures, textbooks, dictionaries, encyclopaedias, etc.; on the
> one side, those who invest above all in production and, secondarily, in
> the work of representation which contributes to the accumulation of a
> symbolic capital of external renown. Indeed, those richest in external
> prestige could be divided again according to the proportion of their
> time which they devote to production properly speaking or to the
> direct promotion of their products (especially working in the academic
> import-export trade colloquia, symposia, conferences, reciprocal invi-
> tations etc.).

(Bourdieu 1988: 99)

Bourdieu argues that there is a principle of division between older and
younger professors with the former endowed with more academic titles and
signifiers of prestige than the latter. He also maintains that a similar form of
distinction is evident between different types of institutions. In the French
university system this would be between, for example, the College de France
on the one side and the Ecole des Hautes Etudes and the faculty of Nan-
terre on the other.

The academic field, therefore, is highly differentiated according to type
of institution or faculty, discipline and sub-specialism and age and status of
professor or academic staff. Academic staff can be located according to
their position within the different hierarchies and their possession of the
types of capital discussed above. All of these criteria determine their value
or the extent to which their symbolic capital has power or is recognized
within the academic field. The struggle to determine the classifications
within the hierarchies, the construction of 'value' by which judgement is

made, is the struggle for 'symbolic life and death' (Bourdieu 1988) of agents in the academic field.

The trajectory of agents within the academic field is principally determined by what could be termed the 'academic habitus', the 'feel for the game' which they have. This refers to their 'practical sense' of the principle of hierarchization discussed above and their attempts to maximize their symbolic profits by accumulating the necessary capital. It must be re-emphasized that these strategies are intended to maximize the specific symbolic or social profits within the academic field and cannot be equated with an economic reductionism. Furthermore, Bourdieu is at pains to emphasize that these strategies or practices should not be interpreted as a cynical calculation of ends and means. The strategies are more an unconscious attempt to realize one's potential in the academic field than a form of rational choice or conscious decision making.

Critical to the correspondence between habitus and practice is the concept of 'illusio'. The idea is that agents involved in the 'game' within a social field do not perceive it as a game. They believe in it; they take it seriously. The strategies and systems of values within a field may appear illusory to anyone outside of the field. For example, the philosophy field and its concerns may seem alien to the economist. However, the participants of the field have an intense involvement with the rules of the game. It is an investment in a social field that Bourdieu argues could equally be described as a form of 'libido'. It exists as a means of social expression and form of legitimization for the players involved. Indeed, it is their struggle to 'augment their social being' in an expression through this game which is both socially instituted (objective/field) and is incorporated in their bodily self (subjective/habitus). These ideas are key to the current study. Bourdieu describes it thus:

> What is experienced as obvious in *illusio* appears as an illusion to those who do not participate in the obviousness because they do not participate in the game ... Agents well-adjusted to the game are possessed by the game and doubtless all the more so the better they master it. For example, one of the privileges associated with the fact of being born in the game is that one can avoid cynicism since one has a feel for the game; like a good tennis player, one positions oneself not where the ball is but where it will be; one invests oneself not where the profit is, but where it will be.
>
> (Bourdieu 1998: 79)

For Bourdieu's theory of practice, therefore, agents have strategic intentions but these are rarely experienced as conscious intentions. Agents have a 'practical sense' of the game, they do not consciously manoeuvre and calculate their aims. When they are involved in a social field or game, they are 'possessed by the ends' of that field and 'they may be ready to die for those ends' (Bourdieu 1998).

In his analysis of higher education policy debates in Australia in the

1990s, Zipin (1999) utilizes Bourdieu's ideas to demonstrate how the values underlying debates over the 'main game' or purpose of higher education are polarized between an 'ideological fiction of ... a (higher order) "spirit of inquiry", versus (lower order) "practitioner" skills and that engagement in this debate 'indicates its dangerous half-truth appeal to the deep structural reality that diverse university activities are not equal in status and power' (Zipin 1999: 22). The appeal by university representatives, particularly those from the elite, sandstone universities, to the 'main game' of liberal, autonomous inquiry into knowledge serves to distinguish these institutions from the more vocational, economically oriented institutions. Zipin (1999) echoes Bourdieu's insistence that opponents in a 'game' concur with each other despite the apparent opposition. They concur at least with the idea that the 'game' is worth playing and they agree on some level with the terms of debate.

> That is, those who jockey powerfully for position within a field complicitly share certain implicit appreciations. They share a sophisticated insider sense of the real diversity of the field's institutions, staff and projects. But they also appreciate that power relations run across differences. They thus share incentives to play a game that rhetorically simplifies that range of differences and power relations, in terms that privilege one's own field positioning over others. Insiders ... know that the complex terrain of higher education can never fit the fictional purities of either a 'higher inquiry' or a 'vocational' logic. In defining an exaggerated binary opposition, they know deep down (and sometimes, I suspect, quite consciously) that their rhetorical constructions are less about describing real complexity than about affecting the power balances that structure this complexity.
>
> (Zipin 1999: 26)

Struggles to define the purpose and values within higher education can be seen, therefore, as a necessary power struggle to determine the worth of institutional and individual activities within the field of higher education. These struggles, however, may not be seen simply as a cynical calculation for personal benefit or as some form of institutional will to power, but as struggles born of passionate commitment and belief. Staff are not 'motivated simply by job survival or crude power lusts' but that promoting 'the value of one's work within a field is also an identity investment in one's self worth' (Zipin 1999: 28).

Despite the possible seduction of this passionate commitment, indeed individual embodiment of structural goals, there has been much questioning of the consciousness, or not, of individual action and strategy (Mouzelis 2000). Before engaging in the varied critiques of his work, however, it is necessary to also elaborate a bit more on the importance of the reflexive positioning inherent in the study of higher education systems. Indeed, Bourdieu's study of the academic field was not done purely to investigate the subject matter. He also believes that research of this kind is absolutely necessary in order to ensure the truly 'scientific' credibility of social *science*.

The need for a reflexive study of universities and academic life

> When research comes to study the very realm within which it operates, the results, which it obtains can be immediately reinvested in scientific work as instruments of reflexive knowledge of the conditions and the social limits of this work, which is one of the principal weapons of epistemological vigilance. Indeed, perhaps we can only make our knowledge of the scientific field progress using whatever knowledge we may have available in order to discover and overcome the obstacles to science, which are entailed by the fact of holding a determined position in the field.
>
> (Bourdieu 1988: 16)

Bourdieu intended to study the academic field not simply to provide an interesting sociological study of this area of social life, but because he believed that this kind of analysis is imperative for a truly 'scientific' sociology. Sociologists cannot hope to understand or represent the social world without first understanding the conditions of possibility (i.e. conditions under which knowledge is produced) of speaking truthfully about the social world. To this end he advocates a 'reflexive' sociology which understands its own position in the social order (academics as a dominated section of the dominant class). Sociologists should not attempt to stand outside society and study it 'objectively' from a distance but should be more 'reflexively' aware of their own position in the social order, the structures of power and the forms of interest which motivate them. The desire for a more reflexive social science has been called for by many sociologists now and in the past (Gouldner 1973).

> What sociologists now most require from a reflexive sociology, however, is not just another specialisation, not just another topic ... not just another burbling little stream of technical reports about the sociological profession's origins, educational characteristics, patterns of productivity, political preferences, communication networks, nor even about its fads, foibles and phonies ... I conceive of reflexive sociology as requiring an empirical dimension which might foster a large variety of researches about sociology and sociologists, their occupational roles, their career 'hang-ups', their establishments, power systems, subcultures and their place in the larger social world.
>
> (Gouldner 1971: 489)

Gouldner advocates, therefore, the importance of a reflexive sociology that is willing to question and investigate the role of sociologists and academics more generally, as part of the social world.

However, Bourdieu is critical of much of the sociological work which has been carried out under this direction of reflexivity, arguing that the end result is of classifying sociologists and academics into different 'types'. This kind of analysis results in the 'concept-as-insult and the semi-scholarly stereotype – like that of the "jet sociologist" – become transformed into semi-scientific "types" – consultant, outsider – and all the subtle indices where the position of the analyst in the space being analysed is betrayed' (Bourdieu 1988). Bourdieu refers to the classifications given by Gouldner (1971) of for example, the 'locals', the 'cosmopolitans' and the 'empire builders'. Similarly, Clark Kerr (1963) describes the 'teacher', the 'scholar-researcher', the 'demonstrator' and the 'consultant'. Bourdieu argues that these classification types, although 'superficially convincing', do not capture the complexity of an individual case which a truly scientific understanding would produce by being 'more distant from the immediate representation of the real given by ordinary language or its semi-scholarly translation' (Bourdieu 1988: 13).

Bourdieu's reflexive sociology, therefore, has three components. Firstly, it is the study of the power relations within the academic field in terms of the forms of symbolic capital, which are operative and the principles of hierarchization (faculty, discipline etc.), which determine the social positions within the field and, in turn, interests and motivation. Secondly, the sociologist must analyse her own position within the field and in the social world generally in order to understand the principles of her own self (determination) and forms of interest. This implies a process of socio-analysis and self socio-analysis of the kind referred to by Bourdieu in the quotation which opened this chapter. This second form of reflexivity is also important for understanding the role of the sociologist in the research process, for example, the social position adopted by interviewer and interviewee in an interview situation. The third significant focus of reflexivity is on an 'interrogation of the scholastic point of view' (Schirato and Webb 2003) or 'the practice of reflexively situating and historicizing the space of one's point of view as a scholar and sociologist' (Kenway and McLeod 2004).

Bourdieu puts his faith in the scientific field to enable the development of what he terms a 'realpolitik of reason' (Bourdieu 1998). To be truly scientific, however, involves a reflexive analysis which includes taking the field of 'science', alongside that of the academic and intellectual field, as an area of study and particularly a questioning of the norm of disinterestedness (Merton 1996) of scientific activity. For Bourdieu, intellectuals (or scientists or academics) have 'disinterested interests' or an 'interest in disinterestedness' (Bourdieu 1993). The particular issue at stake within the scientific field is that of *scientific authority*, the struggle to impose one's own definition of 'science' or what is collectively recognized as scientific work.

It is the scientific field which, as the locus of a political struggle for scientific domination, assigns each researcher, as a function of his position within it, his indissociably political and scientific problems and his methods ... Every scientific 'choice' – the choice of the area of research, the choice of methods, the choice of the place of publication ... is in one respect ... a political investment strategy, directed, objectively at least, toward maximisation of strictly scientific profit, i.e., of potential recognition by the agent's competitor-peers.

(Bourdieu 1984: 262)

In order to produce a truly scientific 'science' one must ignore the 'official fiction' of 'pure disinterestedness' which is claimed to operate within the scientific field. Instead one must analyse in detail the 'struggles and strategies, interests and profits' which structure the field. A truly reflexive science would involve the sociologists' own stakes in the 'game' and identify the structural position from which they make claims. This uncovering of the interests of scientists, Bourdieu believes, may result in a disenchantment but it is a necessary step towards what he terms a sociological utopianism which would be a 'rational and politically conscious use of the limits of freedom afforded by a true knowledge of social laws and especially of the historical conditions of validity' (Bourdieu 1989).

Bourdieu does not want to encourage disenchantment with scientific aims but instead wants to strengthen the possibility of scientific knowledge of the social world. Similarly, he does not want to expose the 'interests' of academics as a means of limiting the power of the academic field and the institutional bases of that power, but to strengthen its claim to the authority of legitimization awarded it. This will be instituted only by the continuation of a scientific field which rewards scientific activities and strategies, but also includes a reflexive study of that field and the constant epistemological questioning demanded (Bourdieu 1998). He intends to question the disinterestedness of the academic scholar, unsettle the notion of the scholastic point of view and ensure that this perspective is 'alive to the character, lineage and space of other points of view' (Kenway and McLeod 2004). Bourdieu is right to make such a plea for the need for reflexivity in all of the ways described, particularly in relation to better understanding the multiplicity of different vantage points of positioning of researchers and researched, and for academics to see themselves as fully enmeshed in the complexities of social life and not by definition able to hold a privileged perspective. Such a position is hard won rather than bestowed and demands a constant process of reflexive questioning.

With regard to this charge of a taken-for-granted disinterestedness, which characterizes academic belief, however, it may be possible that Bourdieu has overstated the case. His concern that homo academicus would be a 'book for burning' because of its potential to expose the enchanted world of academia was perhaps an exaggeration. It is possible to argue that academics are more than capable of reflecting on their interests within the academic world, for themselves, their institutions and their discipline despite a propensity to make claims otherwise. Reflexivity in at least some of these forms is more commonly considered within higher education research (Becher and Trowler 2001).

Despite the immense potential and generation of new ideas for looking at the social world that Bourdieu's thinking tools provide, they cannot be applied unproblematically. There are many unanswered questions and complex issues that arise in attempting to utilize these concepts and it is worth exploring some of these in more depth.

Limitations and possibilities for applying Bourdieu's 'thinking tools'

There are few studies which have attempted to replicate a similar type of analysis to that done in Homo Academicus in different national contexts. However, as stated earlier more use is now made of his ideas in applying them to the study of higher education (Robbins 1993; Zipin 1999; Deer 2003; Naidoo 2004).

In attempting to engage with and utilize his thinking tools, there has been as much critique and questioning as there has insight and revelation (Calhoun, LiPuma et al. 1993). These critiques will be explored in-depth in order to raise further questions about how Bourdieu's ideas can be usefully engaged to explore systems of higher education.

The first issue concerns the idea of 'structure' or 'field' which simultaneously seems to cover a wide variety of social arrangements from 'small regularities through to massive institutions' (Grenfell and James 1998). Similarly, it is not always clear how a particular field is defined. Part of Bourdieu's form of analysis is to look at the boundaries between fields and the means by which they interrelate. However, it is not always clear, given Bourdieu's insistence that it is necessary to bracket the common sense (doxic) or semi-scientific categorizations of the social world, exactly how 'fields' should be delineated. For example, one can talk of the 'academic field', the 'university field' and the 'intellectual field'. At the same time there can be sub-fields such as the 'philosophy field' and the 'biology field' but can the social relations and groupings of a sub-specialisms of biology also count as a sub-field, and where can you draw the line? Grenfell and James (2003), for example, refer to educational research as a field, a complex delineation which can be seen as a subset of the field of education in terms of methods and methodology or as a field which traverses the variety of educational areas and sub-specialisms.

Obviously, for Bourdieu, fields are not fixed and indeed, the changing boundaries and definitions are one of the main subjects of sociological study. However, it is not entirely clear how one can make the argument for the existence of a particular field. This process also seems tautological in that a field is defined as a space where there is a social struggle for symbolic capital and the forms of capital for which agents compete is defined by the field. Likewise, it can be argued that since anything can be defined as symbolic capital then nothing (or anything) can be discovered.

Naidoo (2004) also makes the point, as others have done, that the 'arbitrariness of content' within a social field and what is deemed as being worthwhile 'capital' can be problematic as there is no firm grounding for understanding what counts as socially meaningful and valuable within a field, as it is constantly in flux. This is an undoubtedly valid critique of the concept of field and its relationship to symbolic capital and one which does not produce any unproblematic resolutions. Naidoo (2004) is right to point to the use made of Bernstein's work to better understand the complex relation between the substance, the content of a social field and the social relations within that field. However, critiques have also been made of work such as that of Becher, which to some extent reduced an understanding of these communities to the 'epistemological characteristics of the knowledge domains' and was verging, therefore, on essentialist notions (Becher and Trowler 2001).

In order to understand Bourdieu's reluctance and refusal to resort to any foundational concepts or essential features of any aspect of the social world, we must return to the fundamental belief in a relational understanding of the social world and what Fowler calls his 'perspectivally enriched realism' such that, he argues, the 'real is relational'. There is a reality, there is a knowable social world but this can only be accessed and reported on from a particular perspective, a certain vantage point and ideas and events can only be understood in relation to what surrounds them. For Bourdieu, the only constant in any field is that it is a site of struggle but the terms and conditions of that struggle within any given field have to be periodically explored and investigated.

The problem, claim Dreyfus and Rabinow (1993), is that, firstly, Bourdieu must give up the notion that the struggle for symbolic capital is the sum total of what constitutes human beings and the social world, and secondly, that he must abandon the claim to be doing 'scientific sociology'. There can be no 'objective', scientific position from which the sociologist can speak, or can illuminate the 'true' motivations behind social action which does not simply claim 'scientific (and therefore symbolic) profits' for the sociologist. Many of these arguments become circuitous and tautological but one clear aspect is that Bourdieu is consistent in his thinking and, therefore, does not resort to essentialist or foundationalist means of providing explanations.

A further problem in Bourdieu's work leads to the issue of dispositions (habitus) and the extent to which it can be argued that the 'natural bent' driving the motivation of agents is conscious or unconscious. The awareness of the determinations of their actions may only be partly experienced by agents so that it is semi-conscious. Bourdieu argues that agents have an understanding and attach meanings to their action in the social world, which is legitimate, but for him this is only one part of the truth of the social world. Interviews with social agents, therefore, offer insightful discourse on a particular point of view but it is a 'point of view' and the social scientist must uncover the forces, which are driving the discourse (the struggles and strategies within the field(s) within which the agent is positioned). The scientist must provide a point of view on a point of view.

This issue of the consciousness that individuals have of their motivations and interests driving their action in the social world is a complex and contested one. Sweetman (2003) argues for the idea of a 'reflexive habitus', whereby individuals are consciously more able to reflect and to some degree override and change the determining processes of their primary habitus. He even uses the example of the RAE as a process that on the one hand reduces the autonomy of academics, while on the other encouraging them to be more reflexive about their positioning within the academic field. Mouzelis (2000) in particular has provided a useful critique of this confusion over the semi-conscious awareness of motivation and interest, which as he argues is also linked to Bourdieu's 'highly idiosyncratic' use of the term 'strategy'.

> Neither is it surprising that he uses the notion of strategy in a highly idiosyncratic manner ... stressing the fact that strategies for him have a non-conscious, non-calculating character ... Bourdieu argues in response the most profitable strategies are usually those produced without calculations, and in the illusion of the most absolute 'sincerity', by a habitus objectively fitted to the objective structures. The strategies without calculation produce an important secondary advantage for those who can scarcely be called their authors: the social approval accruing to an apparent disinterestedness.
>
> (Mouzelis 2000: 752)

This implies, therefore, to some degree, that Bourdieu would accept that individuals have 'semi-conscious' strategies and calculations to accumulate forms of capital but perhaps that not only are the most 'profitable' strategies those which are produced without conscious design because the field will reward those who appear to be without interest, but furthermore that the subtleties of 'knowing' how to position oneself in order to maximize the profit demands a more than conscious understanding of the symbolic capital within the field. For Bourdieu, individuals are 'sincere' about what they are doing – the substance and the content of their field has meaning for them as do the social profits of that intense and passionate involvement.

A further point which Mouzelis (2000) argues is that three levels must be addressed in order to understand social action. Following Bourdieu, he identifies the 'normative logic of my position' and the 'practical logic of my habitus/disposition' and to this he argues that a third must be added, which is the 'rational-strategying logic of the unfolding interactive situation'. This unfolding interactive situation is for Mouzelis the events that happen within institutions. It demands to some extent a fuller understanding of the material conditions and everyday practices by which individuals negotiate their positions and strategies within significant interactions. Mouzelis (2000) illustrates his arguments in relation to his own position with the

London School of Economics (LSE) and his fictitious but plausible attempts to reform the assessment practices within the institution (the examination reform game).

> Given this unfolding game between reformers, radicals and supporters of the status quo, my actual practices in relation to this game will be shaped not only by my position or my dispositions, but also by the dynamics of the interactive situation. Given a certain balance of forces between the three groups, I might decide (together with equally-minded colleagues or students) to put into action a rational-purposive plan of building alliances between reformers and radicals, while at the same time creating divisions in the conservative camp. In order to explain my engaging in this type of activity, the notion of habitus is not enough.
>
> (Mouzelis 2000: 755)

Naidoo (2003) also argues that Bourdieu does not give enough 'illumination of university practices'. There is definitely a case to be made that individuals are not just the embodiment of their dispositions and likewise they do not just hold fixed positions but have to defend and negotiate the terms of their positions against an ever-changing and fluid landscape. To this end, therefore, an analysis of individual and institutional practices or, as Mouzelis outlines it, the active or syntagmatic strategying becomes significant.

This argument is also made by Hallett (2003) who analyses symbolic power at the meso level of organization culture by combining the work of Bourdieu, focusing on 'practice' with that of Goffman, who theorizes 'interaction'. He is interested in the ongoing 'negotiated order' that is played out within institutions and argues that, 'embedded in context, valued practices become the basis of legitimacy, legitimacy that negotiators deploy as the symbolic power to define the situation and influence future practices' (Hallett 2003: 136). These debates are central to this project as the main focus of study is the institutional practices and interactions within universities and university departments.

Explicit use is made of Bourdieu's thinking tools within this study. However, the critiques and reservations raised by those who have engaged with his work have raised new and interesting questions. Three significant areas of debate will be engaged with (but perhaps not definitively answered). Firstly, in relation to the concept of 'field', the system of higher education will be taken as a field but within this can appear distinct disciplinary fields and it is assumed (as Bourdieu would argue) that no field is fixed but can be understood only by the continuing struggles to define and delimit membership criteria. Secondly, in relation to the different forms of capital, the key forms of capital to be utilized will be academic capital and research capital (adapted from scientific capital), these will broadly remain within the definitions provided by Bourdieu that academic capital shall include all the necessary roles and status involved in the reproduction of the higher education system and research capital will involve all aspects informing prestige and status in knowledge production. Finally, there is the question of the conscious or unconscious strategying of individuals as a means of constructing and expressing their academic habitus. Given the critiques (Mouzelis 2000, Naidoo 2003, Sweetman 2004), it seems clear that the subjective experiences of the academic habitus cannot be separated from an understanding of how that is determined by the macro level but also that of the university institutional meso level and so this issue of strategying must be explored at the conscious as well as the perhaps unconscious level.

The UK higher education field and the RAE: dispelling 'illusio' and creating an embodied RAE academic practice?

The central concern of this book is the changing structures and management of UK higher education institutions, particularly in relation to research and the conditions of academic work and academic identity in response to significant policy changes, such as, the introduction of the RAE. One of the central guiding questions in this book is: to what extent has the RAE served to dispel the 'illusio' of academic life? How far has the game of disciplinary research or the game of university life been taken over by the performative demands and criteria of the RAE game? In relation to this, in what ways has the academic habitus been influenced by changing rewards, or prizes. How far has the symbolic value of the RAE taken over so that it has now been established as the 'main game' that determines university status and the value of academic work? Has there been a disenchantment of the 'unconscious bent' of the academic habitus such that the accumulation of symbolic capital has become a more 'conscious' and 'rational' process? To what extent can this be evidenced in the rational-strategying of university managers and academic staff in their response to demands of the RAE? These questions will be investigated through an analysis of the practices and interactions of academics and academic- managers within Royal County University and Golden County University.

5
Institutional Management of Research: the game of reputation and resources

research has been an unmanaged activity in the past and it is becoming managed now because of this kind of impulse. But I am not sure, well I think the heart of the thing is that institutions themselves have to decide on what strategic management of research involves. The trouble is that at the moment the RAE is a tool ... it is the only management tool they have because it gives you a set of criteria, it gives you a kind of output measure, it kind of is a way of running it. And if it didn't exist I don't know what you'd do. But I mean it isn't, I think you have to be concerned that that is something in a sense really that is run by us to assess and fund, which is the fuel for their strategic missions.

(Senior HEFCE official, speaking prior to the 2001 RAE)

we have all been guilty of using the RAE as a lever to get change and to get people to do things and to focus on things. I think it is not the RAE in itself, but probably the way it has been used. There can't be any heads of department up to vice-chancellors who haven't at some point gone on about the RAE and the importance of research and getting a research profile etc.

(Vice-Chancellor, Royal County University)

There is much evidence from literature cited in Chapter 2 that universities are now more managed institutions, although much of the research has also demonstrated the complexity of characterizing the different forms of management and in terms of understanding the coexisting dualities of the competing ideational structures of collegiality and managerialism as they are expressed though individuals such as the manager-academic (Deem et al. 2001) or the professional manager or in the idea of management administration (Bargh, Bocock et al. 2000).

This chapter addresses the role of management of research within the case study institutions of Royal County University and Golden County University. As indicated, however, the question of management within universities is a complex one and I explore the continuing role of the collegial ideal with these institutions and at least some of the departments. At the time of my fieldwork in 1997–9, institutions were to some degree still at an embryonic change towards what might be termed 'new' managerialism (Deem et al. 2001). It is an interesting time to study, therefore, as it is possible to see the beginnings of change and the struggles and competing interests at work, which at the time of writing (2005) may be less apparent as managerialism within universities has perhaps a much tighter grip. Middlehurst (2004) contrasts the 'stronger corporate sector models, favouring executive management structures (over committees)' championed by the Lambert Review (2003) versus the organically grown 'university entrepreneurialism' posited by Clark (2004). Perhaps the backward nod to collegial ideals is already a distant memory at the beginning of the twenty-first century but it is perhaps instructive to look in more depth at the struggles evident and the changing discourses apparent at a time of immense change in the late 1990s.

This chapter focuses on the institutional managers and the role of university research committees in relation to research management and policy. This analysis highlights the competing struggles between managerialist forms of organization and collegial ideals evident at the institutional and department level and their implications. Much of the previous research looking at university research policies and strategies has relied on questionnaire surveys to collect data. The aim here is to provide more in-depth, ethnographic detail to institutional life. Each university is discussed in turn and then the focus is on individual departments. The analysis is based on data collected from interviews with senior managers and attendance at university and departmental committee meetings as shown in Table 5.1.

Table 5.1 Details of interviews with senior management and research committee meetings attended at each university

Institution	Departments	Data Collection
Golden County University		Vice-Chancellor
		Pro Vice-Chancellor for Research
	Biology Department	Head of Department
		Department Research Committee
	Sociology Department	Head of Department
		Department Research Committee
	English Department	Head of Department
Royal County University		Vice-Chancellor
		Dean of Research
		University Research Committee
	Biology Department	Head of Department
		Department Research Committee
	Sociology Department	Head of Department
	English Department	Head of Department

As argued in Chapter 2, the political model of the university may also prove fruitful in understanding the complexities and struggles of decision making in university life and in understanding the university field as a site of struggle of different ideational and managerial structures (Bourdieu 1988). A good demonstration of the highly politicized and competitive environment of modern universities was given during my meeting with the VC of Golden County University, when upon my arrival he was quite sceptical and wanted to ask me some questions before proceeding. The first question was which other universities I was researching, to which I replied that this was confidential. This became almost the standard question that was asked of me the minute I sat down in someone's office. When I gave my usual reply to one head of department, he replied 'good, otherwise you would not be researching here'. The VC of Golden County University, however, had many more questions that he wanted to ask, so his interview continued as detailed in my field notes:

> He then asked a variety of questions including what use would be made of the research, who would see it and who had I spoken to in the university, what was the procedure? It wasn't clear to me at this stage exactly what he was getting at so I talked about the steps I had taken to ensure confidentiality and how I had spoken to the Pro V-Cs for research in the first instance in each case, the head of departments and then academics ... He seemed only slightly reassured by this. He further explicated that this kind of information [being asked for in the interview schedule that I had sent him in advance] was very political and that we are operating in a competitive environment. He said you are from the sociology department at Warwick, who are interested in the RAE and what other people are doing. It was at this stage that I realized the implication of what he was saying, that I was potentially a spy for the sociology department at Warwick. I was rather stunned by this and had no prepared answer. I think he could tell that I was genuinely shocked. He mentioned that my supervisor at least would see the data and I knew there was no simple answer to this except to reiterate that confidentiality was taken very seriously.
>
> (VC fieldnotes, Golden County University)

There certainly are ethical issues involved in this and the VC had legitimate concerns, but this does also highlight the extent of competitive behaviour endemic within universities in relation to the RAE. Perhaps, not surprisingly this VC did not want the interview to be recorded and by necessity of his busy schedule the interaction was fairly brief but by the end of the interview rather amicable.

In light of McNay's (1995) table of university models (including collegium, bureaucracy, corporation and enterprise), the political model possibly sits most easily with the corporate one. It is interesting to explore, therefore, the extent to which other characteristics of this model (reliance on a senior management team, leadership of the Chief Executive, working parties and performance indicators) predominate at each of the case study institutions (see Table 2.4).

Institutional management of research at Golden County University

Golden County University is a pre-1992 institution and has been successful in the RAE and so in the 'main game' of research eminence would certainly position itself as a research intensive university. The VC of Golden County University proclaimed that his vision for the university was that it was currently a successful research-led university and the aim was to continue to improve on this. In terms of how this was to be achieved, he argued that a long-term plan must be in place such that any department not able to reach the highest grade by the next RAE would be aiming to do so in the subsequent one. The common perception of staff interviewed in this university was that the VC expected all departments to be aiming for at least 5 rating.

A significant university policy on research had been to 'invest in professorial appointments' and he believed that the key to a successful RAE submission is 'good staff', and these were primarily 'innovative research workers'. These ideas were echoed by the pro-VC for research at Golden County University, who talked enthusiastically about the need to take a long-term view for creating research excellence within departments and in particular creating a positive 'can do culture' within the university. He was keen on the importance of creating a critical mass of researchers and for them to work in teams, which can provide a more 'collegial rather than competitive environment'. Despite the rather guarded and suspicious introduction by the VC, both these senior managers at Golden County University minimized talk of the competitive element potentially induced by the RAE and possible attempts by the university to engineer or use particular strategies to win in the RAE game. In some regard these responses could be analysed as an attempt to distance themselves from any perception of involvement in conscious RAE strategying with attempts to align themselves more clearly with greater symbolic capital accrued by the more 'unconscious' pursuit of research excellence.

There is obvious concern by the V-C and Pro V-C to ensure that the current success in research continues and improves. In a more self-assured and confident manner they had their eye on the longer term as players who know that they are likely winners and the only question is by how much they will win. As Bourdieu argues, like a good tennis player they watch not where the ball is but where they anticipate it will be. There is less emphasis in the discourse of these two individuals on the need to organize and manage research in a strategic way to meet demands for the RAE.

As I was not granted access to the university research committee meetings at Golden County University, and the interviews with senior managers were by necessity short, it was difficult to get a sense of the formal decision-making process in terms of research. However, disagreement over the RAE submission for the biology department demonstrated a conflict with the biology HOD and senior management. Professor Meggitt, the HOD at the time of the 1996 RAE submission took a leading role in the biology RAE submission and policy formation and was described by one member of staff as being 'obsessed' with getting a high rating for the department in the RAE. Professor Meggitt himself maintained that he had made a 'personal declaration' to increase the research rating of the department after becoming head.

He related the events of the RAE submission and the decisions surrounding it almost as a personal crusade with him steering a steady course of decision making, faced with disagreements both from the university research committee and the biology department research committee. He took the final decision on the RAE submission believing that 'it was my responsibility to present it and I was going to take the flak and so I did it the way I thought I should'. He had calculated that the income for the department would be six times greater if the department increased their rating in the 1996 RAE. For this reason, Professor Meggitt felt justified in taking what he believed to be the best decisions for the department in order to maximize income. This could only be done at the cost of submitting a smaller number of staff, thereby achieving less financial return with a lower number of staff submitted. He believed that this was of lesser significance than the overall quality rating which was considered to be the most important goal. Professor Meggitt explains the disagreements over this decision in the following way:

Professor Meggitt: And so we ended up missing a total of seven people off the submission out of xx so we submitted xx instead of xx because in our judgement that gave us the best overall return ... we viewed it as a game where (a) it was essential to become a higher rating, and (b) it was essential within that to maximize income. And we viewed it as exactly that and the strategy was to achieve those aims and we viewed that as more important than the university or the Vice-Chancellor's desire to have it as a full department representation. Keep asking...
Interviewer: So you just went ahead in terms of the ...?
Professor Meggitt: Well, we said we were going to. I sent a letter to the university research committee saying that we were intending to do that and they said you shouldn't, and we said we should. And another department ended up following our example. And I think the result shows that we were quite right because we will be known as a [highly] rated department ... [and income was increased]. So for all reasons it was the right strategy. But that was one that was made basically by me as head of department, I would have done that, eh, I didn't have total support in the department. A lot of people felt that is was really bad

news for the seven missed off and we had to deal with that but it seemed to me that that was the right strategy.

(Professor Meggit, HoD, Biology, Golden County University)

Other heads of department at Golden County University testify to the steering from the VC and the research committee on putting forward a full complement of staff in their RAE submission and concurrently aiming for the top RAE grade. Achieving both these aims was extremely difficult as the HoD was quick to point out and as the example above demonstrates. In the conflict surrounding how best to achieve the highest score, the HoD was determined to struggle for the interests of his department. The desire to increase the symbolic capital and the economic capital return to the biology department created disagreement at the different managerial levels, although there was no conflict of interest but a conflict over how best to achieve the mutual interest of biology achieving a high RAE grade with the optimum number of staff submitted. As the latter part of Professor Meggitt's explanation indicated, however, this did cause major conflict within his own department. This point will be returned to in Chapter 6.

Once the RAE grades were awarded and universities given the commensurate funding, there was further conflict and disagreement at Golden County University in terms of how this money was distributed (or not) back to departments. Struggling to gain this reward seemed to be related to ability to argue one's case with the VC and senior management, but it was not easy for me as a researcher to access the process, nor even to get accounts of it. The HoD of the sociology department retorted indignantly, when questioned about the redistribution of research money back to departments, 'What money, I haven't seen any money!'

The line of command in terms of research strategy and organization at Golden County University seemed to be quite centrally determined with respect to the expectations placed on departments to meet the research plans of the university. And despite the Biology HoD's insistence on ignoring the demands of the university research committee that he submit a full representation of his staff, decision making seems highly centralized. The distribution of research funding also seems to be very tightly guarded and controlled. The mode of operation seems to fit very well with the corporate model (McNay 1995). The central directive is the power of the chief executive and the senior management team and, in relation to the RAE, a clear performance indicator with all departments being expected to achieve a high rating. The political and tactical underpinnings of this are clearly demonstrated, although it is denied that strategic positioning was influenced merely in response to RAE demands.

The strategies appear to have been extremely successful as Golden County University attained significantly improved RAE ratings in the 2001 RAE, as shown in Table 5.2.

The main improvement was in departments moving from a 4 to 5 rating with over 30% of departments getting a 5 or 5* rating in the 1996 RAE

Table 5.2 Overall change in institutional RAE grades from 1996 to 2001 at Golden County University

Grade	% of awards in 1996	% of awards in 2001
5*	9%	13%
5	26%	65%
4	48%	13%
3a	9%	9%
3b	9%	0%
2	0%	0%
1	0%	0%

compared with over 70% in the 2001 RAE. Strategies put in place to boost research after the 1996 RAE were certainly successful. Funds invested in infrastructure, new appointments and research expenditure were targeted well and the vast majority of departments improved their rating.

Institutional management of research at Royal County University

Royal County University was described by the vice-chancellor as 'having emerged from the old polytechnic sector . . . with a reputation that is largely built around teaching.' In terms of a research profile, the VC stated that 'we are not doing badly as a university, but it is still an emerging part of the university's profile and it is one that we are currently focusing on a lot more than has happened in the past'. However, he also argued that in terms of the research profile of Royal County University, it is primarily an 'applied university . . . not a blue skies oriented university', so he maintained, 'we have got to recognise our niche, our potential, which is primarily in applied areas'. This belief is echoed by the pro-VC for research, who said, 'I don't want to be hung on this being exclusively true because it's not, but by and large the nature of our research is far more strategic and applied than it is, eh, what I suppose you might describe as blue skies.'

There is recognition, therefore, given the historical circumstances of the institution, that research was not necessarily the main strength of the institution and where research success does exist it would tend to be more applied than pure or 'blue skies' in orientation. There was also a strong belief that the developing research profile of Royal County University could be greatly enhanced, despite significant limitations and the lack of research strength within particular areas. The VC proclaimed that despite a modest research profile, there was a 'determination for it to grow' and 'it is now a very important part of our strategic plan, which we will do something about'. But it was clear that any plans must be long term, as the VC explains:

And it is not just aimed at RAE, that's about development of the institution and to some extent not worrying about the next RAE because we won't have gone a huge way by then, it is the one after I suppose, as more adds up and the one after that I would like to see mainly 4s and 5s ... I think one thing we have got to do is identify areas where there is a chance of doing well ... So I am optimistic that we will have a better profile in the RAE next time but it is not the key driver, I think it is a useful signpost to see where we have got to but our research development plan must be longer term than that ... It will be useful when we get to that signpost and see how we are and I would hope that we have improved quite a lot in a number of areas. But it will take a bit longer to get to where we want to be.

(VC, Royal County University)

Despite the realistic expectations and recognition of institutional strengths and weaknesses the VC at Royal County University had similar expectations for research success as the VC at Golden County University, although recognizing that it may take a little longer. This may suggest that most, if not all, institutions aim for success in the RAE not just within clearly identified areas of strength but as far as possible across all departments. If this ambition were to be magnified across most, if not all universities, then clearly this would not fit with the HEFCE plan of further research selectivity. The VC argued, quite clearly, that the RAE encourages convergence of institutions rather than diversity. The optimism was surprising, particularly since the VC at Royal County University was quite candid in articulating the obstacles that might impede this development both in terms of the external constraints caused by competition, scarce resources and the currency of research capital and institutional status that was evident and the internal constraints, including the need to build up research active staff, generate more income by applying for research funds and lack of funds to generate more research activity.

Professors in my view are research leaders and it takes time to build them up, it takes time for them to build up their research teams and so on. So it is a slow process and we are not in a position ... to go out and buy people in, put large amounts of money into supporting new research initiatives. We can't do that and we haven't got the money to do it. It is one of the things that new universities haven't got and old universities have.

(VC, Royal County University)

The lack of funds also meant that the university was unable to buy people out, to give golden handshakes and retirement pensions as some universities have been able to do, so it was accepted by the VC that it will be a slower process for Royal County University, but the end goal remains the same, that is, to achieve high grades for the maximum number of departments in the next (2001) and/or future RAE. What was the major strategic research plan, who made decisions and how was it implemented? There are two major issues that I would like to explore in relation to this: firstly, the role of senior managers in directing activities and research strategies within departments and secondly, the role of the research committee in taking decisions on research strategy.

As with many of the examples discussed in this book, at all levels of management within the universities studied, there was a dual rhetoric of research planning, strategy, direction and the extent to which this can be achieved with a light touch or a 'soft' management touch. The major strategies include, conducting research audits, which can help to give a clear idea of where each department stands. The Pro V-C will aim to take an increasingly more prominent role in working closely with HoDs in terms of their planning and giving feedback and direction:

> then that is built into the planning process also in terms of providing concrete feedback ... in terms of what (the departments) are doing, whether they are likely to reach their aspirations, whether we are happy with the way in which we are moving. I think we have been probably until now, lightish touch on where they are going or how ... We are a very devolved university. It is always difficult in devolved institutions to give a sort of direction than in a more centralized organization. So we are starting to become a bit more, not such light touch on the tiller as it were, we are starting to get a bit more intrusive.
>
> (V-C, Royal County University)

He argued, that it was not about giving direction but perhaps giving a 'push or a steer' to help departments to focus more on the strategies they were developing and decisions they were making, for example in relation to new appointments in particular research areas within a department.

Having access to the university research committees at Royal University also allowed for the possibility of obtaining some insight into the process of decision making on major issues concerning research strategy and planning. Or perhaps the correct phrase would be decision-informing since this research committee was described as the forum by which the Central Management Group (CMG) could be advised. One particularly significant discussion took place at many of the research committee meetings that I attended. This was in relation to how to distribute the Quality Research (QR) funding to departments. One scheme was to give the funds back to departments more equally and in proportion to their achievements in the RAE (and numbers of research active staff). Another idea was to further top-slice the funding and to give extra resources to those departments who had performed well in the RAE, thus operating a process of selectivity. A fairly long-running debate took place at the research committee on this issue and in the final instance participants were asked to vote for, or against, the alternative policy of top-slicing. The decision on this policy was to be taken by schools and not the CMG. The voting went 11 against the alternative policy, 4 voting in favour and 1 abstention. One participant argued contrarily that the top-slicing should be taken from the 'winners' and distributed back to the lower RAE rated departments. Another was concerned about the effect on the 'many' who had not achieved a high RAE score. Those voting in favour of the policy were the ones most likely to gain. But there was some anger that the possible funds promised from CMG to match the top-slicing were not to be made available so the actual amount was significantly reduced. There follows an extract from the discussion highlights the issues faced.

Participant 1: Strong argument for Top-up Policy. If university is serious about improving research profile then departments have to be supported. It is difficult enough for high-rated departments to stand still. 8% doesn't seem a huge sacrifice for something that could yield substantial returns.

Participant 2: It is a democracy here but my sympathies lie with [what has just been said]. My individual position, with £200,000 per year you cannot be very effective, need to push 3 and 4 [RAE rated] winners. You need £500,000 to be effective.

Participant 3: Argument for [Alternative] Policy is for investment not for robbing low rated departments. May gain 2 or 3 [departments rated as 5] but will endanger other lower-rated departments from starting off. Overheads – large amount for infrastructure but the rest for something else. That is not investment.

(Royal County University, research committee meeting)

There were clear differentials in positioning of staff across departments and their place within a high- or low-ranking department may have clear implications for what they perceive as 'fair' in funding distribution. There were conflicting interests and strategies, therefore, in terms of how best to allocate research funding across different departments and these were clearly articulated within these research committee meetings. However, in this particular instance, it would appear that the decision was taken fairly democratically or collegially, by the representatives at the research committee (as a model of restricted collegiality, Bush 1998).

The strategies and policies for research at Royal County University worked to improve the ratings of departments in the 2001 RAE as shown in Table 5.3.

The percentage of departments gaining less than a 3a dropped from 75% in 1996 to 37% in 2001, whereas the percentage gaining a 3a/4 rose from 25% to 48% and a modest 11% with 5/5* grades. So almost 60% of departments gained a 3a or higher in the 2001 RAE compared with only 25% in 1996. The trajectory of improvement was certainly quite substantially in the direction that the VC had planned. However, a change to the funding mechanism of the 2001 RAE meant that departments rated 3a or lower received no funding at all and for those rated at 4, the amount of

Table 5.3 Overall change in institutional RAE grades from 1996 to 2001 at Royal County University

Grade	% of awards in 1996	% of awards in 2001
5*	0%	4%
5	0%	7%
4	7%	22%
3a	18%	26%
3b	30%	18%
2	30%	15%
1	15%	4%

funding was reduced relative to 1996 levels. This change in policy would have had serious implications for Royal County University and other universities like it, in that all the hard work and effort put into gaining higher grades would have been financially disastrous. Only 33% of departments achieved grades that would attract QR funding at Royal County compared to 91% of departments at Golden County University. Furthermore, those departments in the 33% at Royal County getting grade 4 or more were all relatively small and would, therefore, attract only minimal funding, given that the funding mechanism is calculated based on the numbers of research active staff submitted.

There are many differences in leadership styles and processes of decision making between these two institutions. Interestingly, despite the claims of collegiality by some within Golden County University, the evidence in this example seems to confirm a more collegial spirit in terms of decision making (although necessarily restricted by some degree) at Royal County University, concurring with previous arguments made that this more egalitarian decision making can be found at the post-1992 institutions (Reay 2004). It seemed a more common practice, at least with regard to research, that decision making at Golden County University would take place within smaller more elite committees and groups than at Royal County University where committees seemed larger and more egalitarian (Bush 1998). However, my access to committees was more restricted at Golden County University so it is difficult to make any definitive statement. This links perhaps with the significant difference between the two universities in terms of how research funding is redistributed back to departments, with Golden County University having a less transparent approach, dependent, one would assume, on overall university strategy; and to some degree at least, the more transparent and equitable system at Royal County University.

At this level of institutional organization, both universities seem to come remarkably close to the corporate model (McNay 1995), where even the more devolved decision making at the research committee forum at Royal County University is restricted to a position of *decision-informing* rather than *decision-taking*. The examples given here are clearly too limited to make generalisations but they at least provide some insight into the behind-the-scenes processes and struggles at each institution.

It is necessary to emphasize that in looking only at policies and organizational strategies in relation to only one of the major roles of the institution – research – a one-sided picture may perhaps be represented. It seems clear that the symbolic capital afforded by success in the RAE is of primary importance to these institutional heads and managers. Within the higher education field both institutions are struggling to position themselves in relation to the 'main game' of research intensity or research success (reputation). For this reason, perhaps, there seems to be a tightened control of research strategy and policy at each institutions, with the pro-VC and the research committee taking a directive role. Central to the strategies for success are the mobilization of relevant forms of economic/material capital in terms of generating more income for the university and distributing of funds, and social capital in terms of appointments, creating a critical mass of researchers and where necessary (and if possible) making redundancies or changing contracts (resources).

How was this received within departments? It has already been illustrated how one HoD successfully battled against the strategic rules set down by the research committee. What, then, does research management at the departmental level involve? It is this question that I now address, taking in turn the three disciplines. The following section focuses only on the management structures and organization of research within each of the departments. Department research strategies are explored in more depth in the Chapter 6.

Management of research activities in the biology departments

Golden County University biology department

At Golden County University there was a close direct relationship between departments and central management. The central role played by the head of department indicated a more managerial form of decision-making within the department. The previous chairman of the Teaching Committee from 1992 to 1996 described a parallel existence of two forms of power structure within the department, the 1960s 'democratic organization' of the subject committee and the 1990s 'line management' style of leadership by the head of department. Rather than fitting into either a 'collegial' or 'managerial' model of decision making, therefore, it is possible to see how both can be seen to operate in different ways and at different levels within this department.

In the Biology department at Golden County University, the research committee was responsible for monitoring the research activity within the department, with the head of department taking special interest in those members of staff who are 'struggling' with their research agenda. Professor Meggitt described this process as follows:

> I mean first of all there is making sure that the staff know what is expected of them. And for that the research committee sees each member of staff each year and basically, eh, basically gets that member of staff to have drawn up a plan for their research for the year with their goals on it and to discuss that with them. Some years I have seen a member of staff as well and I would certainly expect to see members of staff who were having trouble in producing the quality of output that they should be and talking naturally with them. So there is quite a lot of making sure people know what the expectancy is and where that should be going.
>
> But the intention is, I don't know what other people in the department will tell you, but the intention is to do it with as light a touch as possible and to intrude in that when it seems necessary. There is quite a strong direction given I think in what people are expected to achieve but, eh, there is a great deal of freedom in how they achieve it.
>
> (Professor Meggitt, HoD Biology, Golden County University)

This form of monitoring is testament to the increase in what has been referred to as 'managerial surveillance' (Harley and Lowe 1998) of academic work. There are conflicting metaphors used by Professor Meggitt to describe the managerial process, with a 'light' touch being used to guide the activities of members of staff at the same time as a 'strong' direction was given as to the ends those activities should meet. The opposition between the professional ideal of autonomy and self-determination within academic life is increasingly being questioned as new management structures and practices are introduced. It is argued by some commentators, that these management structures are 'predicated on weakening professional control structures' (Parker and Jary 1994). These practices include the monitoring and controlling of academic work. The extent to which academic staff experience or perceive their work to be controlled by themselves or outside influences depends crucially on their position within the department and their engagement in research activities.

In the biology department at Golden County University a small elite group formed the research committee. This was made up of seven members of staff, the 'research stars' of the department as they were referred to by one member of staff. The seven members were mainly senior staff and were all successful researchers. Members include the head of department, five professors and one lecturer.

The research committee in the biology department at Golden County University was an important forum for decision making with regard to the 1996 RAE submission, as discussed in Chapter 7. The committee was responsible for the management and direction of research funds within the department, the formation of research policy, particularly the review of research activity within the department and the monitoring of research activity of individual members of staff. Decisions were taken on issues such as research funds for equipment, grant money, 'pump priming money' to encourage new research, and travel expenses to conferences.

Royal County University Biology Department

In the biology department at Royal County University, the decision was taken after the 1996 RAE to appoint a director of research. Prior to this the head, Professor Laing, had assumed major responsibility. Despite the fact that a director, Dr Niven, was appointed in 1996, Professor Laing made the comment during an interview that 'in some ways it is difficult to see what exactly I do now that I have everyone else doing jobs for me'. But he adds, 'I am responsible for whatever goes on in the school. Even though I have got a Research Director, I am still ultimately responsible for research.'

The research committee was formed by a group of representatives, with a member of staff representing each of the different sub-section areas. The research committee had responsibility for deciding on research strategy for the school and critically how research funding (particularly QR funding) should be utilized. The institutional policy at Royal County University was as far as possible for research funds from the RAE to be redistributed to departments (based proportionately on their grading and numbers of research active staff – after a 'top slice' had been taken by the institution). Schools were then able to decide their strategy for using this money. This contrasts with Golden County University where 'core funding' to a department is decided by the University research committee and central administration.

The level of funding given to Royal County University was much lower than that awarded to Golden County University. At Royal County University, therefore, decision making primarily centred on the funding of post-doctoral positions and funds for travel to conferences. The decision over departmental funds hinged on the extent of selectivity over who should be supported. A discussion at one research committee meeting proceeded as follows:

> *Dr Niven* maintains that the priority of the school is to ensure that the research base is solid first of all . . .

> *Dr Lockwood* says that people should outline what their own require-ments are.

> [Everyone agrees.]

> *Participant* says that everyone may not want the most expensive options.

> *Dr Niven* emphasizes that the discussion must include everyone not in the group.

Dr Summers argues quite emphatically that the department wants to achieve a (higher rating) next time and therefore must increase the international reputation. Also must 'maintain the core' or 'backbone' of the department in order to achieve this. Must look at what these people need, not as a reward but in order to maintain this core.

These 'core' people are named.

(Research committee meeting, Biology, Royal County University)

The issue of degrees of selectivity as a significant research policy is mirrored in the complex decisions faced by central management within universities and then again at the departmental research committees. Within the biology departments the issue of funding and how to distribute funds was important. The cost of equipment and maintenance of laboratories ensured that the distribution of funds remained a primary concern. The significance of material capital necessary for laboratories and also for appointing new staff is apparent within both departments and is central to the decision-making processes.

Management of research activities in the sociology departments

Golden County University Sociology Department

but you would have to be crazy to want to, I mean, the job has changed beyond recognition even in the few years I have been doing it. I can remember when it used to be a glorified office worker. Now you are expected to be a senior manager. I mean, I am supposed to be preparing a business plan, that is what it is called a business plan ... to be a glorified accountant. All the time they are trying to push administrative decisions and executive decisions down onto the department because it cost so much to do ... It has become more bureaucratic ... So we have problems getting people to agree to be head of department in the first place.

(Professor Davenport, HoD Sociology, Golden County University)

The sociology department at Golden County University was relatively small and most members of staff had been in this department for a large number of years. It was perceived by some as informal and friendly and united by a 'concern with teaching and students'. The HoD quoted above is aghast at the expectations of his role and also finds it difficult to 'manage' in any way the research activities of the staff in the department. One professor argued, that 'some staff would appreciate research advice but most are established and set in their ways'. This problem was clear during the interaction of members of staff at the departmental research committee meeting.

1st participant: OK ... em, and sorry I should have had any other business here, are you aware of applications (for funding) and stuff happening?

2nd participant: No, well in the sense that no one has asked me to sign any so I can only assume that there aren't any which is bad news.

1st participant: Yes, I mean Bob and I are developing two at the moment.

2nd participant: Right, I have been pondering about how to deal with this and in a sense the logical thing to do is what we do anyway which is send something round asking people if they are thinking of putting in grant applications and have they done so and if so how many did they apply for – that sort of thing. I am reluctant in a sense to do it because you get half the replies and you wait six months for the other half and . . .

(Research Committee meeting, Sociology, Golden County University)

There was evidence, however, that the head of department and other members of the research committee feel a sense of frustration with the lack of urgency shown by some members of staff towards the research work and the research profile of the department. For example, they discussed what to do about the lack of applications made by staff for funding.

There was clear frustration on the part of the HoD, who felt powerless to effect any change. The culture within the department, therefore, was one of individual autonomy where lecturers are left to decide on their personal research plans. As Professor Morrisey explained, it is not the 'research committee's business to determine those things'. Members of staff are seen as being well established in their field and it is for them to decide on their research strategies. Suggestions are given in relation to publications and funding but it goes no further than that. The members of staff in this sociology department have been there for a long time and so there was a strong sense (or at least expectation) of egalitarian collegiality and individual autonomy with little managerial direction.

In terms of the organization of the department and decision making there would seem to be little evidence of 'managerialism'. Although the department may not fit the description of 'pure collegiality' (Bush 1998) in the instance of research policy, there was little central (managerial) direction. The common sense of purpose revolved mainly around teaching activities and decisions over research were left largely up to the individual so long as minimal requirements for RAE submission were met. However, some radical changes were made prior to the 2001 RAE and a substantial number of new staff were employed, something which had not happened in more than 10 years. These changes resulted in an improved RAE grade for this sociology department.

Royal County University Sociology Department

The management structure at Royal County University operated more at faculty rather than department level. Departments in the social sciences are small and so managerial direction is organized mainly at the faculty level.

No, no, no, we have a [faculty] structure here which has got a federation of different departments, one of which is sociology. Em, there is some departments with a management structure introduced with the more senior staff. Sociology partly because of its values and partly because of its small size has always resisted the view of having one person being a hierarchical person and we always invest in the Chair [HoD] a lot of day-to-day power particularly for students.

(Professor McGowan, HoD Sociology, Royal County University)

In the sociology department at Royal County University, everyone was involved in the research committee, which made decisions on how research funds will be spent. It also took decisions on study leave and funds for conference attendance for members of staff. However, all of these decisions have to be approved by the HoD and must demonstrate a continuing relevance to the overall research strategy of the department and faculty. The process participation in decision-making is open to all members of staff and so in principle a form of collegial relations operates within the department, although this is subject to further managerial direction at faculty level.

Further monitoring of research activities was carried out by distributing a questionnaire to check staff progress. As Dr Nicholas explains:

As part of the planning that is going on now we distributed a questionnaire to every individual member of staff in sociology asking them to state what publications they have in the pipeline, what publications they are intending to make in the next couple of years, what external grant applications they are planning to make, where they saw their strengths, where they saw weaknesses, where there were barriers. Em, that, so, has given us baseline information on everybody and we've all agreed that we will send that questionnaire around again once a year to monitor how people are doing, whether they have achieved what they had expected. Em, and we will use that information to make decisions about who goes into the next research assessment exercise. Well, anyway, that decision will be made closer to the RAE but we can use that information to make judgements about supporting research ... If someone said that they would have certain articles submitted in the next year and it turns out in our monitoring that they haven't done that then...

(Dr Nicholas, Deputy HoD Sociology, Royal County University)

Reactions by staff to this form of monitoring largely depend on how they were positioned in relation to the expectations for research activity and whether they perceive this as supporting or threatening. The general feeling within the department was one of collegiality but this was confined to the small number of sociologists who work closely together and, generally, all participate in department meetings and can be contrasted to the rather larger and bureaucratic forms of monitoring and management that are carried out by the faculty management team.

The sociology department at Royal County University would appear to adopt a more managerial approach, compared with Golden County University. There is certainly closer monitoring of research activities at Royal County. However, the small size of each of these departments helps to create a sense of a collegial and inclusive environment, which would be perhaps impossible in a larger department.

Management of research activities in the English departments

Golden County University English Department

In the English department at Golden County University, there was an often stated belief in collegiality and respect among colleagues. The English department at Golden County University scored a high rating on the 1996 RAE. Members of staff that I spoke to believed that this result was achieved without strong managerialist pressures. This belief was reiterated by members of staff and seemed very important and critical to their self-perception and that of the department. Mr Wright, for example, compares his experiences at Golden County University with his previous institution.

> I mean, the last institution I was in really was a rather brutal one and there was a lot of the rough end of what the research assessment exercise was all about there. You know, internal rivalry and nastiness and brutal attempts to get rid of people and so on, and so on. And that really did strike me as being a very unpleasant result. Here I think it is a much more interestingly benign institution. I think in lots of ways it has been much less touched by the horrid hand of the eighties than many places. The management is much more civilized. It is interesting that, you know, it is a very good university in research terms. It is not that one model produces results and another one doesn't. This one seems to manage to be relatively civilized and be a very strong research-based university.
>
> (Mr Wright, English, Golden County University)

Mr Wright contrasted what he saw as the strong managerialist tendencies of other institutions with the relative civility of the collegial relations at Golden County University. This kind of 'contrastive rhetoric' (Hargreaves 1981) is common in many of the interviews that I conducted, where the member institution is contrasted favourably against other institutions and institutional practices. However, it is interesting to analyse the extent to which this idea is shared by other members of staff in the department and the extent to which reported practices within this department bear out the claim to collegiality.

It is not so much that staff do not believe that managerial strategies operate within the English department at Golden County University but that it was perceived to be a form of 'humane management' (Dr Ballard, deputy head of Department). In making this claim Dr Ballard was talking specifically about the university policy of having all staff research active. He stated that there was a possibility of a 're-engagement package' (teaching-only status) for those members of staff who are not research active. Just as all members of staff were expected to teach, therefore, all were expected to be research active. Professor Hadfield maintained that a full return of staff was being planned for the 2001 RAE, although not all were returned in the 1996 RAE. There was little said by Professor Hadfield or other members of staff on the decision-making process of who would and would not be included in the RAE. There was little evidence of dissent over these decisions by staff that I interviewed. Professor Pearson was the only member of staff who discussed this issue in relation to one particular person not included in the 1996 RAE. Professor Pearson, however, also reiterated the belief in 'humane management' of these issues.

However, beyond the sense of harmony present within the department was the possibility that this has been achieved by excluding non-research active staff resulting therefore in the exclusion of explicit conflicting interests within the department. Little mention is made of the number of staff (approximately one-third) who left the department to go elsewhere or had retired just before or just after the 1996 RAE. A comment from one member of staff indicated that these individuals were not research active for RAE purposes.

Well, we have meetings with our mentees outside and we have lunch with them or whatever and then we report back to the research committee. It is not terribly ... and we just say, yes, Bloggs is not a problem or whatever. I mean in our department the people who are problems have been got rid off and you know I have to say I think the whole scene is quite ghastly and no doubt you ... however, so you know the people that I am mentor for are all beavering away like mad and producing just as they should do. So the kinds of conversations that we have, in fact I can't remember back to before 1996 so I don't know if I can be of any use to you. I think we have got all this in place much more firmly after the 1996 RAE than before. I think before the 1996 RAE we did have this system but it was more haphazard and was less successful in that we had a whole lot of, a number of research inactive people. Well I think they have all gone.

(Professor Rosewall, English, Golden County University)

The expression of community and collegiality within the department may be strengthened by the more 'strong managerial' pressures from outside, the 'us' and 'them' of the department and central management of the university. The existence of a collegial spirit, therefore, may exist in a variety of forms and at different levels of institutional organization. Within the context of the English department at Golden County University, collegiality was dependent primarily on equality, particularly equality of the division of labour and equality of the worth given to these different activities. All members of staff must be involved equally in all activities and for research practices, these are defined by the importance of RAE criteria. Those individuals unable to meet these criteria would find their position very difficult and in many cases might be 'got rid off'. The 'hard end of managerialism' in relation to the RAE does therefore perhaps exist in this English department, despite the perceptions of many staff to the contrary.

As in other departments, the HoD held a database on staff research activities and the research committee required that all staff submit details of their research activities annually in the form of an 'RAE questionnaire'. So a significant amount of monitoring of research activity of staff was evident in this department, although the system of mentoring is intended to provide a culture of support rather than of monitoring.

Royal County University English Department

The English department at Royal County University like that of the sociology department is fairly small and was experienced by staff as having been friendly and collegial. It was described by one member of staff as being a department that was a 'cosy, amiable backwater', that became a place with 'tensions between colleagues generated by competitiveness', although still perceived as 'relatively civilized'. The department was managed by the faculty in terms of research activities and processes and having done relatively badly in the 1996 RAE compared with other departments, was under close scrutiny. More financial help was being given to the department to help boost research activities but this resulted in greater monitoring and high expectations from staff.

At the time of data collection, there seemed to be no clear leadership within the department (only at faculty level) and I was not allowed to attend departmental committee meetings (there was no separate research committee meeting) so it was extremely difficult to get a sense of the culture and organization of the department. However, reporting by some staff seemed to indicate that research priorities and decisions were discussed within committees where all members of the department were included. For example, issues such as the allocation of research money, time off for sabbaticals and other issues would be discussed. There seemed to be a sense of inclusiveness with regard to decision making within the department. However, one member of staff, Mr Booth commented that the notion of collegiality was a 'platonic ideal' and that this idea more realistically represents a 'sense of responsibility to each other'. He also argued that the department was on the 'brink of differentiation' with enormous tensions between those doing mainly teaching and those doing mainly research within the department. Much of this was perceived to be a result of having done badly in the 1996 RAE. The organization and management of the department was to go through substantial changes in the run up to the 2001 RAE and these are discussed further in Chapter 6.

Collegial or corporate: managing research within universities

The notion of 'collegiality' seems particularly important to the members of academic staff in the two English departments. Whether it is a successful department in terms of research, such as English at Golden County University, or not so successful, such as English at Royal County University, the desire for a collective with regard to responsibility and decision making seems to be strong. However, it becomes very apparent that this collegiality exists as part of a 'negotiated order' (Hallett 2003). Staff perception, particularly in the sociology and English departments, was that collegiality best described the relations between staff in the department. This view was expressed despite evidence that decision making particularly in relation to research policy and RAE assessment was not 'open to all' and where quite apparent 'hard managerialist' decisions were being taken with regard to staff contracts and employment. What is significant is the way that academics resist or at least reinterpret forms of managerial intent and so it becomes a 'negotiated order' by collective (or not) interpretations of social cultures and procedures within departments. Thus, for example, mentoring and monitoring of research activities of staff within departments is interpreted as support for those activities. This was particularly the case in the English department at Golden County University.

The 'collective fiction' of collegiality is an important one for the identity of academic departments and one that most academics struggle to maintain. However, signs of managerial organization within universities were evident both at GCU and RCU. The role of the departmental head in the biology department at GCU illustrates one example of the increasing authority structures. Similarly the management of activities throughout the institutions and the extent of *strategic* planning within institutions and departments including the monitoring of staff activities, particularly in relation to research, are all evidence of increasing managerialism (Parker and Jary 1994) and managerial surveillance (Harley and Lowe 1998).

There is clear evidence of increasing managerial authority and control in the organization of research within the departments at these two universities, particularly within the biology departments. Within the sociology and English departments, this seems to be less so. However, the interviews were taking place at a time of rapid change and, to some extent, capture a period when relationships and strategies were changing within departments. In order to become more successful in research the old more relaxed notion that people could have autonomy over their research activities was beginning to disappear and new staff and new organizational, managerial and ideational structures (Grenfell and James 1998) were being negotiated within these departments.

At the departmental level, there seemed to be a mix of collegial and bureaucratic forms of organization (McNay 1995), whereas at the institutional level, a corporate model of organization seemed to be evident. Institutional leaders seemed to be fully engaged with the 'main game' of research success and fully conscious in their strategying to enable positioning of the institution with the higher education field. The setting of targets for departments in relation to their expected performance in the RAE was a particular strategy adopted at Golden County University and to, some degree, also at Royal County University. The reputation of the institution was being built primarily in relation to research at both universities and the generation and deployment of resources to this end were paramount. The means of achieving this aim, however, was more complex at the departmental level. Struggles both to implement and also to resist the senior management research policy and the imperative of the research 'main game' within the university were evident in each of the departments. The extent to which these struggles were mobilized to produce successful research policies and strategies within the departments will now be taken up in Chapter 6.

6

University Departments: the game of research struggles, strategies and stakes

> in the humanities one's work is awfully personal to one. We do, of course, have common projects but really in the humanities it is still very personal. It is like a marriage with an idea that you live with for a long period of time and very often divorce is very painful. Em, so, em, and that is very difficult because you are looking at, it is not just, em, work in terms of production. You are looking at what people have thought about and lived with for many years of their lives and this is very precious to them. It is not just a commodity and you can't treat it as such it is just so insulting.
> (Professor Hadfield, HoD English, Golden County University)

There was a dramatic increase in RAE scores from 1996 to 2001 across the higher education sector in the United Kingdom. In this chapter, this phenomenon will be explored in depth in relation to the case study departments. The issue of RAE submissions and strategies for each of the departments of biology, English and sociology will be addressed. This includes decision making on how these submissions were constructed, who was involved in the key decisions and to what extent staff members were consulted. What were the strategies and plans for research activity being enacted both in terms of reflection on the 1996 RAE submission and in preparation for the 2001 RAE submission? The research strategies and policies of the case study departments can be analysed only as moving and ongoing processes that change over time as personnel and conditions change and develop. In the interviews conducted, individuals were talking about decision making on the 1996 RAE submission, how the vision for the department was now being constructed, and plans being put in place for RAE 2001. What insight can be gleaned in looking more closely at individual departments and their particular struggles and strategies?

The evidence attempts to provide an close-up perspective on the decision making by heads of department and research committees on the priorities for research and the details and substance of the 1996 RAE submission. It is argued that the RAE submission and the research strategies and plans for each department are underpinned by the accumulation of perceived forms of 'research capital' within particular disciplinary contexts that are necessary to acquire status and prestige in each of the fields of biology, English and sociology. The different forms of capital, mainly symbolic and material and social, are explored.

It is possible to look in greater depth at the case study departments within Golden County University and Royal County University to better understand the detailed research strategies and plans relating to the 1996 and 2001 RAE. The data represent staff reflecting on the 1996 RAE submission and discussing plans for the 2001 exercise. Insights may be gleaned, therefore, on how improvements in rating were gained by these case study departments. However, the purpose of this study was not simply to study the 'rationale' behaviour of institutions and UOAs in their RAE submissions and research strategies and plans. The aim was also to situate this within the socio-cultural environment of specific institutions and departments and gain a better understanding of the negotiations and struggles over research strategies and indeed, wider values and beliefs held about the purpose and priorities of academic research and teaching work. Bourdieu (1989) would argue that strategies and struggles must be analysed in relation to positioning within the academic/disciplinary field as well as the dispositions of one's habitus. But as Mouzelis (2000) also argues, there is also a need to understand the 'rational-strategying logic' of the 'unfolding interactive situation'. This links also with Hallett (2003), following Goffman and the idea of a 'negotiated order' within institutions and social situations.

The analysis presented in this chapter relates more to the conscious strategying of departmental managers in relation to increasing research activity and potential rating in the RAE where they are attempting to engage with the stated rules and criteria given by RAE panels. As shown, however, there are varied interpretations of these criteria and decisions are taken within a 'negotiated order'. And this negotiation is based on the underlying assumptions and beliefs of values within disciplines and within academic work. The engagement of values, therefore, as Bourdieu suggests, is not necessarily experienced as conscious strategying by individuals in relation to achieving a set goal but is related more to their passionate belief in the value and worth of research or other academic practices.

The values within disciplinary cultures is also important in trying to understand both the qualitative evaluations and judgements that are made in relation to academic research work and the passionate participation and values which individuals hold in relation to their work. Each discipline is analysed in turn, looking in detail at some of the decision making in the departments on the 1996 RAE and their research plans for 2001. This is further explored in relation to the importance of specific research capital that is operative within each discipline and each department and how in much of the discourse of academic managers at least, these different forms of research capital are perceived in relation to RAE criteria and the extent to which the focus and energy within departments lies in aiming to meet RAE criteria.

Research strategies within the biology departments

One significant change in the biology landscape, alongside other disciplines, is the significant increase in RAE gradings, with the numbers of 5 and 5* UoAs at 41 (54%) in 2001, as shown in Table 6.1, compared to only 18 (22%) of UoAs that received those gradings in the 1996 RAE.

Table 6.1 Number of biology departments with 1–5* grades in RAE 1992, 1996 and 2001

Grade	RAE 1992	RAE 1996	RAE 2001	1992	1996	2001
5–5*	8	18	41	9%	22%	54%
4	15	20	17	17%	24%	22%
3	25	26	12	29%	32%	16%
2–1	38	18	6	44%	22%	8%
Total	86	82	76	100%	100%	100%

Source: Higher Education Research and Organisation (HERO), www.hero.ac.uk

This dramatic improvement in RAE gradings begins to look even more impressive when some individual university biology profiles are examined. For example, one university in the North of England achieved a 4 in 1992, dropped to a 3a in 1996 and then jumped to a 5* in 2001. Similarly another university in the North of England achieved a 3 in 1992, a 4 in 1996 and a 5* in 2001. What is perhaps surprising about these two examples is that in each case the numbers of research active staff (RAS) also increased from 21 to 67 in the first case and from 38 to 68 in the latter. Despite possible assumptions that higher grades had perhaps been achieved by submitting lower numbers of staff, this was not shown to be a factor in many cases, indeed the opposite seemed to be occurring (Sharp 2004). A possible explanation is that departments expanded by recruiting new members of staff or, more likely, within the departments, which increased substantially, mergers of departments or units within institutions took place.

However, this was not universally the case as a few institutions did achieve a higher grading with a much reduced number of RAS submitted. Another North of England institution reduced its RAS submission from 50.2 to 19.0, with a correspondingly successful rise in RAE grading. Different strategies were therefore evident in different UoAs in terms of the RAE submission. The grading for the two biology departments did not make any dramatic shift from 1996 to 2001. Biology at Golden County University held on to a high grade and at Royal County University made only slight improvement in their modest grading but lost out significantly in terms of funding in 2001, where they had previously gained substantially in 1996.

Decision-making and the 1996 RAE submissions within the biology departments: the HoD takes charge?

We play the game. We try and maximize the benefit to the department by the rules set on us. At least I do. And there are people in the department who say that it is absolutely silly. And I am afraid, I think, as head of department the job is to maximize the resource in the department and to try and get it running well. You know, so you make decisions based upon these things. You learn the rules and you work to them, I am afraid. I am a shamed player of that game. If the government is going to play games with us and say this is the right work, I respond, and, eh, whether I approve or not is irrelevant.

(Professor Meggitt, ex-HoD Biology, Golden County University)

Professor Meggitt was the head of the biology department at Golden County University from 1990–97 and was, therefore, in post prior to the 1996 RAE. He describes the department as having been 'run under me' indicating a highly individualized role compared to the possibility of an 'executive committee' style of leadership which he says might be instigated by the incoming head. It is evidenced by many members of staff in the department that Professor Meggitt took the lead in the RAE and made it his personal responsibility. The example of his struggle with the university research committee was detailed in Chapter 5 and he made it very clear that he was determined to secure a high RAE grading. And as discussed, he succeeded in his battle with the university research committee to exclude seven members of staff from the 1996 RAE submission. As Professor Meggitt acknowledged, however, not all staff were in agreement with the decisions that had been taken. Those members of staff who had not been put forward in the RAE were unhappy with the outcome and there were others who supported their objections. However, Professor Meggitt went ahead with his decision.

For the biology RAE submission at Golden County University, one of the main criteria for exclusion and inclusion of staff was their ability to be classified as having an international reputation. The main determinants of this were, for example, invitations to speak at international conferences and collaborations with members of staff at universities abroad. This was the key distinction which stopped Dr Merrygold from being put forward in the submission for the department since he was not deemed to have an international reputation.

It was not a question of publications. I had plenty of publications. It was a strategy decision. This department [was] trying [for a high RAE rating], you know that, of course, the question was how many international, em, committees were you on. It wasn't a question of publications, there were plenty of publications in good journals but it was a question, em ... probably as you know for a [high grade] everybody ... everyone has an international reputation ... or some do and some have a national reputation. We had to state what international committees are you on, have you worked abroad, eh, where have you been working abroad recently and what international meetings ... I couldn't show sufficient international meetings...?

(Dr Merrygold, biologist, Golden County University)

A decision not to put a member of staff forward in the RAE submission may be, as Dr Merrygold suggests, no more than a strategic decision to maximize the grade awarded to the department. However, the implications of these kinds of decisions extend beyond the RAE submission. They imply an important site of struggle of classification within academia over the determination of a legitimate claim for researcher status.

Further examples of difficult and conflictual decisions being taken by the head of department can be found in the biology department at Royal County University. Professor Laing worked with a small group of senior staff but he took a leading role in the decisions for the RAE submission.

One of the main decisions was how many staff to put forward. Professor Laing argued that they wanted to put forward only the 'best staff' but also the maximum number possible. The conditions for inclusion that he lists are as follows: that the candidate must have four publications, an established reputation within their peer group; and how the research presented would 'look to a panel of classical biologists'. The result was a submission of just over 50% of staff in the school. A critical policy in the 1996 RAE submission was the return of staff under a particular UOA. A number of staff were returned under a different UOA from biological sciences. In terms of classifications, therefore, decision making centred both on those members of staff deemed 'research active' and also under which UOA they would be submitted. Of the members of staff interviewed at Royal County University there seemed to be most disagreement from those submitted under a different UOA from biological sciences.

Interviewer: So from your point of view you just submitted...?

Dr Freeman: [I] also supplied information on scholarly activity ... that was it basically ... It was kept very shrouded, for instance, I actually was submitted as [UOA] rather than [biological sciences] submission in this department and I am very clearly in [biological sciences] ... I assume they saw me as more fitted with the [UOA] which I don't agree with and also our [UOA] was very weak and because I had a lot from a research and publications point of view ... I think they used me to bolster the submission. I realize it is a game that they are playing but on a personal basis I don't wish to be considered [that kind of scientist].

The decision-making process around the RAE submissions for these biology departments provides evidence for increased managerial leadership, particularly in the role of the HoD at Golden County University. Staff were consulted to some degree but the main decision making within this process was taken by the HoD and senior research committee members in the case of Royal County University. All of these decisions were taken based on the perceptions of how RAE panel members would evaluate and judge the work being done in the department. What is important, therefore, is the underlying assumptions and values behind the decisions being made. In particular, the significance of an 'international reputation', definition of being 'research active' and differing values given to particular research areas within biology. These issues will be explored further in relation to different forms of research capital operative within biology.

Research strategies and plans for the 2001 RAE in biology

Each of the two biology departments had strategies and plans in place to increase their RAE rating for 2001. Directions from the vice-chancellor and senior managements for each institution were discussed in Chapter 5. At Golden County University the expectation was for all departments to become, where possible, top rated in 2001. At Royal County University the aim of top rating was seen as a longer-term project but all departments were expected to increase in 2001 to perhaps a more moderate rating.

In the biology department at Golden County University there was a concern to hold on to a high RAE rating. The research strategies of the department, therefore, reflect this in the emphasis on increased funding to support an expanding and expensive department and on the significance of staff having not just a national but an international reputation. The key strategies for this department are shown in Table 6.2.

The key features of this strategy included; giving pump priming funding to get individuals started on research projects, but then a strong emphasis on the need for individuals to win research grants, on creating a critical mass of researchers and expertise in particular research areas and appointing new staff in these areas and directing research activities more towards RAE expectations and ensuring that there was an administrative system in place to monitor research activities. There was also a specific fund to encourage international collaborations and an effort to publicize and increase the international profile of the department.

The biology department at Royal County University, on the other hand, had a moderate research record, which it wanted to improve. In line with what the vice-chancellor of the institution was saying, there were big

Table 6.2   Selection of research strategies and plans in biology at Golden County University

Research strategies and plans
Direct research activity towards RAE expectations
Encourage grant applications
Pump priming funds
Grants for conferences and to develop international collaboration
Reduced teaching loads for new members of staff and 'deals' for light teaching loads
Policy to have new, young, research active staff
Create a critical mass of staff in specific research areas
Peer review of research activity and individual meetings with staff to determine research activities
Questionnaire for staff on research publications and funding
Database held of publications and grants
Research Administration Office
Create team spirit
Encouragement and constructive monitoring
Publicising research activity
International visitors to department
Investment in Technical Staff
Increase research at expense of infrastructure

aspirations within the department but also an acceptance of specific limitations and a recognition that achieving a top grade may take longer. However, a moderate grade in the 1996 RAE earned them a substantial amount of funding. Indeed, Dr Niven exclaimed that the result of the 1996 RAE 'transformed us', since the additional funding had allowed them to invest in new researchers and research projects. The key research strategies of the biology department at Royal County University are shown in Table 6.3.

These research strategies do not differ markedly from those of biology at Golden County University. A similar emphasis was placed on increasing the amount of research funding, appointing new staff where possible to strengthen research areas and increased monitoring of research activity. Each institution emphasized a need for lower teaching loads for staff engaged in research projects. At Golden County University, this process was enacted by negotiation, whereas at Royal County University, a banding system was being put in place to distribute differential teaching loads depending on research activity of staff. Given the more moderate funding at Royal County University the emphasis was also on using these funds for studentships and technical support staff to help researchers get projects off the ground where there was, as yet, no external funding available.

There seems to be no doubt, in talking to staff in these departments, that increased emphasis was being placed on research activities and on the means by which these activities were supported and monitored, and that this was directly in relation to working towards RAE 2001. These strategies

Table 6.3 Selection of research strategies and plans in biology at Royal County University

Research strategies and plans
Increase research output and income
Research groups to get technicians and PhD students
Internal funds for research
Use money for studentships rather than teaching assistants
New appointments on research strengths
Set targets for income generation
Monitoring research income and expenditure
Create a biotechnology group
Banding for teaching and research duties
Invite visiting professors
Appraisal interviews
Promotion for successful research active staff
Appointing younger staff within specific research areas

cannot be presented as simple, rationale decision making but must be placed in the context of an understanding of the assumptions and values that lie behind some of these strategies, the differentiations and the struggles within them. The biology field is a site of struggle over the significance, importance and meaning of the forms of capital and the stakes involved in the field.

Struggles and stakes in capital accumulation in biology

Symbolic capital: research areas, publications and the importance of being international

Becher (1989) describes biologists as a rather heterogeneous group with a variety of subsets of research areas. Indeed, along his taxonomy of hard/soft and convergent/divergent as a means of categorizing disciplines, biology is found to lie in the intermediary area. Thus for example, certain specialisms fit into the category of 'hard' science (for example, molecular biology) and 'soft' science (such as ecology). Similarly, biologists are found to be fairly harmonious and convergent in their interests despite the variety of research areas. As Becher argues: 'there is a mutual antagonism between those who study structure and processes and those whose concern is with organisms or communities. But the subject is not prone to "deep and permanent divisions"; there is 'more intellectual unity than the structural diversity of the subject suggests' (Becher 1989: 156).

The distinction between 'hard' and 'soft' refers to the way that the discipline or research area is characterized in terms of its organization. Becher (1989) maintains 'hard' knowledge

has clearly defined boundaries; the problems with which it is concerned tend to be very narrow and circumscribed. It focuses on quantitative issues, and tends to have a well-developed theoretical structure embracing causal propositions, generalizable findings and universal laws. It is cumulative in that new findings tend to be linear developments of the existing state of knowledge.

(Becher 1989: 153)

'Soft' knowledge has the opposite characteristics of 'unclear boundaries, problems which are broad in scope and loose in definition, a relatively unspecified theoretical structure, a concern with the qualitative and particular, and a reiterative pattern of enquiry' (Becher 1989: 153).

The other dichotomies referred to by Becher (1989) are those of pure/applied areas of research and urban/rural forms of research organization. 'Pure' research is seen to be of higher value within scientific research than applied. Bourdieu (1988) provides a diagram of the divisions between pure/applied and theoretical/empirical. Within the science faculty he places biology in the middle between the two scales but leaning towards practical, applied and empirical, impure research. Becher (1989) also argues that biology lies in an intermediary area between hard/soft and pure/applied research with some specialisms such as ecology on the soft/applied side and others such as microbiology on the hard/pure one. It is perhaps best to think of these as a continuum rather than a dichotomy with most disciplines positioned somewhere along this continuum rather than definitively on one side or the other.

It is clear from the interviews I conducted that research areas could be differentiated along certain scales of evaluation. One example of this can be cited in the interview with the head of biology at Royal County University, Professor Laing. He used the term 'classical biology' to describe the kind of research areas which might be highly esteemed by a biology panel. He discussed one particular research area that is placed in the 'soft' and 'applied' sections of the continuum and compares this to, for example, molecular biology, which would be towards the 'hard' and 'pure' side and, therefore, accorded more value.

But this [research area] is not looked upon very highly in terms of the high academic biological scientists who were sitting on the [RAE] panel ... And in general we thought that if you were a really top-rate molecular biologist, for example, which a lot of the panel members were, they would not look particularly favourably on this [research area]. So although I take that particular person who was slightly upset at not being included [in the RAE submission], I think we probably made the right decision given the nature of the panel.

(Professor Laing, HoD biology, Royal County University)

A hierarchy of research areas that can be loosely coupled around the dichotomies of pure/applied and hard/soft can be shown to exist within the discipline and this is perceived to be important to the judgements made within the RAE. However, some members of staff question whether this 'pure' research is universally awarded greater value within the institutional context. Dr Lester, for example, a research fellow at Golden County University argues that 'applied' research was also highly valued because of its ability to attract greater levels of funding from charities and commercial sponsors. Thus, he believed that his own research, which would be characterized as pure research was less valued because of low levels of funding. Although areas of research such as molecular biology were highly esteemed within the research community and also attract high levels of funding, this equation of esteem and funding is not always so clearly drawn. For this reason, therefore, biology departments like the one at Royal County University look to develop their research potential in areas that are both highly valued and capable of attracting funds.

> An [eminent professor] pointed out to us that all of the five-star departments in biological sciences are very big in biotechnology. So if we want to move to a [higher grade] then we have to move in the direction of biotechnology. So we are currently trying to find a way of bringing a biotechnology group into the department.
> (Professor Laing, HoD, biology, Royal County University)

What is important is the extent to which there is a conflict over the principles of evaluating different forms of research. There was certainly a perception by some that it was more profitable to make a move into more 'urban', high intensity areas of research, which were more likely to attract funding. Working in such areas may also provide possible opportunities for publishing in high impact, prestigious journals.

There was little doubt that for biologists, in common with other scientists, the primary mode of publishing research work was within journals. There were very few authored or edited books or other forms of publication in the 2001 RAE submissions (as shown in Table 6.4). The significant issue was which journals are the main vehicles of publication and which appear to carry the highest prestige? There is a clear differentiation between departments that are highly rated and those not. *Nature* comes out as the most prestigious journal and this accounts for 281 (10%) of submitted outputs for the 5 and 5*; and for departments rated 4 there are a total of 41 outputs in *Nature*, whereas for departments rated 3a and below there are very few (4 in total). This pattern continued for all of the next most prestigious journals, including *Journal of Biological Chemistry, Proceedings of the National Academy of Sciences, USA, EMBO Journal* and *Science*. Although panel members were judging the quality of articles, there was also some correspondence between the award of a high RAE scores and publishing outlets of staff from those UOAs.

There was a clear perception from most of the biologists interviewed that

Table 6.4 RAE submission 2001 for biology UOA, by type of publication

Grade Band	Authored book	Edited book	Chapter in book	Journal article	Conference contribution	Other	Total
5*	0%	0%	0%	99%	0%	0%	100%
5	0%	0%	1%	98%	0%	0%	100%
4	0%	0%	1%	98%	0%	0%	100%
3a	1%	0%	1%	97%	1%	0%	100%
3b	0%	0%	2%	97%	0%	1%	100%
2	2%	1%	3%	93%	0%	1%	100%
All	1%	0%	2%	96%	0%	1%	100%

Source: Higher Education Research and Organisation (HERO), www.hero.ac.uk

they would like to publish in the most prestigious, high impact journals and indeed that this would be an important for the RAE. Dr Summers at Royal County University stated that she had changed her research areas because her current research area would never be accepted by the most prestigious high impact journals. However, there was also much resistance from some staff, despite the pressure, to the idea that one should try to publish in prestigious journals. Dr Lewis at Royal County University stated that he would 'publish where it would be read' and 'didn't give a damn about the RAE'. Others felt that the prestigious journals were dominated by the United States and so researchers were forced to compete even where they may prefer to publish in European journals. Dr Freeman at Royal County University called it the 'publication game', which you have to play but one that he disliked. The pressure to play in the publications game and strive to submit to journals of high international standing, was felt equally in pressure to attend international conferences and to raise the international profile of one's work.

Research workers can also be divided into those biologists who, as Bourdieu maintained, 'invest above all in production and secondarily, in the work of representation which contributes to the accumulation of a symbolic capital of external renown' (Bourdieu 1988). Given the important national and international distinction used in the RAE, the incidence of conference attendance and other activities to boost 'external renown' is evident among the biologists interviewed. Some lament the pressure put upon them to chase such acclaim when they feel that they are more successfully engaged productively in the laboratory.

Research funding: the importance of material 'capital' for biology

I think [from] the departments' point of view they are very interested in money. I think that is, although there is denial of this at the highest levels, I think money really is important. If you can bring in large grants that is what eventually gives departments a huge boost. It is regarded then by people higher up the ladder as being a successful department. As such research papers by themselves don't bring in the grants, don't bring in the money. The grant applications, the successful grant applications bring in money. And I work in a subject that is 'pure' research. There is no way that I can get money from Unilever or such like. Other people working in more 'applied' research can get money in from industry and industry tends to provide a lot more money. And I think that there is a danger there that those of us who try and work on pure research are actually going to be squeezed out because it is better to employ people who work on applied research because they bring in more money than people who work on pure research who depend, particularly medical research, who depend on medical charities.

(Dr Lester, biologist, Golden County University)

The total research funds for all biology departments submitted in the 2001 RAE is shown in Table 6.5. There was a clear difference in the amount of research funding awarded to departments and this correlates with the RAE rating. Departments rated 5 and 5* have a significantly higher level of research funding than those rated 4 and below.

Table 6.5   Total research funds for all biology departments submitted in the 2001 RAE, separated by grades

Grade	Number of Departments	OST funds	Total funds	RAS FTE	OST/FTE	Total funds/FTE
5*	11	9.114.010	27,482,484	41.5	219.706	662,504
5	30	8.467.436	19,685,744	43.2	195.957	455,576
4	17	2.534.161	6,545,934	23.9	106.108	274,084
3a	8	1.601.012	4,634,644	22.7	70.413	203,833
3b	4	87.896	431,172	7.5	11.778	57,778
2	6	93.402	523,545	7.6	12.236	68,587

Source: Higher Education Research and Organisation (HERO), www.hero.ac.uk

The amounts of funding received by Golden County University and Royal County University were very different with Golden County University receiving almost 10 times the amount of research council funding as Royal County University, 12.5 times more funds from UK charities and almost 10 times more funds from UK industry and commerce. Dr Lester's quote at the opening of this section implied that there was a move towards greater reliance on funding from industry. It was argued in Chapter 2 that limited funding to universities has forced a reliance on commercial funds, creating a form of 'academic capitalism' (Slaughter and Leslie 1999). However, there was little evidence in the interviews of a concerted move towards attempting to win more commercial money. In both of the departments the most substantial amounts came from the research councils, with approximately 10% of total funds from UK business and commerce. The contribution is, however, not insignificant and the implication appears to be that this might grow as departments become more starved of government funding.

The cost of research in biology is high and departments struggle to maintain the level of resource needed to sustain the infrastructure, laboratory technicians and facilities that are necessary. Some directors of research groups like Professor Mulligan at Golden County University had a research group of about sixteen staff, comprising research assistants, a laboratory assistant and postdoctoral researchers, all of whom he has to supervise. Other members of staff such as Dr Malone and Dr Martin had no laboratory and no research team to direct. For Professor Mulligan, who spent much of his time writing grant proposals, there is great pressure to continue the flow of funding so that he can maintain the staff and facilities to keep doing the research. For others such as Dr Martin and Dr Lester, quoted at the beginning of this section, the need for grants is much less since their work is smaller in scope and demands fewer facilities and staff. As Dr Lester explains in the quotation above, however, some individuals feel that their research, however worthy, may be less valued because it does not attract large research grants. In many ways, therefore, there is the real need and struggle for biology departments to maintain funding levels that can support them. There is also the perceived 'symbolic value' of attracting large research grants that can bring more researchers into the department and create a critical mass within particular specialisms. Dr Waterman at Golden County University stated that he believed the department was more interested in 'research money input than research output'.

Following Bourdieu, one can determine the specific forms of scientific power, which individual members of staff possess in terms of their accumulation of research (or scientific) capital. The example of material capital within biology would refer to the material representations of research 'wealth' such as well-equipped laboratories, qualified research staff and substantial research funding. Struggles over equipment and laboratory space were referred to particularly in research committee meetings and it was reported that there was more competition and division over the use of resources within the department.

There was a large variation in the distribution of such forms of material capital and evidence of attempts to accumulate this form of capital was found among most, but not all, of the academic staff interviewed. For some it was not considered important or necessary for their research work but for others it was vital to the continuation of their research laboratories and employment of research staff. However, it seems clear that the symbolic as well as the obvious material benefits derived from funding awards were considered highly important, at the very least by academic managers, and served at least in some cases to inform the direction of research being done.

Social capital: conference and collaborations

Science is predominantly a social activity. Researchers tend to work in groups and there is a great deal of co-dependency involved in terms of expertise, facilities and working together on projects and publishing. The common perception may be of the individual scientist as genius but the majority of scientific success is born of the collaborative effort of groups of people working together. Research strategies at both institutions involved creating a unified strength of teams of people working in specific research areas that would give a critical mass of expertise and capacity.

The accumulation of social capital within research areas can also be evidenced. In biology there were a number of collaborative projects with people working together between national and international institutions. Some areas of research necessitate a form of collaboration when a particular researcher or research group has expertise or facilities that need to be utilized. Where competition is created it can be difficult for researchers to collaborate. Social capital, therefore, is extremely important within the sciences as one is often reliant on the goodwill and expertise of other researchers.

The importance of international conference attendance has been discussed previously and similarly importance is placed on international collaborations on research projects. As Dr Lester from Golden County explains the importance of social connections can be vital to getting one's work known.

> Yeah, em, we would try. In fact I am going to America soon deliberately to publicize work, to be seen by the potential reviewers of my next [UK charity] application and I am honing down going to British conferences in order to go to American conferences. It is entirely down to profile and being seen by the people who matter. At the moment I am told that a good sixty of the reviewers for [a UK charity] are American so you stand a good chance if you hit the right conference of being in the right place where the people matter. And it means going up to people and introducing yourself and trying to make your talk or presentation as exciting, innovating and eye-catching as possible. And because you can only go to say one or two of those conferences you have to make an impact there.
>
> (Dr Lester, biology, Golden County University)

Many see attendance at academic conferences as a necessary part of publicising their work and getting to hear about new research, but feel resentful at the pressure to build up social capital in the way that Dr Lester described. Dr Battersby at Royal County University explained that he would now probably go to conferences that he would not normally go to in order to raise his profile with certain people. Dr Merrygold, who was discussed earlier as he was not put forward for the 1996 RAE because he had not attended any international conferences or had sufficient international collaborations, argued that it was pointless for him to go travelling round the world when his laboratory and his work are in the department.

There are significant issues here in terms of the need for collaborations as a vital and necessary means to carry out research work and the need for social connections in order to ensure a reputation within a particular field. The former is clearly important and there is some evidence from these departments that the competitiveness and divisions both between departments and within departments partly instigated by the RAE has damaged to some degree these vital relationships. The need for social connections, on the other hand, leads to a contrary set of responses with some members of staff resentful of the perceived need to engage unnecessarily in these activities, while others recognize their importance.

Research strategies within the sociology departments

Table 6.6 shows that there was not such a marked increase in top-rated departments within the sociology UOAs. UOAs had improved but there was more of an equal spread across the different gradings. This was a common pattern among a few of the social science subjects including education and social policy (Fisher and Marsh 2003; McNay 2003), where there was no dramatic increase in numbers of 5 and 5* star ratings as there had been for the biology UOAs. Indeed, within the sociology field ratings went down for a number of departments.

Table 6.6　Number of Sociology departments with 1–5* grades in RAE 1992, 1996 and 2001

Grade	RAE 1992	RAE 1996	RAE 2001	1992	1996	2001
5–5*	6	9	18	9%	15%	38%
4	12	15	10	18%	25%	21%
3	20	27	16	30%	44%	33%
2–1	29	10	4	43%	16%	8%
Total	67	61	48	100%	100%	100%

Source: Higher Education Research and Organisation (HERO), www.hero.ac.uk

Equally, there was no discernible pattern in terms of numbers of staff submitted and whether this may have impacted on ratings. Size of department may have some impact as many of the highly rated UOAs had between 20 and 40 staff submitted in the 2001 RAE compared to some lower rated UOAs with fewer than 10. However, this was not universally the case as one university in the south of England submitted almost 30 staff but gained only a 3a grade.

Both sociology departments at Golden County University and Royal County University improved their rating in the 2001 RAE. I look now at some of the strategies and plans that helped to achieve this.

Decision-making for the 1996 RAE submissions within the sociology departments: creative story-telling?

> Well, I took over as head of department only twelve months before [the RAE submission] and as far as I can tell there was no strategy leading up to it. I mean we more or less kind of found ourselves having to do the return without very much ... There was a realization that people needed to have publications but by that time it was almost too late to do very much about it. It would be wrong to say that we had any kind of real strategy leading up to it. I had a strategy in mind when I was writing the return and the only other things that we were trying to do that we were doing anyway was building up graduate numbers ... I mean, to prepare for these exercises you need a strategy to start years before so it was very much a ... and in my own mind I see it very much as a somewhat cosmetic exercise, trying to put things together to present the department in the best image. It is a creative piece of copywriting is how I saw the exercise really.
>
> (Professor Davenport, HoD sociology, Golden County University)

Professor Davenport took over as head at a late stage in the process and found himself putting together a submission that had been preceded by a limited, even non-existent amount of strategic planning.

In terms of research policy there seemed to be widespread consensus within the department that, particularly with regard to the RAE, there was no special research strategy or organization of research activities. The head of department, Professor Davenport, who was also one of the key authors of the RAE submission, claimed that the main form of strategy was to write the submission in order to present the department in the most positive way. This 'creative copywriting' earned the department a moderately high grade in the 1996 RAE.

> In other words, a way of presenting the department to make it more obvious that what we were doing were good things, like the scholarship and research thing. I mean one way of looking at that is to say this is a department with a poor research record, you know, very few research funds and not a good research record. What I tried to do was present it in a different way and say, well, actually what it is, is a department with a strong scholarship record that feeds into the research. And that is what I meant by creative copywriting ... what I tried to do was to take features of the department and present them in such a way as to make

them look as if, well as if they were policy decisions but as if they were actually advantageous. I identified research ... So we had these identifiable substantive research groups and also theory and methods groups. Em, that was a strategic decision we took early on about how to present the department ... So it was just ... I presented it to other people as putting really the best light on the department possible without actually telling any lies.

(Professor Davenport, HoD sociology, Golden County University)

Professor Davenport, therefore, took very much a leadership role in creating and constructing the RAE submission, but more reluctantly than the exuberance exhibited by Professor Meggitt in the biology department. His decision making centred on how best to present the structure and organization of the research (and scholarship) activities of staff in the department. Where conflict arose in his situation, it was over which pieces of research work to include for members of staff who were in disagreement with how he was presenting their work. As all but one member of staff was included in the submission, he had fewer difficult decisions to make over which members of staff to put forward.

There was no significant leader directing the 1996 RAE submission in the sociology department at Royal County University but a research committee was set up to plan for and write the submission and this committee has continued, meeting once or twice per term. As one member of staff explained:

Well in the past, em, perhaps also I was ... no it wasn't so much of a you know we didn't have meetings to say right who's research active who isn't, who's going to do this, who's going to do that, what about bidding for some funds to support that piece of research. That wasn't, three, four years ago that wouldn't have been part of you know, well certainly I didn't know about it. It wouldn't have been devolved to the department in the way those discussions are now.

(Ms Chandler, sociology, Royal County University)

In both of these departments, therefore, there appears to have been very little strategy in place or preparations for the 1996 RAE. The major work, therefore, was in putting together the submission, which was mainly the work of Professor Davenport at Golden County University and a more collaborative effort at Royal County University. Both departments as a result gained disappointing grades in the 1996 RAE, although, in terms of planning for the 2001 RAE, much had changed in both departments.

Research strategies and plans for the 2001 RAE in sociology

At Golden County University, as discussed, the expectation was that all departments should achieve a top rating in the RAE. The sociology department had received a moderate rating in 1996 and despite the aspiration to gain a higher grade, it was felt by the HoD and some members of staff on the research committee that staff in the department were not feeling the necessary urgency to develop strategies to aim towards a higher grade. The key strategies developed are shown in Table 6.7 and include, building up research strength and staff numbers in specific areas and developing research groups.

Table 6.7 Selection of research strategies and plans in sociology at Golden County University

Research strategies and plans
New appointments in specific research areas
Strategic publications in journals
Create teaching only appointments
Stimulating academic environment
Strengthening research groups
Pump priming money
Mentoring for new staff
Research term scheme
Increase postgraduate numbers

There was little evidence of monitoring of research activities in the sociology department at Golden County University. The decisions taken by the research committee were seen to guide the research activities within the department but there was no formal monitoring of staff activities or direct pressure put on them by the head of department (as seen in Chapter 5 with the discussion at the research committee). This can be shown both by the comments given by members of staff and by comments from the head of department and the research committee. As one senior lecturer explained:

> Yeah, I think there might have been information about the sorts of criteria, which would be relevant. So I seem to remember dimly that you know the RAE before had included all one's publications or something and it was moving to a best four [publications] or some such and I think that we were informed about this change, so I suppose ... Now I didn't feel it because I get four without, I mean four isn't a problem for me. If you are someone who isn't publishing regularly and four is a problem then in a sense hearing that it is four is rather like a suggestion or a nudge to, em ... you would interpret it as a nudge. I didn't because I already had the four on whatever so I never, I mean it didn't impinge in any particular way ... Otherwise there was no kind of particular strategy.
>
> (Dr Leighton, sociology, Golden County University)

There was no mechanism to compel people to do research but there were 'little chats' and some 'encouragement to publish'. To a certain extent members of staff did not perceive any specific research policy within the department and did not feel any particular pressure with regard to the RAE. The 'managerial surveillance' (Harley and Lowe 1998) of research activities was not reported in this department. However, most people within the department were research active and were entered in the RAE. The one person who was not included was given other duties (including a half time administrator post for the university) so that person did not count in the percentage of staff included.

However, the university policy on research at Golden County University was for all departments to be awarded the top rating in the RAE. The head of department was realistic about the chances of this for the sociology department. He argued that not everyone in the department was necessarily capable of achieving the highest grade for their research activity and he reasoned that the assumption was wrongly made that continual improvement was always possible in the same way that standards in education are always expected to increase. Moreover, it was difficult to impress upon staff the implications of going for the highest grade.

> But the other thing I found a bit distressing about it was that [members of staff] were thinking about it in terms of four publications and when I pointed out to them that they should be thinking about it in terms of four quality, high-quality publications, not four publications, em, they were sort of taken aback. In other words, they hadn't really accepted the fact that it isn't four publications it has to be four publications just to remain [at the same grading]. If you want to get to a [higher grading] we are talking about high-quality publications, however these are assessed by the panel.
>
> (Professor Davenport, HoD sociology, Golden County University)

Despite the more collegial relaxed feel of the sociology department at Golden County University, it was apparent that things would have to change if a higher RAE rating were to be attained. As a result new members of staff were brought into the department that expanded the current research areas and more established groups were developed from the 'loose groupings' that had existed, which included recruiting more research fellows and research assistants. At least five new members of staff were appointed prior to the 2001 RAE and this included one member of staff who brought substantial funding to set up a research team. The appointments were all made to strengthen and develop the research areas within the department. It seems apparent, therefore, that central funding was made available in order to resource these appointments and so the head of department obviously engaged in successful negotiations, despite his earlier reservations about no money making its way back to departments.

Some changes were also made in the sociology department at Royal County University, and strategies were similar in some way to Golden County University but with some differences, as shown in Table 6.8. Starting from a fairly low number of research active staff, the sociology department

Table 6.8 Selection of research strategies and plans in sociology at Royal County University

Research strategies and plans
Appointment of new research active staff
Establishment of a research centre
Increase postgraduate numbers
Defining research areas and appointing promising new staff in these areas
Increase part-time appointments
Mentoring system for new research staff
Encourage staff to publish in prestigious journals
Encourage staff to apply for research funding
Research links with other departments
Study leave for staff
Establishment of the research committee

was concerned to increase part-time appointments of staff to full-time appointments and encourage more research activity and attract new staff to the department that could enhance research specialist areas. Key to this was the development of a research centre.

Unlike the more collegial, autonomous situation of sociology at Golden County University, there was a greater sense that staff research activities were being directed more strongly from the management of the faculty as well as the department, in that they were being encouraged to apply for research funding and raise the number of publications. However, Professor McGowan emphasized that the pressure put on staff was more 'moral pressure than strong pressure'. Despite the sense of collegiality and autonomy within these departments, the RAE push had obviously caused quite a substantial cultural change with regard to organization and management of research activities. But was this also true of the changes to the values and forms of research capital within sociology?

Struggles and stakes in capital accumulation in sociology

Symbolic capital: research areas, publications and the importance of being international

It emerged from many of my interviews that the distinction between work carried out under the umbrella title of scholarship, or perhaps theory, and work which is empirical or applied was central to the definition of the kind of research work being done by individuals within sociology. There would also seem to be a specific value attached to both of these forms of research. Typically 'pure' or theoretical work is accorded a higher value across academic disciplines, specifically within the sciences (Becher 1989). However, the interview data collected from the sociology departments within this study would seem to indicate that applied, empirical investigation which attracts, or at least has the potential to attract outside funding was also becoming more highly valued, at least within institutions.

> I have noticed that the research emphasis here is not just simply the RAE, but of course that is a big factor and of course the RAE is publication above all else, but the other thing that has happened is the emphasis has been to generate funds and of course the way to generate funds is to do projects that appeal to the ESRC, that sort of thing ... why I am defensive about what constitutes research is because I clearly don't do research that is easily fundable and I clearly don't do field-work in the orthodox sense ... I don't know if, I imagine there is still because somehow if you are not a researcher then you are just a teacher or something or somebody who just reads books and that's not quite the same. So I wanted the definition that doing research is original thinking and it seems to me that some of the best stuff in sociology comes like that.
>
> (Professor McGowan, sociology, Royal County University)

Interviewees at both Golden County University and Royal County University gave evidence of a struggle to endorse the primacy of the scholar, the generalist, the theorist. The importance of this for the sociology department at Golden County University was demonstrated in the RAE submission, which showed that a majority of staff would be placed in the category of scholarship (as opposed to 'research'). A claim was made for the value of this kind of research activity within sociology.

> ...emphasize that the departments' activities were a combination of scholarship and research and tried to make that a distinctive feature and strength of the department because the way the thing is all written up it rather presumes that academics do research, scholarship doesn't appear anywhere in the material or the discussions ... it is a mistake because in the social sciences one of the strengths, in sociology, one of the strengths has always been that it bridges in a way the social sciences and the humanities. That is very true of this department and always has been. So we made a point of putting that in the return, that we had people who were dedicated to scholarship in the department and people doing research in the department and tried to make that a distinctive feature.
>
> (Professor Davenport, HoD, sociology, Golden County University)

There was a perception of differentiation in the valuing of particular forms of sociological research work, although it was emphasized in the RAE criteria that 'most highly valued will be those works that contain significant or innovative research (whether theoretical or substantive)'. This implied that no greater value would be placed on either theoretical or substantive/

empirical work but would instead concentrate on the main indicators of the 'quality' of publications and a vibrant research 'culture'. It is unclear whether this was also the case for different forms of research output. Table 6.9 shows the types of research output for the 2001 RAE.

Table 6.9   RAE submission 2001 for sociology UOA, by type of publication

Rating	Authored book	Edited book	Chapter in book	Journal article	Conference contribution	Report for external body	Others	Total
5*	18%	4%	22%	53%	0%	1%	2%	100%
5	19%	4%	23%	52%	1%	1%	0%	100%
4	15%	5%	28%	50%	0%	2%	0%	100%
3a	14%	5%	24%	55%	0%	1%	1%	100%
3b	14%	6%	24%	53%	1%	2%	0%	100%
2	12%	2%	30%	48%	1%	5%	2%	100%
1	–	–	–	–	–	–	–	–

Source: Higher Education Research and Organisation (HERO), www.hero.ac.uk

A small percentage of edited books and a majority of journal articles were included as research outputs. However, journal articles only accounted for around 50% of output with authored books around 15%. A significant proportion submitted, around 25% of outputs, were book chapters. There was some differentiation between departments that are highly rated and those that are not, with slightly more authored books and slightly fewer book chapters for the highly-rated departments. *Sociology* came out as the most cited journal with *British Journal of Sociology* and *Work, Employment and Society* following. More than 30% of submissions from 5 and 5* departments appeared in these journals, with over 20% of submissions in these journals in 3 and 4 rated department, but none in submissions rated lower than 3. The issue to note here is that these journals are UK based and, therefore, the judgement of 'international' quality may be difficult if there is reliance on the journal as an indicator of international excellence.

Members of staff in these two sociology departments were clearly aware of a hierarchy of prestigious journals but there was less of the same emphasis on particularly 'international' publications or in attending international conferences. In sociology at Golden County University some members of staff clearly worked with international collaborators and individuals were being invited to international conferences to give presentations. In sociology at Royal County University, on the other hand, there was less talk about attending international conferences or their importance. There was perhaps a recognition of the need to do this but maybe not the funding to support it. Perhaps this was also an indicator that much significant work done within sociology and perhaps other disciplines like education or social work could be more important within the national context than the international, although it may be of a quality comparable with international standards of research. The central distinction between national and international relevance of research is the key criteria utilized in the RAE but despite numerous critiques, the concept of 'international' is left largely undefined. This continues to be the case for RAE 2008. This may, however, go some way towards explaining why sociology departments did not experience an increase in 5 and 5* departments unlike disciplines such as Biology. Research funding may be another significant factor.

Material capital and types of sociologist and sociological research

Some members of staff in these two sociology departments felt concerned about the pressure to raise external funding for research. Despite attempts to achieve this aim, it was difficult for some people, particularly where the research interests do not accord with the kind of research that was likely to be funded by research councils and other funding bodies.

> I'm not an income generator ... some of my colleagues get decent money ... but I just don't see myself doing that sort of work but I feel pressure, is it peer pressure? It is from above too, I mean, clearly the university says that too, we must increase our research income. So the priority is that department sets figures, not sociology, schools set figures and we have a figure that we have to reach and [deputy head of department] keeps nudging.
> (Professor McGowan, sociology, Royal County University)

It would appear, therefore, from the perceptions of some staff in sociology departments at least that empirical work was increasingly becoming more highly valued especially where it attracts funding from outside bodies.

> Somebody like [famous sociologist] who is an internationally renowned scholar, has had relatively few research grants but, I mean, the quality of what he has produced has been highly regarded. So that it, you know, gets money. Instead of doing it on the cheap we have got to get money and do that kind of research that involves people like you rather than, if you like older fashioned forms of scholarship where people sit down and read books and do it themselves.
> (Dr Leighton, sociology, Golden County University)

However, the more traditional hierarchy that places theory and scholarship at the apex is still defended by certain sectors of the academic community within sociology. However, institutions need to secure research funding and for this reason it might appear that the accumulation of research capital has become more *material* than *symbolic* (Bourdieu 1988). Therefore, the 'alleged cleavage' within sociology between theory and empirical research may give rise to different scales of evaluation where one is no longer dominant.

The amount of research funding available within sociology is significantly smaller than that of biology. However, it is clear from the data presented in Table 6.10 that levels of research funding correlate quite strongly with rating in the RAE with 5* departments in particular attracting more research funding. However, the pattern is not clear cut and it would appear that low rated departments of 2 and 3 grades, although not successful in gaining research council funding, were able to attract funding from other sources.

Table 6.10 Total research funds for all sociology departments submitted in the 2001 RAE, separated by grades

Grade	OST funds	Total funds	RAS FTE	OST/FTE	Total funds/FTE
5*	2,155,648	4,605,576	32.2	66,977	143,097
5	630,524	1,532,190	20.7	30,455	74,007
4	399,359	1,186,605	18.6	21,502	63,889
3a	46,474	604,847	13.1	3,559	46,316
3b	23,438	132,410	10.6	2,211	12,491
2	2,387	778,096	8.1	295	96,061

Source: Higher Education Research and Organisation (HERO), www.hero.ac.uk

Unlike the biology departments, there was no substantial difference between the two sociology departments in terms of research funding. Both had similar amounts of funding from the research councils, with Royal County sociology department gaining substantially more funds from UK charities and central government, while sociology at Golden County gained more from EU government bodies. In terms of funding, these two departments are perhaps not typical as neither is large (greater than 20 staff) and so perhaps do not compare with the very large sociology departments that receive significantly more funding. However, they are interesting to compare since they provide examples of how within the social sciences, the amount of research funding given to low and high rated RAE UOAs (and, indeed, comparing old (pre-1992) and new (post-1992) universities) does not necessarily correspond and that all types of departments are capable of attracting funding. There does seem to be a question, therefore, given the fewer number of sociology departments given high ratings in the 2001 RAE (compared to other UOAs), whether the apparently highly differentiated but perhaps less hierarchical sociology field has multiple principles of evaluation with regard to types of research outputs and distinctions between national and international esteem. The differing values attached to sociological work, therefore, may make it more difficult to establish forms of hierarchical distinction. Furthermore, the possibility of conducting sociological research without significant research funding may mean (with resources to support academic research time) that such work could be carried out across all institutions, with less differentiation between new and old universities.

Social capital: conference and collaborations

Using his categories of convergence and divergence to describe the commonality and diversity of sociologists, Becher puts sociology firmly in the
divergence category describing it as 'fissiparous and fragmented' (Becher
1989). This finding would seem to be supported in the light of discussion of
scholarship and research, along with the many and varied forms of sociology (different theorists, methodologies, research areas). However, when
one looks specifically at research interests within departments there is evidence of a convergence of commonalities specifically with regard to
research interests. At Golden County University there were three identifiable research groupings within which staff had common research interests.
Likewise at Royal County University a new research centre had been
developed to which over half the staff in the department were affiliated. As
indicated by research strategies in Tables 6.7 and 6.8, there was a concerted
effort to consolidate research groupings within these departments.

> But as it turns out, it happens that there are people working in these
> identifiable groups, particularly in the [research area 1] and the
> [research area 2] where although they are groups with only two people,
> they are the ones that have most graduate students and postdocs. And
> then the rest is in a sense a much looser group, em, part of the
> coherence comes from the fact that we offer this [postgraduate course]
> and most of the other people teach on that course ... Em, but we
> realize that in a sense we have got to make a pitch for research
> coherence from the point of view of appealing to the research assess-
> ment exercise and also appealing to the university ... we know that we
> have to specialize, we can't pretend to do everything and we have a
> fairly naturally ... falling into these research groupings.
> (Professor Morrisey, sociology, Golden County University)

There would appear to be a concern to establish areas of expertise within
sociology departments, which has meant that research groups have become
more pronounced. This gives the impression of a greater convergence of
research interests. When questions are posed as to what a research group or
a research centre means effectively, in terms of practice, the idea of convergence is not quite as straightforward.

> Yeah, I mean by agreeing to disagree about more or less everything the
> staff get on pretty well. So [particular group of sociologists] think a lot
> of the other sociology is unsystematic and unpainstaking ... So it is not
> that we all agree what the future agenda for sociology is but that we
> recognize that all of us are probably pretty good at the thing that we do.
> (Professor Morrisey, sociology, Golden County University)

The sociology department at Royal County University had a new research
'centre' to which a large percentage of staff are affiliated, and their research

interests have converged on a particular research topic. They research and publish together, organize conferences and meetings and have regular contact. However, the introduction of such centres within sociology does have other important implication. Winsborough (1992) uses the term 'centrifugal' to indicate that research centres may 'fracture the disciplinary core'. One result of this is the move towards centres of specialization and a shift from 'GP sociology'. Professor McGowan gives one example to illustrate this.

> *Professor McGowan:* And to go back to the question of how does it fragment? It clearly, some people in this [department] ... are pursuing their research which is quite focused and specialized. They have to be very focused to do fieldwork that gets funded and that takes them away from general questions and it makes them, I think, not very keen to come to the seminar as we had the other week ... on the Origins of Sociology [by professor from LSE]. I mean it is fascinating stuff for sociology ... but if you are interested in a contemporary [empirical research] area ... it doesn't appeal ... And I do think the general question is, well I think of myself, I like that term, it's not mine its [professor from another university] who calls himself a GP sociologist. Did you ever see that article?

> *Interviewer:* No.

> *Professor McGowan:* And I think that is partly because of teaching, teaching undergraduates and I think I have made a virtue of it but this notion of having a wide interest again doesn't quite fit with funded research where you have to focus right down.
>
> (Professor McGowan, sociology, Royal County University)

Some members of staff were concerned that the emphasis on specialized research groups and funded research on narrow areas of expertise could result in the loss of the GP sociologist, the scholar, the theoretician. Perhaps these dichotomies of general and specialized are too strictly drawn but they do emphasize an area of struggle and tension over the 'social' nature of sociology. But in order to build up a research profile and reputation of expertise, it was recognized that departments have to be organized into research groups.

There was certainly a reluctance to engage in any form of active gathering of social capital in terms of attending large international conferences with Dr Leighton exclaiming that he did not like to 'network at large conferences'. There seemed to be a preference by some staff for smaller conferences and networks that Professor Davenport described as 'chummy'. He also made the claim that sociology can be quite 'insular', which may explain a relative lack of concern for social presentation and social prestige on the international stage – an interesting comment but one that would need further substantiation. In general, like the biologists, some sociology staff were not willing to engage in the social circuit of conferences, and others clearly saw it as central to their work.

Research strategies within the English departments

In contrast to sociology, the English UOA's demonstrate a huge increase from 1996 to 2001, particularly in 5 and 5* departments, much like biology, as shown in Table 6.11, with the number of 5 and 5* star rated departments rising from 11% in 1996 to 46 % in 2001.

Table 6.11 English departments with 1–5* grades in RAE 1992, 1996 and 2001

Grade	RAE 1992	RAE 1996	RAE 2001	1992	1996	2001
5–5*	7	10	41	10%	11%	46%
4	13	18	22	18%	20%	25%
3	24	31	23	34%	34%	26%
2–1	27	32	3	38%	35%	3%
Total	71	91	89	100%	100%	100%

Source: Higher Education Research and Organisation (HERO), www.hero.ac.uk

There were no discernible patterns in terms of number of staff submitted. But one interesting and significant difference is that a much larger percentage of post-1992 universities received high ratings in the 2001 RAE. In English, 63% of post-1992 universities gained a 4 or more rating in the 2001 RAE compared with 27% and 7% in sociology and biology respectively in the post-1992 university sector. The pre-1992 universities gained 96% of grade 4 and above in English with 85% and 95% for sociology and biology, respectively. It is interesting to compare the two English departments at Golden County University and Royal County University as it provides a contrast between an old and new university and their research strategies and submissions for the 1996 and 2001 RAE.

Decision making for the 1996 RAE submission within the English departments: a 'humane' form of management?

Professor Hadfield was responsible for drafting the 1996 RAE document for the English department at Golden County University. This was done in consultation firstly with the research committee and secondly in discussions with the directors of the research schools and with individual members of staff. Professor Hadfield emphasized the consultative nature of this process.

He maintained that, 'I did various drafts of the documentation which I passed around to people on the research committee and the directors of the schools and so we just worked on the plans together. But I was the one in charge of the overall drafting.' In terms of deciding on the submission of individual publications, Professor Hadfield talked directly to members of staff.

> In the other part of the RAE, the lists of publications, well, obviously that was a case of me speaking to each of the people and saying or agreeing what were the four best publications to put forward because just about everybody had far more than four and the issue was what weighs more, an edition or a monograph. That got very tricky because very often it was unclear in the rules as to quite which was best. I mean I can talk to you about that if you like but, eh, basically the way that was actually handled, which is what I think you are asking me about now, is that I saw everyone individually and talked through this with them. And we agreed on what was best to put forward. You know, em, I would never dream of telling anyone you must put forward these four. It was more a matter of a discussion, sharing the problem and seeing how it would look from the outside and we agreed on that.
>
> (Professor Hadfield, head of department, English, Golden County
> University)

Little was said by Professor Hadfield or other members of staff on the decision-making process of who would or would not be included in the RAE. There was little evidence of dissent over these decisions by staff that I interviewed. Professor Pearson was the only member of staff who discussed this issue in relation to one particular person not included in the 1996 RAE. Professor Pearson, however, also reiterated the belief in 'humane management' of these issues, as discussed earlier.

> I think we have managed it fairly humanely ... [long pauses]. There have been, I suppose, painful pressures on people who are not producing. One or two people who are not producing ... have been demoralized. Now I am thinking of one colleague in particular who is rather a special case. He was deemed by the criteria to be research inactive and in fact he was very productive and research active in a different form. He did a lot of editorial work and he contributed to other people's research through his editorial work and kept his own knowledge fresh and growing. But for reasons partly ... he was not actually producing any original work. Now he was a very useful member of the department. A creative mind in terms of research and in terms of thinking and in terms of teaching but it had a very bad effect on him because he didn't fit the criteria. It also discourages creative work since creative work isn't valued in this kind of exercise in the same way that ordinary scholarly research [is].
>
> (Professor Pearson, English, Golden County University)

Most of the staff interviewed were extremely positive about the 'supportive environment' for research within the department. These comments came mostly from the professorial staff but also from the lecturers and senior lecturers. For example, Mr Edmunds enthuses that the 'atmosphere is encouraging and positive'.

For the English department at Royal County University, I was not able to gather any data on the 1996 RAE submission. The result for this department was low with very few members of staff submitted. However, a significant increase in rating was achieved in 2001 so the strategies put in place to achieve this evidently had a significant impact.

Research strategies and plans for the 2001 RAE in English

The key research strategies within the English department at Royal County University summarized in Table 6.12 included: the further strengthening of research centres and groupings within the department, increased monitoring of research activities and mentoring of staff and supporting staff in terms of providing time to research and funds for conference attendance and library visits.

Table 6.12 Selection of research strategies and plans in English at Golden County University

Research strategies and plans
Staff have equal teaching loads
Strengthening of centres and research groups
Mentoring for all staff
Progress reports on individuals given at research committee
RAE questionnaire to be completed by staff
Database of research activities, publications, funding
Research leave for staff
Rich research culture
Encouraging interdisciplinary research
Funds for conference attendance and library visits
Teaching buy-out time
Reduced teaching loads for newly appointed staff

The support given to staff in terms of research included sabbaticals, whereby everyone was entitled to one term off in every seven to do research. Professor Hadfield made it clear that the award of a term off for members of staff was now strictly for research purposes, 'with a capital R'. In the past such time could have been used to develop a course or engage in other forms of scholarship but now it is designated for research purposes only. Staff were expected to outline what they intend to achieve during their time away and then a report is produced which is given to the research committee.

The positive attitude towards staff and the 'sense of understanding' was expressed by the head of department and other professorial staff, of the pressures which individuals are under and the belief in the pride which they have in their work. Professor Hadfield, for example, was insistent that asking members of staff for four publications in four years is not 'particularly onerous'. He talked about having trust in staff to know 'the right thing to do'. Furthermore, as indicated by the quotations used in the opening of this chapter, he understood the personal involvement, which academics have with their work.

The English department at Golden County University, however was planning for RAE 2001 from a strength in research and a high rating in RAE 1996. The English department at Royal County, on the other hand, was struggling to increase its rating and as a result there was a radically increased concern with research activity within the department and research strategies being put in place, as summarized in Table 6.13.

Table 6.13 Selection of research strategies and plans in English at Royal County University

Research strategies and plans
Creating clusters and groups of research areas
Creating a research centre
Departmental seminars and conferences
Teaching relief for research active staff
Research leave for staff
New appointments made in specific research areas
Increase external funding
Report on research activities
Invitation of visiting scholars
Funding to provide teaching buy out
Mentoring
Monitoring of staff progress against targets

As Dr Groves at Royal County argued, 'there is now a strategy and forms of monitoring of research in the faculty' and 'both at the faculty and the department level there is active intervention to increase research output'. The key features of these interventions related to staffing, funding and monitoring. The faculty had sought to increase appointments where possible through the use of both internal and external funding. In the English department at Royal County University staff submitted in the 2001 RAE were substantially different from those submitted in the 1996 RAE. More than five new appointments were made prior to the 2001 RAE, all of whom were research active and brought new areas of expertise to the department.

The inclusion of these new members of staff in the 2001 RAE submission obviously served to increase the rating awarded.

There was also a mentoring system within the department to enable members of staff to begin and develop their research. Professors played the role of mentor to a member of staff and would meet with them to discuss research plans and generally to talk about how things were going and give advice or guidance on any research issues. The 'research culture' of the English department at Royal County University was promoted by mentoring within the department. Unlike the English department at Golden County University where mentoring took place on an individual one-to-one basis, the emphasis at Royal County University was on 'collaborative and/or interdisciplinary research programmes' within the faculty. This involved research mentoring of those departments with a high RAE rating and those with a low rating. So it was more a strategy of merging research interests across disciplines than having one-to-one discussions on development.

The faculty at Royal County University had an interdisciplinary research centre that ran conferences and regular lectures, seminars and lunch-time meetings, which served to bring together researchers with common inter-ests and to serve as a promotional and instructional forum for research activities within the faculty.

The pressure was certainly felt by some members of staff in the English department at Royal County University, however, particularly those who were on part-time contracts and expected to engage in research activities at a level equivalent to full-time members of staff. As Dr Casey argued, part-time members of staff are 'paid half but expected to do the same as other people in terms of generating research'. Many staff felt under pressure and there was, according to Mr Sawyer at Royal County University, 'a kind of divisive, competitive spirit' in relation to those who are mainly teaching and those who are doing research, which created lot of tension between col-leagues. However, he was also keen to emphasize that the English depart-ment is 'still a relatively civilized place'. This was also the claim for the English department at Golden County, as well as the belief in the existence of a 'humane form of management'. In many of the views expressed, there certainly seemed to be greater concern with the personal nature and involvement in research and respect for individual autonomy. Where exclusions of non-research active staff were made, these were perceived to be regrettable.

Struggles and stakes in capital accumulation in English

Symbolic capital: research areas, publications and the importance of being international

Evans (1993) posits a tension between two schools of thought within English studies, one beginning in the 1920s and the other in the 1970s. The first is the Leavisite school of English. Also referred to as 'Cambridge English', the Leavisite view can be summarized as a desire to establish the importance of the 'great' literary works and make them fundamental to the study of English, to portray English as a serious discipline of study rather than a frivolous, amateurish activity and further to place English at the centre of human life: 'The belief was that studying English would make people more moral and would enable them to lead better lives amid the pressures of the modern world. English was redemptive' (Evans 1993: 131). The Leavisite position can be seen as a key development in the professionalization of the discipline (a process started, according to Evans (1993) by philology in its break from the classics) for it to be accepted as a legitimate and important area of study, critical to an understanding of human existence and providing a guiding moral force.

Most universities offer an area of study for English but there are a number of variations as to what these particular departments may be called. Some universities have a department of English or English studies, some have the more inclusive titles of English and related literature, while others make the distinction between English language and English literature. These different names given to the area of study, which is English, point to the complex history of the discipline and the particular specialisms or interests within individual university departments.

The evidence presented by Evans (1993) showed English studies to be a discipline with a multitude of cleavages and points of division. This is also attested to by the different names given to English studies departments. In many of the 'new' universities and some of the 'old' universities there was now a growing concern with English studies and its relationship to cultural studies. Also, the importance of multiculturalism within English studies has questioned the exclusive study of 'English' literature. Many universities have English language and related literature, which broadens the scope to include other non-English literatures; this was the case at Golden County University. Within the English department at Royal County University there was an interest in cultural studies and multiculturalism. As Dr Millen argued, at Royal County University the emphasis was on English studies 'because it is English from a broad cultural perspective'. The disciplinary organization of English, therefore, contains multiple divisions and processes of construction. These also have a strong influence on the organization and ideational structures within university departments.

The key determinants of research excellence outlined within the RAE process were that of research defined as 'original investigation' and the categories of national and international excellence. However, the English panel made clear that the different forms of output and publications would also be taken into consideration. It was not a straightforward process for the authors of research submissions to decide which forms of output were more valued than others. At Golden County University, for example, Professor Hadfield outlined the difficulties of making judgement on academic 'value'.

Interviewer: Did you look closely at the criteria set out for the English . . .?

Professor Hadfield: Yes we did but it is not terribly helpful you see because, em, if you are worried about what particular biases may be in the RAE panel. I mean, if you have an edition, you know how scholarly and how important does an edition have to be in order for it to weigh more than a single authored monograph and there is a kind of half joke, half truth about the RAE as it does single authored monograph over everything else and, therefore, you could have an extremely scholarly edition but you know it is felt rightly or wrongly that that doesn't quite weigh as much as a single authored monograph, because that has got your name on it, even though it might not be all that good, as it were. We can discuss the issue of quantity versus quality if you like but that was a problem. Then there was the issue of how to present certain things. I mean if you are an editor or a co-editor of an anthology and you got a major article in that anthology, is it better to put in the article or is it better to put in the anthology? And in my view it is better to put in the article and you can always . . . You may recall in the last RAE that there was this line or two that you had for extra information and I always put editor as well as something. . . .

Evidence from the research meetings at Royal County University also indicated how they are attempting to judge the relative importance of what has been called the 'second order reading of the signs' of reputation (Bourke 1997), namely the specific journals or publishing houses through which the research is published. At the staff meeting they discussed in detail the possible hierarchy of publishing houses such as the university presses and 'reputable' international publishers. Using these signs of reputation, they attempted to calculate their own collective publications within the department and the potential 'value' based on RAE criteria. They also discussed ways in which those publication outlets that were rated most highly can be the target for members of staff in the department. Ultimately, however, there was no absolute certainty as to the 'value' placed on some forms of publication over others (and these are not explicitly stated in the RAE criteria).

Of the three disciplines studied here, English demonstrates the greatest variety of research output, as shown in Table 6.14. There was also less differentiation between types of publication and different rating awarded to UOAs. The 5* UOAs submitted outputs across the range of journal article, chapter in book and edited book, as well as authored book. The two most cited journals in the 2001 RAE submission were *Review of English Studies* and *Textual Practice*, with 11% and 8% of outputs in 5 and 5* UOAs being located in those journals. However, there was no discernible difference between rating of UOA and the location of outputs in particular journals. It was also more difficult to establish international rankings of these journals in a way that would be possible in biology.

Table 6.14 RAE submission 2001 for English UOA, by type of publication

Rating	Authored book	Edited book	Chapter in book	Journal article	Others	Total
5*	22%	11%	31%	28%	8%	100%
5	22%	10%	30%	29%	8%	100%
4	26%	9%	30%	28%	7%	100%
3a	16%	5%	29%	39%	11%	100%
3b	17%	9%	33%	35%	6%	100%
2	17%	2%	19%	37%	25%	100%
1	–	–	–	–	–	–

Source: Higher Education Research and Organisation (HERO), www.hero.ac.uk

The distinction made between national and international standards of excellence proves a difficult process of differentiation for the individuals involved in writing the RAE submissions. The struggle over classification of 'international' can be centred on one's external reputation. At Golden County University, for example, the participants at the research meeting concluded that simply attending international conferences, giving papers or chairing discussions do not count. In order to demonstrate an international reputation one must be invited to address conferences (particularly as a keynote speaker) or be invited to present special lectures. There is an ongoing debate over definitions being used by panels particularly in relation to the category of 'international' and this was clearly an aspect of the evaluative criteria which academics struggled to interpret, often producing contrary views.

The relative (in)significance of material capital for English departments?

In terms of material capital, fellowships (particularly those granted from the British Academy) and other sources of research funding are the most prominent. At Royal County University staff made little mention about applying for external sources of income. Dr Groves had received research fellowships that covered travel and subsistence to do research work abroad, but apart from travelling to gather research sources, there was little need for Dr Groves to have research funding. His research, as he described, relies on 'scholarly solitude', the greatest currency for this is *time* to read and write. The solitary, book-based nature of research work within English means that there is no real need for substantial material funds. Most of the funds granted are used to release time from teaching and for travel to conferences or to specialist institutes to search archives.

The total amount of research funding given to English departments was obviously small compared to other disciplines. There is also a marked difference in funds awarded to departments rated 4 and above from those rated lower (see Table 6.15).

Table 6.15 Total research funds for all English departments submitted in the 2001 RAE, separated by grades

Grade	OST funds	Total funds	RAS FTE	OST/FTE	Total funds/FTE
5*	113,601	475,888	35.2	3,224	13,506
5	42,403	172,839	19.6	2,164	8,821
4	27,905	75,624	15.0	1,866	5,058
3a	746	9,718	8.1	92	1,199
3b	0	1,160	4.8	0	243
2	0	23,125	5.0	0	4,625

Source: Higher Education Research and Organisation (HERO), www.hero.ac.uk

For the period 1996–2001, research funding awarded to these two departments was fairly small compared to other disciplines. However, there is a clear difference between the two departments, with Golden County University being awarded double the amount of money as that given to Royal County University from the Arts and Humanities Research Board (AHRB). Golden County also received 15 times more funding from UK charities than Royal County. Material capital is clearly not central to the ability to conduct research in English. However, as indicated by Dr Groves, it can afford more time to spend on research and provide funding for conferences and international travel.

The relative (in)significance of social capital for English departments

The solitary, individual nature of much research in English also determines the forms of social capital. These can be identified as research groupings within and across departments; specific groups within a research specialism; and also attendance at conferences and meetings. The RAE submission for both departments has 'groupings' of staff within particular research areas.

At Golden County University they were divided into five areas and at Royal County University they were divided into four areas. The extent of research collaboration between individuals, however, was variable with many obvious research connections but also many staff working on their own.

Participation in national associations of research specialisms was common in the field of English. At Golden County University, for example, Mr Wright was a member of a research association so that he had a large number of contacts in his research area. This grouping was, however, as he described, 'too informal to call it a grouping but there are just a number of people who happen to be working in somewhat similar areas at several universities. It is as loose as that'. Interactions between members take place at 'day conferences, committees and also the circulation of regular bulletins'. It is within such specialist associations, however, that one can substantiate a reputation for one's work, which is outside of the institution. This can be further enhanced by the attendance at conferences and specialist meetings.

Research struggles, strategies and stakes: comparing across different disciplines

The movement of ratings from the 1996 to the 2001 RAE across all subjects was significantly upward. However, the extent varied across disciplines and it has been shown here how biology and English UOAs increased the numbers of 5 and 5* departments much more than sociology UOAs. There were also disciplinary differences in the extent to which the status of the university impacted on the likelihood of higher grades. English UOAs at new universities were able to attain high ratings in the 2001 RAE and to a much lesser extent this was true of sociology UOAs. However, highly rated biology UOAs were predominantly found in the old university sector. The findings reported by Sharp (2005) and others, that old universities perform better in the RAE, is supported but there are minor variations across a minority of disciplines. It is also important to note that these English departments would likely be fairly small and so would attract only a small proportion of RAE funds through formula funding. A high RAE rating, therefore, may bring symbolic rather than material rewards. When looked at across the sector, an elite of old universities are awarded the majority of research funding, as shown in Chapter 3. The point perhaps remains, however, that at least within some subject areas, excellent research can flourish across all institutions, particularly where there is less reliance on large grants to support research work.

In the small sample of university departments investigated here, there was substantial improvement in RAE ratings from 1996 to 2001 or at least a retaining of the same score. Each department has provided a unique insight into the complex processes that enabled developments in research activity.

Beginning with the views presented on the submissions for the 1996 RAE, it became clear that some departments were very organized and had adopted conscious strategies and plans in preparation for the submission, namely the biology departments at Golden County and Royal County University and the English department at Golden County University. All of these departments performed well in the 1996 RAE. The sociology department at Golden County performed moderately well but clearly had little strategic design in place prior to the 1996 RAE. The sociology and English departments at Royal County University had little, if any research strategies in place prior to 1996 and their ratings were unsurprisingly low. This situation had changed substantially in the lead up to the 2001 RAE and this was clearly reflected in the 2001 ratings.

The emphasis on the importance of research activity within all of the case study departments after the 1996 RAE was indisputably high. Organization of research activity and the amount of effort and forward planning given to the strategies for the 2001 RAE submission across all the case study departments give testimony to this. There were many commonalities within the strategies outlined by departments on the plans for RAE 2001. Particularly significant for those departments that substantially increased their rating was the employment of new staff. These staff were all research active and were predominantly employed strategically to strengthen areas of research within the department. The common and effective research strategies evident within these departments can be summarized under three key headings:

1   Creating areas of research strengths
    • making new appointments in those areas,
    • encouraging groupings of all staff within research areas.
2   Management and Organization
    • having a departmental research committee,
    • monitoring and mentoring the research work of staff,
    • creating time for research (and reducing other responsibilities),
    • providing start-up funds for staff research,
    • holding a database of information on research activities and setting research targets.
3   Research environment and culture
    • encouraging applications for research grants,
    • encouraging staff to publish,
    • encouraging all forms of research publicity including attendance at conferences,
    • increasing the numbers of postgraduates,
    • invitations for international colleagues,
    • encouraging a departmental research culture with seminars, conferences etc.

When set out like this, the research strategies seem remarkably simple and may be perceived as demonstrating fairly common-sense principles.

However, this list of relatively straightforward strategies is placed on top of a complex mire of disciplinary values. The RAE process and the academic and disciplinary fields within which it operates are enmeshed in complex and contrasting forms of hierarchies of evaluations and judgements, which have no necessary objective or clear 'criteria'. In each of the different disciplines the understanding and articulation of different forms of symbolic, material and social capital were explored in relation to the complex and often contradictory socio-cultural values. The significance of material capital for biology was highlighted alongside the importance of social capital in relation to internal and external collaborations and social networks and reputation. This was true to some degree for sociology, but for English, the necessity of material capital was less urgent and also to some degree social capital.

Common to all departments, however, were the complex struggles and decision making to determine what would be most valued by the disciplinary peers who make the judgements on the RAE panels. Evidence was presented of research areas being advanced that would be looked upon favourably by a panel, struggles over what work would be considered 'international' and how this would be judged. Much of this supports the findings of previous research that the RAE has impacted on the direction of disciplinary development (Harley and Lee 1997), with some researchers changing their research area to one which would be more likely to merit inclusion in prestigious journals and departmental heads attempting to change or modify research areas within departments to more closely fit the possible perceived biases of RAE panels.

Arguably, the most significant issue within biology and, to some degree, also the sociology departments, was the necessity of winning external funding. For biology departments, this was a necessity in terms of meeting the ongoing costs of laboratories, technical staff and research assistants. More than this, however, was the symbolic value accrued in relation to increasing material capital. This led in some cases to the expectation that all academics should be applying for and receiving (large) research grants, whether their actual research required it or not. In the sociology departments, there was a clear perception by some members of staff that there was an expectation that they should be engaged in empirical research that again would be able to attract research funding. Within sociology, and this would also be the case in the English departments, research funding was seen as crucial to departments being able to expand their numbers of researchers and of funding staff time to conduct research. The stakes are high because failure to attract funding would mean the inability of departments to develop their research capacity.

But what does this mean for the academic and research work of individual members of staff and their career trajectory over the period from 1996 to the 2001 RAE and beyond? In what ways do they respond to the departmental and institutional research strategies and what are the individual stakes for them in terms of their academic work and academic identity?

7

Academic Struggles for Recognition: the game of publications and priorities

> And remember at the beginning of the 80s we were talking about a situation where roughly most academics would do 70 per cent teaching and 30 per cent research. I mean, there was variation but everybody was funded around that level, to a situation where selectivity has meant that that no longer can be the case, that everybody can do 70/30 ... They no longer have the funds for every member of staff to have the kind of job description that they had previously. So that is the fundamental problem, is that for institutions that have not had sufficient quality, they can't ... they are gradually getting to a situation where they can no longer sustain a traditional academic job and that is the hard part.
>
> (Senior HEFCE official speaking prior to 2001 RAE)

What has happened to the traditional academic job? In the analysis presented in Chapter 6, it was clear that expectations had changed and priorities moved towards research even in those departments that had previously been more teaching-oriented. Some academics in these departments are struggling to accumulate the kinds of research capital deemed necessary to be classified as research active and to be deemed worthy of inclusion in the RAE while others are struggling to redefine what research active means or to widen the categories of academic judgement away from purely research activities. The classification of research active or research inactive is central to an understanding of academic identity and the positioning and valuing of academic work across all the departments. Given the symbolic capital associated with research success and the emphasis given to research by institutional leaders and managers, no department will want to be labelled as teaching only and so will struggle to maintain the 'traditional academic job' for all members of staff where possible, in other words, ensuring that they are research active as well as teaching. But not all academics in these departments can fit the ideal model the institutional research strategists want. What happens to them? What can their experiences tell us about the changing academic landscape and the changing demands of academic work? And what happens to the notion of a 'traditional academic job'?

Structural positioning and the construction of an academic 'habitus': changing dispositions and practices

The academics within these departments at Golden County University and Royal County University do not simply reproduce the ideational structures and research strategies within the university and disciplinary field, they also construct and resist them. This chapter looks at how these structures and forms of organization are mediated through the experiences of the academics situated within the case study departments. This analysis also includes a discussion of the perceptions that they have of the RAE and the way in which the demands of this process, again mediated through the context of a particular university department and discipline, affects their dispositions and practices.

Bourdieu's concept of 'habitus' is a complex one but put simply, it refers to the internalization of the social structure of individual agents. Academics are situated within a myriad of institutional and disciplinary structures. The field is the site of construction of strategies and struggles based on the *interests* and *dispositions* inherent within the habitus. Agents in a particular field are endowed with a 'practical sense' or a 'feel for the game', which orients their actions. This is no mechanical process where individual agents are conditioned or predisposed to act in a particular way since there are multiple configurations of possible social action in any field.

In order to look at the academic habitus one can study the many social and cultural influences that shape a person's 'practical sense'. In this study, I focus only on the immediate institutional and disciplinary location of academics. The competing strategies and struggles for the accumulation of academic and research capital (symbolic, material and social) undertaken by these academics, based on their position within the field, form the main focus of analysis.

Each of these academics can be considered a 'case'. They all represent one possible example of a social location within the myriad institutional and disciplinary structures. Thus, the individuality of the academic and their social positioning can be grasped and the institutional and disciplinary field context within which they are situated (Grenfell and James 1998). Some of the academics within the study are discussed in more detail in order to expand on the themes presented in the previous chapters. These include the principles of differentiation of academic and research work, the specific forms of academic and research capital and the struggles for classification within each discipline.

A biological habitus: changing dispositions and practices

Seventeen members of staff were interviewed in the biology department at Golden County University and 19 members of staff interviewed at Royal County University. The staff sample from each of the positions within the departments comprised professors, research professors, principal lecturers, research fellows, senior lecturers and lecturers. Of the 19 academics interviewed at Royal County University, 13 were considered research active and submitted for the RAE. Of the remaining 6, Dr Forster, Dr Francis and Dr Davies would consider themselves not research active whilst Dr Conway, Dr Jennings and Dr Castello are engaged in research. Of the 17 members of staff that were interviewed at Golden County University, 11 were submitted in the RAE as research active. The remaining 6 would all consider themselves research active despite their non-inclusion.

Individual cases of staff form two groupings, those classified as research active and those classified as non-research active for the purpose of the 1996 RAE submission. The members of staff in each biology department who were submitted as research active in the 1996 RAE are shown in Table 7.1. Their subsequent inclusion, or exclusion, in the 2001 RAE and whether or not they are still a member of staff in each department in 2005 is also shown in Table 7.1.

This form of differentiation of academics in terms of research active or non-research active is an important classification in terms of individual identity, but also, as will be argued, the valuing of academic work. The sample cases include four members of staff from the two departments who are classified as research active (for RAE purposes), including one research professor, one professor, one research fellow and one senior lecturer. From the group classified as non-research active they are all senior lecturers.

A comparison of dates of staff joining the departments (where available) and the status of being research active shows that everyone interviewed in each of the biology departments who was classified as research active and submitted for the 1996 RAE, joined the department after 1979. On the other hand, all of the staff interviewed who were classified as non-research active joined the departments between 1965 and 1975. Two members of staff who joined during this period were classified as research active. These cases show perhaps that newer members of staff are more research oriented (at least in terms of the criteria measured by the RAE) than those staff joining the department in an earlier period. This implies that the 'academic habitus' of newer members of staff in biology may be more disposed to research and that their 'feel' for the research game may be more central to their 'practical sense' of academic work.

Table 7.1   Biology departments interviewees

University	Name	Position in 1997/8	Inclusion in 1996 RAE	Inclusion in 2001 RAE
Golden County University				
	Prof. Meggitt	(Ex) HoD	Yes	N/A
	Prof. McEwen	Prof	Yes	Yes
	Prof. Mulligan	Prof	Yes	Yes
	Dr Waterman	Reader	Yes	Yes
	Dr Dray	SL	Yes	Yes
	Dr Merrygold	SL	No	N/A
	Dr Martin	SL	No	Yes
	Dr Eccles	SL	No	N/A
	Dr Revell	SL	No	N/A
	Dr Stanton	L	Yes	Yes
	Dr Robinson	L	Yes	Yes
	Dr Malone	L	Yes	Yes
	Dr Galloway	L	Yes	Yes
	Dr Sinclair	L	No	No
	Dr Newby	RF	Yes	N/A
	Dr Lester	RF	Yes	Yes
Royal County University				
	Prof. Laing	HoD	Yes	Yes
	Prof. Garrison	Prof	Yes	Yes
	Prof. Warner	Prof	Yes	Yes
	Dr Niven	PL	Yes	Yes
	Dr Lockwood	PL	Yes	Yes
	Dr Castello	PL	No	No
	Dr Richards	SL	Yes	Yes
	Dr Battersby	SL	Yes	No
	Dr Kirby	SL	Yes	Yes
	Dr Summers	SL	Yes	Yes
	Dr Lewis	SL	Yes	No
	Dr Davies	SL	No	No
	Dr Freeman	L	Yes	No
	Dr Forster	L	No	No
	Dr Francis	L	No	No
	Dr Conway	L	No	No
	Dr Jennings	L	No	No
	Dr Morris	RF	Yes	Yes

Biology staff classified as research active

Professor Mulligan (Golden County University)

Professor Mulligan joined the biology department at Golden University in the 1990s, having previously held academic posts at other universities. At Golden University he concentrated his efforts solely on research. His title was research professor and he was employed explicitly to make a direct contribution to the research activity within the department. He did no teaching in the department except for a nominal few hours of postgraduate teaching, which he described as 'fun'. This contact with students and other teaching staff (in meetings) also gave him some sense of being included within the department, as he often felt rather separate in his secluded research environment. He talked of 'peninsular research laboratories'. His lack of what is termed academic capital (in the form of teaching and participation in teaching committees), however, can be compared to his accumulation of research capital. This includes his position as a member of the research committee within the department, one that few members of staff in the department hold.

Within the institution he has a wealth of research capital both material and social. He was the director of a large laboratory and a research group of sixteen people, including technicians, postdoctoral researchers and PhD students. He described a kind of pyramid structure that characterized the interaction between him and the research staff. He was the director of research at the apex and there was some devolving of supervision with postdoctoral researchers supervising research assistants and research students.

Professor Mulligan does very little laboratory work himself and, indeed, he emphasized that his role was primarily a supervisory one, where often the postdoctoral researcher was the expert and had the technical ability. He said, 'I can focus on what needs to be done and how it needs to be done without knowing how to do it.' His role, therefore, was to manage and direct the activity, the 'the hand-waving person' with the 'big picture view'. He characterizes his three primary roles as being to manage, to write and to raise money. He confesses to having had little training in either managing staff or writing grant proposals, things which he spends a large proportion of his time doing. The time spent is hard to quantify in days or weeks since the activity fluctuates, although the need to ensure a steady flow of funding makes grant applications a constant activity.

The need for a continuous flow of income was felt by Professor Mulligan to be necessary not only to the ongoing production of research but also the employment of his research team. Being the only person with a university paid salary, while all of his staff are on 'soft money' (paid from research grants), Professor Mulligan felt a duty to ensure the continued employment of his staff. Applying for and being awarded research grants, however, is a fickle business and leads to a situation in which he feels 'unrelenting pressure and lack of certainty'. The funding situation within the department where there were very few internal research funds and the huge cost of the research work, including laboratory and staff costs meant that Professor Mulligan was under constant pressure to apply for and be successful in being awarded research grants. For this reason, much of his time was spent on formulating and presenting research proposals to funding bodies.

His other main activity was the presentation of the research work in terms of publications and lectures at conferences and meetings. The importance of publications for the symbolic value of one's research was evidenced both by the criteria used in the RAE and in the general perception of the success of one's work. Professor Mulligan argued that the recognition given to publications in prestigious journal articles (symbolic capital) was imperative for success in receiving grants (material capital), which in turn was necessary for the continuation of research work. He insisted that the primary reason for publication was for the greater good of scientific enquiry but that it also has the added advantage of establishing a 'successfully productive' reputation with funding bodies.

> it is important to make your information public domain so that other people can capitalize on that and the whole field moves forward incrementally as a result of everyone's published things. So if you don't publish you are not part of that no matter how good your stuff is. So, I mean, that's really the reason for publishing and that is why the funding bodies want to see publications because they want to fund research that moves science forward. So, I mean, ultimately it is a good reason. But the short-term reason is that if you have got a nice list of publications every year coming out then people think that you are productive and therefore if you are productive you should be given more funds if you have a good idea.
>
> (Professor Mulligan, biology, Royal County University)

The main activities of Professor Mulligan, therefore, have to be towards the presentation of the research work in the form of publications and conference presentations. This involves the 'work of representation' which contributes to the accumulation of 'a symbolic capital of external renown' (Bourdieu 1988). Professor Mulligan's strategy was to increase where possible this form of symbolic capital. He did not believe this to be the primary goal of his endeavours (as the quotation above suggests, the primary interest is in the development of scientific enquiry). However, the symbolic value of his activities, particularly for funding purposes and for RAE submissions was not to be underestimated.

Professor Mulligan was less involved in the production side of the research work within the laboratory since he had a more distant directorial role in supervising the research team. This freed up his time to be spent in grant applications and presentation of the research work. This distinction between production and presentation, however, is not always so divided, as the case of the next biology professor demonstrates.

Professor Warner (Royal County University)

Professor Warner, unlike Professor Mulligan, spent much of his time in the laboratory. He was involved with all of the research work. This was partly because he does not have a large research team, although he was one of a limited number of people in the biology department to have research staff.

He had two technicians, one postdoctoral researcher and postgraduate students. He also had a large laboratory space that was well equipped. He described himself as having a 'drive for science work' and works very long hours in the laboratory. He never takes coffee or lunch breaks and can be found in his laboratory from early morning until late evening.

Professor Warner: Well as far as I am concerned the normal working day is part time because when I get so enthusiastic, my daughter is doing nursing and sometimes she has a seven o'clock shift at the local hospital so I drive over here about half past six in the morning and it wouldn't be unusual for me to still be here at eight or nine at night the same day. What makes me tired is things not working, you know. I don't actually get tired by the physical effort of the work but worry when things don't go well or worry when you don't get a grant or...

Interviewer: So long as things are ticking over...

Professor Warner: So long as I can see the way ahead I like working in the lab.

Interviewer: So in terms of other duties within the university do you attend committee meetings?

Professor Warner: I'm not a committee meeting person, you can't do everything and I don't try. A typical situation would be that I would go to a board meeting and I'll have a piece of paper with me and I will doodle and start thinking about my next experiment or analysing the results of my last one. I go, I listen when there is something particularly relevant to me but most of the things that are relevant to me are research based, research facilities, funding... em, I teach on [a course] and I enjoy that but there is no way in which I could function at the level I do in research if I had lots of teaching...

He was very hands on and also took part in menial tasks within the laboratory (such as labelling bottles) as a means of demonstrating to his staff how important each individual task is to the overall scientific enterprise. He believed that he has a lot of autonomy in his work, arguing that, 'I am driving myself and not being driven.'

Professor Warner had been at Royal University for over 20 years. After securing a grant from a commercial organization and further grant money from a government scheme, he moved into his current area of research. He described what he sees as a 'fair element of good fortune' in his 'choosing the right topic at the right time' and managing to get funding to support it. This research area has resulted in the work being highly successful commercially. His research was not always so successful and he compares his current situation of a 'charmed existence' to his earlier years when he was always getting 'poor results' from his experiments and 'nobody was interested in (my) work'. He also feels particularly valued within the institution.

Professor Warner played an important role in the research environment of the department. He saw his research as being central to his position. His primary aims were to get grants, write papers and enhance the research profile of the school. He had already accumulated substantial research capital in a variety of ways including, materially with his commercial success, socially with his collaborations across the globe and invitations to international conferences and symbolically with a large number of research publications in prestigious journals.

Professor Warner spent much time in the laboratory due to lack of staff and also his enjoyment of the productive side of science. Institutional circumstances and lack of research funding meant that he was involved in much of the research work in the laboratory. He did believe, however, that more support could be given to his research efforts, particularly in the employment of research staff.

Professor Warner was committed to his research and it is within this area of academic work that he devoted his struggles for recognition. He thinks that teaching can be enjoyed as 'an interesting sideline' and described himself as 'not a committee person' with little time for departmental administration.

Interviewer: So you yourself would feel quite loyal to this institution?

Professor Warner: Oh it suits me, it suits me to a T. When you have been in an institution as long as this, you have been fortunate enough to be well respected by people around you. It is like … once I come in through that door it is my own little world here. Project students come in and out but, em, yeah, I have got a very well equipped laboratory. We have the radio on. We make our own rules. As long as we are producing papers nobody can, nobody would want to attack us or slow me down. I am doing just what the university wants even down to the commercialization.

Professor Warner felt highly valued within the school as his research continued to be successful. Research fortunes, however, can decline as well as rise as the case of the next biologist shows.

Dr Stanton (Golden County University)

Dr Stanton came to the biology department over ten years ago. He was given a reduced teaching load on his arrival so that he could concentrate his energies on building up his research work. The development of his research was aided by a start-up grant of £20,000, which was modest in terms of the necessary finance for molecular biology (approximately £10–12,000 per year is needed for consumables alone). Dr Stanton went on to receive multiple grants from a variety of sources including the Biotechnology and Biological Sciences Research Council (BBSRC). Like Professor Mulligan, therefore, he was dependent on the awarding of funds from research councils and charities so that his research could be maintained. When research funding becomes limited research capital is quickly diminished. For example, he had a group of 12 research staff working with him on these various research projects. However, at the time of the interview he had only two grants and his research staff had been reduced to four: one technician, one research student and two postdoctoral researchers.

Dr Stanton produced a lot of publications that were mainly multi-authored. He was criticized for this in the department. However, his research, firstly, was dependent on one particular professor (at another university) for the materials he needs for research. So this person must always be cited in his work. Secondly, he felt that he should help people in their careers. So he included the names of his research staff. 'People say it is not the best way to operate but they can like it or lump it,' he maintained. Given his changing fortunes he is uncertain of his success for the future. His accumulation of research capital was not consistent with the demands of the department and particularly RAE criteria. He had too many multi-authored publications, which were believed by the authors of the RAE submission for the department to be accorded less value for RAE purposes (although this is not stated in the panel's list of criteria). His research funding has been reduced and subsequently he has fewer research staff.

Other biologists, however, have difficulties obtaining funding at all, for a number of reasons not least of which is the type of research that one is engaged in. The following biologist demonstrates the problems involved.

Dr Lester (Golden County University)

Dr Lester has been a member of staff in Biology at Golden County University for over ten years. He worked as a postdoctoral researcher with a professor in the department for six years and then won a fellowship. He was not involved in teaching since his fellowship stipulated that he should be totally dedicated to research work.

> Having a [fellowship] grant also prevents you from applying for any other research money. Their aim is to focus you entirely on doing bench work yourself and not to become an administrator or a teacher and so they are particularly keen for people not to get side-tracked into doing paperwork for the department. Very much they want the scientist to remain at the bench doing practical work and to remain creative.
>
> (Dr Lester, biology, Golden County University)

The stipulations given by his fellowship are contrary both to his potential integration within the department and his ability to build a research grouping by applying for further research money. Dr Lester felt that his position within the department was rather contradictory since he was both a valued member of the department (his fellowship is a valuable asset) and also a rather marginal figure in that he had no official teaching or research status. This placed him in a difficult position with regard to departmental meetings. It is not entirely clear whether he should attend and what he should know. Since he does very little teaching, he felt there no point in him attending teaching committee meetings. Dr Lester's position within the department was uncertain in terms of both his official status and his future as a member of staff. For example, he did not have his own office with his 'name on the door'. He was led to believe that if he was successful in securing the fellowship he would be given his own office and there was a very strong possibility that he might receive an official appointment. This resulted in him refusing a permanent job offer at another university.

Dr Lester's accumulation of research capital was primarily symbolic (publications). He had no material capital (grants) because of lack of funding for 'pure' research and no social capital (few research staff), although he does have collaborations externally and he presents his work at international conferences. However, due to his unique funding arrangement, much of his time was spent in the laboratory. He was, as mentioned, in a contradictory situation where he had research capital but was not part of the general academic work of the department, nor was he able to increase his reputation in research, particularly through increased external funding.

Dr Lester, however, does represent a particular form of academic habitus, one which is oriented towards research and with a very definite view on the competitive nature of science and expressing particularly explicit strategies and interests. This may be because of his ambiguous position and that experience of this has heightened his awareness of the contradictory expectations and demands within academic life. The following interview extract begins with him discussing the 'politics of authorship' with publications.

> *Dr Lester:* So consequently that it is the way that we are going to proceed. And that again is partly a cosmetic exercise to show again the department and the outside world that you are researching on your own. In actual fact it makes no difference to Professor Bond to have his name on the paper or not. I prefer it if it was because he is obviously contributing some academic input. But then by doing that it then implies that he has the majority academic input which is not correct. So consequently it is easier on occasion to actually leave his name off and just have my name and my staff's name. There is a certain degree of politics involved, a large degree of politics involved, actually. To be seen to be is what is more important than what you are sometimes.

> *Interviewer:* Listening to you it seems obvious that a large amount of thought has to be put into the pros and cons of . . .?

> *Dr Lester:* I think very much so. You have an audience within the department, you have an audience outside the department and you have your funding body, which is difficult. You have to convince all of those people. Obviously to get another research project . . . you have to

show that the project has been successful and the people who review your project will be scientists in or outside the country which drives to a large extent the publications, the number of conferences you go to, which conferences you go to and, as I say, the politics, the authorship of it. That is very, very important.

Dr Lester is struggling to maximize the symbolic value of his work in the form of primary authorship of publications. His predicament as a research fellow and his need to respond to different authorities with their own definitions of research success placed him in many contradictory situations. The ambiguity of demands and expectations, however, was even more difficult where one's work was felt to be undervalued and overlooked. This is particularly the case with members of staff who were not put forward in the 1996 RAE submission.

Biology staff classified as non-research active

Dr Merrygold (Golden County University)

Dr Merrygold had been in the biology department at Golden County University for over 20 years. He had his own research group of five people, one postdoctoral researcher, two research students and two technicians. He spent his time on teaching, discussing research progress with his staff and writing grant proposals. He meets with his technicians every day, research students every two weeks and holds monthly meetings with the postdoctoral researchers.

During the period leading up to the 1996 RAE, Dr Merrygold held a significant post that involved him in a lot of administrative duties. He managed to maintain his teaching and research activity. However, despite his successful research record, funding from a multitude of sources and a list of publications, he was not included in the RAE submission. Dr Merrygold was unhappy about this decision and he was uncertain about how his work was being judged or whether he would merit future inclusion in the RAE. He was informed that his profile was not perceived to be international. In response to this he felt that it was pointless for him to go travelling round the world when his work, his staff and his laboratory were here in the department.

Dr Merrygold had accumulated similar forms of research capital to the other members of staff in the department. He was involved both in the laboratory work (although this is only possible in vacation time), and the presentation and development of his research work, including applying for research funding. The differences, compared with staff classified as research active were that Dr Merrygold held the administrative post, a role which took up more than the allocated 20% of time. For this reason, he had less time to spend on research. Furthermore, this responsibility meant a close involvement with departmental and institutional matters. During the period prior to the 1996 RAE, therefore, he did not have research links with universities from other nations nor had he travelled to international conferences. He did not believe that the possibility of international links was necessarily a constant in research work since it depends on what is appropriate for the development of research in a particular area.

> *Dr Merrygold:* There are certainly some research projects where there are particular groups and there are examples in this department, I think people you have probably talked to, where there are particular people related to them in different countries and it is very sensible. But there is no point in doing it just for the sake of being able to say you are doing it, it is pointless.

> *Interviewer:* So it would only be worthwhile if it was going to further your research?

> *Dr Merrygold:* That's right and in some cases it could do but, em, it depends on the particular field you are in, what you are doing and where you are going and what is happening in other places.

> *Interviewer:* Yes, that's why I asked, when I used the word appropriate I meant as a measure of quality.

> *Dr Merrygold:* I think it relates to quality in the sense that ... (pause) ... the more your international reputation is known the more people will suggest collaborations of various kinds. So I mean it must relate to quality but I am not saying that it is a simple linear relationship. It depends, and there are certainly examples where there are international collaborations, which I don't feel, are particularly challenging or particularly sophisticated. So it relates to quality but it is an over-simplification.

The reason for the non inclusion of Dr Merrygold was that he did not appear to have an international reputation in research. The strategy of the department was to achieve a high rating in the RAE and, therefore, it had to have a majority of staff of international acclaim. However, the precise meaning of 'international reputation' is not at all simple and academics raise the question of whether it is a measure that can be applied at all times to research work. Dr Merrygold resists the possibility of reorienting his practices to include more overseas research work but for this he is excluded from the classification of being 'research active', something, which he felt undermined the value of his work. Dr Merrygold was not included in the 2001 RAE and is no longer a member of staff in the biology department at Golden County University. Other members of staff in the department who were not included in the RAE submission were excluded for different reasons.

Dr Eccles (Golden County University)

On first introducing himself, Dr Eccles presented me with a timetable of events, which had happened to him over the course of the previous few months. They included a recounting of various meetings he had had with the head of department and the personnel department. The meetings with the head were to discuss his research plans specifically with regard to his attempt to secure research funding. The meetings with personnel were to discuss the proposal of early retirement that had been made to him. He was very resistant to the idea of early retirement feeling that he still had scientific work that he wanted to finish. From the point of view of the department, however, despite his possession of the required list of publications he was not defined as research active and was not put forward in the submission to the RAE.

Dr Eccles has been in the biology department at Golden University for over 20 years. He arrived when it was still a 'building site'. He had one graduate student working with him. In the first of a series of meetings he had with the head of department, it was made clear to him that he should be applying for research grants and in subsequent meetings he was asked to provide evidence of this activity. At this time he was particularly busy with teaching and working on a significant administrative role. Despite the fact that these initial meetings were conducted in a non-judgmental and helpful way he felt very pressurized and could not see how it was possible for him to meet the demands.

Dr Eccles suffered from severe stress during this period. He felt unwanted within his department and certainly undervalued as an academic. He had taken pride in a complimentary letter sent to him on his good work done in his administrative role. However, this ultimately held no comfort for him as he felt that due to his inability to attract research funding he was 'in bad grace', despite the fact that his research area needed little money to finance it. His status within the department was uncertain but he intended to remain until at least retirement age.

Dr Eccles did not have large research grants or a research team. He argued that his research is cheap to do and requires little funding to be maintained. He also has no international research collaborations or links, although he was invited to talk at two international conferences. For this reason, his research strategies and interests are at odds with the department, which requires staff to have research capital consistent with RAE criteria. Dr Eccles' research capital, therefore, did not fit with a department aiming for a high rating in the RAE. Dr Eccles was not submitted in the 2001 RAE and is no longer a member of staff at Golden County University.

Even in departments with lower expectations of their possible RAE rating, however, staff not involved in research felt that they are also undervalued, as the next biologist shows.

Dr Forster (Royal County University)

Dr Forster's main activities in the school of biology at Royal County University are teaching and administration. He made a conscious choice to stop doing research because he wanted to concentrate his energies on teaching students. 'Actual research interests, what people regard as research interests I don't have any. So I haven't done active research, experimental research for a long time' (Dr Forster, biology, Royal County University).

He continued with research interests and scholarship that he felt helped to give practical examples and provide a positive link with his teaching activities. He is a section leader within biology and this takes up a large proportion of his time. He is prepared to do more teaching than other research active members of staff but he is concerned that his worth as a teacher is not properly valued. He believes that despite the fact that evaluations for teaching are carried out, they are not used to any effect so that teachers who do a good job are not rewarded or valued within the university.

Dr Forster did not have a high volume of research capital in terms of any of the RAE measures of funding, publications or international reputation. His strategies and interests did not conform to the strategies and interests of the department in terms of raising their research profile and RAE rating. Dr Forster was resistant to change or to modifying his practices and he argued instead for a greater valuing of teaching. The department accepts that not everyone can be involved in research activity that can contribute to RAE measures. So there was a process to differentiate the activities of members of staff (hence the proposed policy of banding of teaching and research loads).

Dr Forster believed, however, that his position and activities in teaching and administration were less valued within the department with no acknowledgement given for work done well.

> I mean, if one has senior administrators and they acknowledge the fact that research, teaching and administration are three prongs that have to be covered and, therefore, different people could be doing that then all three somehow should be monitored and should be evaluated to actually say, look we acknowledge the fact that this person is good at it and that person is bad at it and that credit should be given, it should be publicly acknowledged. Whereas as it is you tend to find that people put in, like our departmental bulletin, you get regular notes saying congratulations to so and so who just got this grant or somebody who has just written up their PhD or whatever, but you don't ever see notes saying congratulations to so and so for doing a good course on, or doing a good job on administering this or setting up something novel in relation to their teaching or administrative duties. And it just seems in that sense, one feels you are pottering around in the background and you may be achieving very nice things but no one is actually crediting that other than perhaps your immediate colleagues, eh, and

even sort of senior folks. It is quite often one would go down the corridor and you can hear them saying what is happening with this research project or what is happening with that thing or that research experiment. But people don't ask you about what happened with that project you were doing in relation to resource-based learning or modifying that course or whatever. And you sit there thinking these things are not on a par even though in principle one says they are supposed to be.

(Dr Forster, biology, Royal County University)

The most salient issue to come through from the cases of these individual biologists is the extent of differentiation between academics in their activities and practices within these university departments. In contrast to the picture painted of the homogeneous profession (Scott 1995), the current situation is more an accentuation of the differentiation of the profession (Halsey 1995). A high percentage of research staff in biology nationally are on temporary contracts (62%), and this is particularly high in departments with high research productivity such as Golden University. The brief profiles on the few members of staff within the biology departments at Golden County University and Royal County University begin to give some insight into the differentiation of academic and research practices that exist within the same discipline, within the same department and even for academics at different points in their careers.

The 'feel for the research game', therefore, the understanding of the multiple forms of evaluation and principles by members of staff in these biology departments was not straightforward. Many of the interviewees discussed the multiple audiences (and therefore evaluators) for their work. Dr Lester, for example, was caught between the demands of the department and those of his funders. Other members of staff struggled to have their research recognized and valued and expressed confusion over the principles governing that evaluation. This was particularly the case for Dr Merrygold. The 'practical sense' and 'feel for the game' of many of these biologists, therefore, has been undermined by the development of research strategies employed by departments in response to demands of the RAE, creating a changing and conflicting landscape for the principles of evaluating their academic work.

One of the main issues raised in this chapter is whether academics are becoming increasingly more polarized between those classified as research active and those classified as non-research active. And whether the struggle for classification of being research active (based on RAE criteria) is changing the practices of biologists and, subsequently, the 'practical sense' and 'feel for the game' of these members of staff. Evidence from the biologists at Golden County University and Royal County University suggests that this is the case. There are significant institutional differences, however, in carrying out the research strategies developed in response to the RAE. At Golden County University only one member of staff who was not submitted in either the 1996 or 2001 RAE was still with the department in 2005. All other staff who were not classified as research active were gone. Some may have been due to retirements but other examples may serve to represent that inability of academics to survive in research oriented departments who do not possess suitable research capital. At Royal County University, on the other hand, there were two members of staff in biology who were not submitted to either the 1996 RAE or the 2001 RAE, and six who were not submitted both times, who were still with the department in 2005. Not being classified as research active did not necessarily mean exclusion, at least in biology at Royal County, but it did have significant implications for the type of work engaged in, the valuing of that work and individual academic identity.

A sociological habitus: changing dispositions and practices

The sociology departments that have been studied at Golden County University and Royal County University are relatively small compared to other sociology departments nationally. One third of all sociology departments have twenty or more staff. The experience and positioning of staff within them, therefore, may not reflect that of staff located in much larger departments. Smaller departments allow for different forms of interaction and cultural construction that would not be possible in much larger departments. However, the changing structural and ideational influences surrounding academic departments are similar for these sociologists.

All of these individuals are located in specific positions within these departments and their practices and 'points of view' reflect these situations. This section, therefore, explores the sociological habitus of the academics interviewed in order to analyse the 'practical sense' or 'feel for the game' that orients the actions of these sociologists.

Five members of staff were interviewed at Golden County University: two professors, two senior lecturers and one lecturer. At Royal County University there were six interviewees, one professor, one senior lecturer and four lecturers. At Golden County University only Mr Robertson was not put forward for submission in the 1996 RAE and, therefore, classified as research inactive. In comparison, three of the staff interviewed at Royal County University, Dr Casey, Ms Chandler and Mr Taylor, were not submitted in the 1996 RAE but as can be seen in Table 7.2, Dr Casey and Ms Chandler were submitted in the 2001 RAE.

In each department only one member of staff interviewed was not submitted in either the 1996 or 2001 RAE. Mr Robertson at Golden County University was still a member of staff in 2005 but Mr Taylor was no longer a member of staff at Royal County University. Unlike the biologists discussed in the previous section, there is no apparent link between the length of time

Table 7.2 Sociology departments interviewees

University	Name	Position in 1997/8	Inclusion in 1996 RAE	Inclusion in 2001 RAE
Golden County University				
	Prof. Davenport	HoD	Yes	Yes
	Prof. Morrisey	Prof	Yes	Yes
	Dr Leighton	SL	Yes	Yes
	Dr Abrams	SL	Yes	Yes
	Mr Robertson	L	No	No
Royal County University				
	Prof. McGowan	Prof	Yes	N/A
	Dr Nicholas	Deputy HoS	Yes	Yes
	Dr Jenson	L	N/A	Yes
	Dr Casey	L	No	Yes
	Ms Chandler	L	No	Yes
	Mr Taylor	L	No	No

at an institution (or in one's career) and the classification as research active or research inactive. Mr Robertson at Golden University and Mr Taylor at Royal County University have been at those institutions for over 20 years. Ms Chandler and Dr Jensen, both at Royal County University, on the other hand, are near the beginning of their career and had recently joined the department. There were fewer staff in the sociology departments who were on research-only contracts than in biology, such as research professors or research fellows.

Sociology staff classified as research active

Professor Morrisey (Golden County University)

Professor Morrisey had been in the department since the early 90s. He had taken on a number of commitments that relate to both teaching and research, including administrative roles in relation to research. He was, therefore, involved extensively in the research plans and policies of the department and in the 1996 and 2001 RAE submission. He had built up a strong research trajectory within his academic career moving between institutions and research specialisms. He spent a lot of time in accumulation of research capital, including national and international collaborations, attending research networks and small (more specialized) conferences (social capital). He was keen to receive research funding (material capital) and was applying for many research grants (currently four in preparation). Research funding was used primarily to employ research staff. Professor Morrisey was the only person in the department to employ a research fellow to work on his research project. Other members of staff have used such research money to 'buy themselves out' of teaching and free up their time to do more research. Professor Morrisey concentrated on the former strategy although he acknowledged that when it is necessary to write up major research projects then he may need to 'drop out' of teaching. This was not always the best option but is seen as the lesser of two evils.

Professor Morrisey reports a high teaching load (approximately thirteen and a half hours per week 'on paper') because his courses are popular. He felt under tremendous pressure and described his basic position as 'frantic firefighting' between the different demands on his time. Given his commitment to teaching, he also had an established accumulation of academic capital in his close involvement in teaching and in teaching committees such as the graduate committee.

Professor Morrisey was intensely passionate, however, about his research work and the convergence of his interests and 'expression of social being' or sociological being. He maintained: 'Well, I have got a position (in research debates) and it is a shame not to have that position represented. I mean it is because I believe in this position that I want it to be out there.' From his own perspective in his research field he was also concerned about the possible clash of values between what is demanded by RAE criteria and what he feels to be the important achievements of his work or ways of reaching his intended audience. This kind of dilemma was faced over publications choices. For example, should he publish in a handbook of research in his area (not highly rated for RAE purposes) or in refereed journals such as the *British Journal of Sociology* (which are highly rated for RAE purposes)?

Yeah, there is a clash partly in terms of two things. There is a clash in terms of RAE and so on because it is fairly clear what counts as reputable in terms of the RAE are books with recognized publishers or articles in the top mainstream journals. Whereas writing chapters for, you know, a book in Lisbon is more or less insignificant ... But it maybe that I am altogether wrong about these other things that I am doing, maybe I am stupid to be doing the handbook and what I ought to be doing not just for the RAE but for the sake of ... maybe people really do just go and read BJS (*British Journal of Sociology*) or *Sociological Review* and if it is in there then it has more of an impact than being in the International handbook. I kind of think not but I don't have the time or necessarily the inclination to try to work out a precise answer to that ... So at my interview I was asked this kind of question by the professor of psychology who said to me, do you know what your next RAE publication is going to be, and I said, well, yes I do, but I don't want to live my whole life as though that were the only thing that you are answerable to. Because there are things that I believe about the way sociology of [research area] should be done and there are people who I believe do [this kind of] sociology very badly and I want to stop them dominating the market. So I am more concerned, in some ways I ought to be more concerned to stop them dominating the market than for us to do well in the RAE. Although I know if we don't do well in the RAE I am not going to have time to do any research anyway so they will dominate the market at any rate. So...

Professor Morrisey's interests were focused on research capital accumulation both institutionally (through the RAE) and disciplinary (through his research specialism). He struggled, therefore, to achieve recognition across these multiple levels of evaluation.

As well as conflicts over what count as 'valuable' forms of publications within sociology, the RAE also offers a definition of research and terms of criteria or definitions of research which may not coincide with other scales of evaluation of academic work such as scholarship and original thought (rather than original research). This, at least, is the perception of the next sociologist.

Professor McGowan (Royal County University)

Professor McGowan had been at Royal University for over twenty years and in that time had built up a reputation within sociology both by holding positions of importance within sociological societies and in terms of his publication record. He maintained that he had little difficulty in attracting publishers for his work and, on the contrary, was often invited to write books. For example, he said that in the last few years he had 'had several approaches from publishers'. However, he was concerned that his kind of sociological research does not easily attract external funding and he said, 'I clearly don't do research that is easily fundable and I clearly don't do fieldwork in the orthodox sense.'

Professor McGowan described a term borrowed from another sociologist of a "GP sociologist", a general practitioner, one who serves to integrate and pull together the different strands of the discipline. He contrasted this with the specialist, the kind of sociologist who is expert in one particular research area but knows little of wider sociological themes and areas of study. He placed himself squarely within the former category. He worried, however, that the value of sociological work was being put more on the latter. Professor McGowan would position himself within the integrative, GP position within the sociological map.

Professor McGowan also argued in favour of 'original thinking' in contrast to the definition of 'original research' used within the RAE process. He gave examples of individual sociologists who would be placed within this category. This form of differentiation can be compared to the distinction made by Bourdieu between intellectual and research capital. It fits also with the idea of an integrative approach to research or scholarship.

A further differentiation can be made between theory and empirical research (see also Merton 1970) and disciplinary and problem based research (see also Gibbons *et al.* 1994). Professor McGowan argued that the empirical, problem-based research is becoming more valued within sociology because of the ability to attract research funding, particularly from research councils.

Professor McGowan, therefore, had spent time accumulating what could be described as 'intellectual capital' rather than research capital. His sociological reputation is based primarily on accumulation of symbolic capital (publications – books and journal articles) and social capital (collaborations with members of staff within the institution, but in different departments, and collaborations outside the institution). He was also keen to improve international collaborations with institutions in Canada and the United States. This struggle to achieve international links and an international reputation was in direct response to RAE criteria of research success.

Professor McGowan's major concern, however, was the difficulty of attracting research funding for his type of research work. Where he has been successful in small grant applications he has used the money primarily to buy himself out of teaching in order to have time to write books.

The difficulty of attracting research funding, however, is not reserved for more theoretically oriented sociologists but also affects more empirically oriented researchers as the following example illustrates.

Dr Leighton (Golden County University)

Dr Leighton was a senior lecturer in the department at Golden University and had been a member of staff for over 25 years. A large part of his time was spent working with postgraduate students (approximately 13–15 hours per week), in comparison with the time he spends with undergraduates (approximately 7 hours per week). He also supervised an 'erratic number' of visiting overseas students. His supervision of these students was related to his research area but the heavy time commitment meant that he had less time for his own research work, and particularly the writing up of his research for publication. His research area was empirically based and, therefore, very time-consuming in terms of collecting and analysing data. There is no time for research during term, as he puts it 'term time is zilch' and not enough time in vacations.

He had a reputation within his field of research and for this reason most of his writing happens in response to prompts and invitations. However, writing is often held up, because he lacks the time to complete it. He used the analogy of a 'camel' to explain how pieces of work can be carried around for a long time before there is finally time to finish writing.

> I have submitted two journal articles. One of which is based on work that I did in 1989 to '91. It was oldish work and I wrote up a draft in about '91 and it took me until some time to get that finished off. And

that has just been published. Another paper was this one that I mentioned that I almost completed the draft in about '94 ... term began and I didn't have time to finish it and came back to it in September [in 1996].

(Dr Leighton, Golden County University)

Dr Leighton reported no well-defined strategy for the presentation of his research work, given that many of his publications arise in response to invitations to write books or chapters for edited collections. However, he was concerned with the 'quality' of journals and implied a certain correspondence between the 'emotional investment' contained in a piece of work and his interest in placing it in a 'quality' journal.

I have been pleased about getting a particular paper in [a journal] because it is a journal that I have long wanted to have something to send them. And I think that with work that I really care about there are certain journals that I would like to get things into. But I wouldn't otherwise have a regular place [to publish].

Dr Leighton's work was interdisciplinary so he maintained collaboration with another department in the university. The main interest in his work was in the United States and so he had a number of collaborations with US colleagues. His social capital, therefore, is primarily with international colleagues and members of staff from other departments outside of sociology. His focus was on the accumulation of research capital rather than academic capital. His interests are working closely with postgraduate students on the 'production' of his research work. His reputation in the field and his publications also ensure possession of symbolic capital. However, he was unable to secure much research funding for his work. Given that his research area was not directly applied, he argues that it was difficult to receive funding from the ESRC. One application he had made was turned down. A shortage of material capital means that he is unable to spend much time pursuing international collaborations or taking time off from teaching to engage in the production and presentation of his research work.

For some members of staff, however, the accumulation of research capital was of secondary interest to teaching and administration; or the accumulation of academic capital is their priority.

Sociology staff classified as non-research active

Mr Robertson (Golden County University)

Mr Robertson was a lecturer who had been in the department for more than 20 years. He was the only member of staff not to be returned in the 1996 RAE and he felt that it was 'like a confession' to say that he 'hadn't published coming up to the RAE'. As a 'tactical move' he was given a position of 60% teaching within the department and 40% working on administration. He had a lot of enthusiasm for teaching. 'I love teaching, I love contact with students and I don't mind administration, you know as long as it is productive administration.' He believed that the RAE, however, has made research the 'be all and end all' of academic life at the expense of what he sees as the historical commitment to the teaching tradition of the institution.

> I have been in the game thirty years and I can see a shift, em, you know in terms of the priority given to teaching and I think that is a very regrettable move because it allows some people basically to get out of those responsibilities and write what I would consider to be academic self-serving articles. That is they write articles for, you know, twenty or thirty other academics to read somewhere else in the world which is . . . it has made us more inward, writing for these particular journals rather than addressing public issues. But I wouldn't say everything in the RAE is bad. I am just getting my chance to moan in early because academics do moan.

Although Mr Robertson enjoys his job, therefore, he felt that he did have much to moan about. His position reflects many lecturers in university departments who now feel undervalued and 'relatively deprived' not only in terms of income but also in terms of the symbolic value of their efforts. His main areas of interest were broadly an accumulation of academic capital, in the reproduction of the academic field in terms of teaching and student administration. The latter task he believed is perceived to be a 'punishment post' within the academic field.

> The official thing is you have got to be as it were outstanding in two areas, administration and teaching or research. I mean, I have been a lecturer now here since 1975 and I have never applied for a promotion and one of the reasons is because I know enough about it to know I wouldn't get it. And I am not going to put myself in the position of . . . every year asking for it, you know, and possibly getting disappointed. So, you know, and feeling relatively deprived. I would sooner just get on with what I am doing . . . because I know a lot of people, who have been quite affected by not getting promoted, hard done by and I can't . . . You know, this is what you have chosen to do. The one thing that is different now is the amount of time it takes your graduates to overtake you in terms of income. I mean I keep meeting these people who graduated about five years ago who are earning £10,000 a year more than I am earning. Bloody hell, you know, who is going to become an academic?

The position of staff who are mainly involved in teaching can be seen to be doubly undermined as the decline of status and income generally for academics (Halsey 1995) is accompanied by a lack of recognition for efforts in teaching and research. It is not so much that institutions and departments do not recognize the importance of these activities but that it remains a compensatory activity in comparison with the symbolic capital achieved through research (Bourdieu 1988). This is true even in departments where staff felt that teaching in particular was a valued activity. Lack of possession of research capital is seen as detrimental to the interests of the department.

Mr Taylor (Royal County University)

Mr Taylor described himself as an 'old timer' having been at Royal County University for over 20 years. He has held an important administrative role in the department four times and has recently been given this position on a permanent basis. It took up a lot of his working time. He also taught for approximately 10–14 hours per week. He believed that the important thing in the context of Royal County University was a 'commitment to teaching'. He argued that 'the old university idea of a lecturer being there to do research and a little bit of teaching on the side ... will not actually meet the needs of the sorts of (students) that (are) coming in now'. He also felt that he was often picking up the supporting side of the teaching role when other members of staff were unavailable. One example he gives is of a student who 'had never actually been able to get to their personal tutor because the personal tutor was never in ... so I switched over as personal tutor and dealt with it'.

Mr Taylor would once have classified himself as a researcher but now, particularly in relation to RAE criteria, he did not want to be classified as research active. He had no interest in accumulating the forms of research capital that are valued for the RAE such as publications and research funding. He passed over all of his PhD students to other members of staff. He felt that it was 'not about research, it is about publication'.

> To be here (in the department) is not work, work is to get published even if hardly anybody ever reads them. The little CV-able items. Teaching and student care, those things are not CV-able. They are not part of the department's achievements and it is the classic thing that you find in any institution, it is the observable things that actually become part of the records of the institution that become important. All the literature on hospitals, any sort of institutions, em, bear that out, that tendency. The things that can't be seen or counted are ignored. Now I tell everybody I think this is a smashing place. I think that those things are tendencies, they are external tendencies and there are responses to them. All the staff that I know are really con-scientious and they will ... they are student centred, they will work on behalf of students ... But what they experience is a putting away the fact that this is unproductive, it is not valid. Things that are valid are the things that appear in the departmental reports as publications.
>
> (Mr Taylor, sociology, Royal University)

Other members of staff in these departments, particularly those joining the department more recently and who are at the early stages of an academic career recognize the importance of research capital for achieving status within the institution. These people, such as Dr Jensen and Ms Chandler are concerned, therefore, to maximize their strategies to develop their research interests.

Ms Chandler (Royal County University)

Ms Chandler has been in the sociology department at Royal County University for five years and is employed as a fractional lecturer. She was just completing a PhD. Her official teaching load took up the whole of her half-time post.

> I lead a module with 200 students this term as a half timer and another module, much smaller, but basically I am fully committed, you know, half of my week is spent teaching tutorials, preparing, whatever. So the research is something that goes on in my unpaid time, em, and I regard the PhD as mine ... as my treat to myself in some way but the department will ultimately benefit from it.

Despite the fact that such a large proportion of her time was spent on teaching, Ms Chandler was keen to develop her research interests and particularly to increase her acquisition of forms of research capital. She was not submitted in the 1996 RAE but was determined to be included in the 2001 RAE. She maintained that 'we are encouraged to be research active and I definitely want to continue to be. I would hate to be just teaching.' She was quite explicit on her research strategy, therefore, which was directly aimed at RAE submission. Her primary goal was to have four publications and so she was working towards this, helped by some internal funding to 'buy more writing time'.

> Em, basically I definitely want to go into the next research assessment exercise ... whenever that might be. I was named as a researcher in the last one but not with enough, sufficient papers. So I am working very much towards having four papers for the next exercise whenever that might be. Em, and already I have a chapter in a book and I have a paper that is with (a journal) at the moment ... Em, and I have funds from a QR fund ... to help me write a paper. Basically, it is sort of buying me in to write another paper but that paper, all of my publications are linked to my PhD. So I am being very instrumental in publishing as I go along which I believe is common practice now. But I certainly aim to have four publications for the next RAE.

Since Ms Chandler was at the early stages in her career, inclusion in the RAE submission had become an important marker of her status as a researcher. Her accumulation of social capital had included attendance at conferences and workshops where research links had been made. Her research was part of the departmental research centre and this also involved collaborations with other members of staff in the centre.

The ways in which all of the individual sociologists discussed are enmeshed within the structural locations of disciplines and institutions ensures that they have unique positions and trajectories which give them particular strategies and interests. The balance of activities and the economy of time spent on research and teaching was different for all members of staff. Although in both department all members of staff reportedly have similar teaching and administrative loads, with the exception of Mr Robertson at Golden County University and Mr Taylor at Royal County University who have additional administrative duties. For those members of staff not submitted in the 1996 RAE there was either an overriding concern to accumulate the necessary research capital and prioritizing of this in order to be submitted in the 2001 RAE (Dr Casey, Ms Chandler), or a significant rejection of the research priorities of the department – a concern that other important activities such as teaching and administration were being undervalued (Mr Robertson, Mr Taylor). A possible gender issue was thrown up in these two departments, where female members of staff were more likely to be working part-time (often with full-time teaching loads) and, therefore, would perhaps be doing research often in their own time (Ms Chandler). For those members of staff who were submitted in the 1996 and 2001 RAE there were still struggles over the valuing of different kinds of sociological research work (Dr Leighton, Professor McGowan). The continuing struggle ultimately is over what it means to be an academic and what is means to be a sociologist.

An 'English' habitus: changing dispositions and practices

The English departments at Golden County University and Royal County University are contrasting in a number of ways with differences in numbers of academic staff and RAE ratings. The English department at Golden County University was much larger than at Royal County University and in the 1996 RAE, their ratings were at opposite ends of the scale. However, by 2001, they were significantly closer together with both achieving a high rating.

I interviewed ten members of staff in the English department at Golden University: three professors, three senior lecturers and four lecturers. All of the staff that I interviewed were returned as research active in the 1996 RAE, except the relatively new members who had joined the department just after finishing their PhD. At Royal County University I interviewed five members of staff of whom only one was returned as research active in the 1996 RAE. This included one principal lecturer, three senior lecturers and one lecturer. All of these individuals had been in the department for over 20 years with the exception of Dr Millen who was a recent appointment, having just finished a PhD at another institution. By the time of the 2001 RAE the situation at Royal County University had changed quite dramatically with only one original member of staff remaining, as shown in Table 7.3.

Table 7.3   English departments interviewees

University	Name	Position in 1997/8	Inclusion in 1996 RAE	Inclusion in 2001 RAE
Golden County University				
	Prof. Hadfield	HoD	Yes	Yes
	Prof. Pearson	Prof	Yes	Yes
	Prof. Rosewall	Prof	Yes	Yes
	Dr Ballard	Deputy HoD	Yes	Yes
	Mr Savery	SL	Yes	Yes
	Mr Edmunds	SL	Yes	Yes
	Mrs Jeffries	L	Yes	N/A
	Mr Wright	L	Yes	N/A
	Dr Honner	L	No	Yes
	Dr Green	L	N/A	Yes
Royal County University				
	Dr Groves	PL	Yes	N/A
	Mr Booth	SL	No	No
	Mr Sawyer	SL	No	N/A
	Mr Bond	SL	No	N/A
	Dr Millen	SL	No	N/A

At Golden County University only one member of staff was not submitted in the 1996 RAE, Dr Honner, but he was submitted in the 2001 RAE. By 2001 two members of staff had left the department, Mrs Jeffries and Mr Wright.

The division of labour for these English academics was closer to that of the sociologists than the biologists. There were no 'research only' appointments and in principle the teaching loads were the same for all members of staff, regardless of status. The classification of research active or research non-active is important, however, for an understanding of the habitus of these English academics and their dispositions and practices in terms of the accumulation of academic and research capital as the individual cases illustrate.

English staff classified as research active

Professor Rosewall (Golden County University)

Professor Rosewall has been at Golden University for a number of years. She was the director of a research centre. Her research interests were varied and diverse, but she claimed to have too many research interests, which she believed was not a sensible RAE strategy. She was a generalist and had research interests in a multitude of areas rather than developing an international reputation in one specialist area.

No, em, you know the book that I am writing now, I want to stop just writing articles or chapters or whatever people ask me to do. Em, and really, yes, and really get a monograph ... a colleague and I are editing a set of essays and we are putting essays in ourselves on one thing. And there is another set of essays I am editing which I will only contribute an introduction to. But the monograph, and then you know then I get just chapters and articles. But the monograph on my [research area], I am really focusing on that. And that is a totally RAE generated, well it is not totally RAE generated but I mean there is a terrible sense with the RAE that you have got to have a monograph for the next RAE. So I am looking to be able to present one alongside other things.

Due to her reputation in a particular research area, Professor Rosewall received numerous requests to contribute to edited collections. However, she was resisting the possibility of having a 'whole research career generated by other people's priorities'. For this reason, she was keen to publish in journal articles and particularly to complete her monograph. Her strategies for research capital accumulation were heavily influenced by RAE considerations and particularly the perception that monographs were more highly rated. This was explicitly stated in the 1996 RAE criteria set by the English panel. She was also keen to consolidate her research interests and be less involved in too many research areas, since she believed that RAE criteria demand an international reputation in a specialist area.

Professor Rosewall also had many teaching and administrative duties which take up her time. She was on a number of departmental and university committees. Her interests and involvement in university and department affairs was wide. Her status and positioning within the department, both in terms of research and teaching was highly regarded and centrally placed. She ran a successful research centre with many graduate students. Her only concern was to ensure the continuation of her research work and to avoid complacency when faced with relative success. She said, 'I have ten more years to go, that one doesn't think well I've got it all in the bank now. I think you have to keep moving forward right to the end.'

Other members of staff, however, when faced with multiple pressures of teaching, administration and research, were more inclined towards retirement even when there was a continued interest in academic pursuits.

Mrs Jeffries (Golden County University)

Mrs Jefferies held a significant administrative role. She had taken over this post for one year only to replace a colleague who took early retirement and changed to a part-time contract. Mrs Jefferies had been at Golden County University for over 20 years, beginning her lectureship before finishing an MA. But she did not have a PhD. She planned to take early retirement but would like to be retained on a part-time contract. She believed that being part time will mean that she has more time for research, particularly in terms of time to spend at libraries, which she argued can be notoriously difficult during vacation but much easier during term time. She would, therefore, continue to teach at Golden University on a part-time basis.

Mrs Jefferies enthused about her research work and talked at length about it. She was included in the 1996 RAE, having four publications but finds it difficult generally to work to timetables. 'My curiosity leads me,' she said, 'and I don't sort of think sufficiently firmly in terms of, I need this length of time to write it up and it has got to be published by then.' For this reason she feels unsuited to the time-bound culture of RAE deadlines.

Members of staff at Royal County University, particularly those not active in research, also see retirement as a possibility for escaping the pressures of academic life.

English staff classified as non-research active

Mr Sawyer (Royal County University)

Mr Sawyer joined the English department at Golden University over 20 years ago. He currently holds an administrative post, which involves chairing meetings, distributing teaching loads and day-to-day administration. A substantial proportion of his time, therefore, was spent on these activities, which serve to reproduce the academic system, and consequently, he accrued academic capital in his position. As compensation he had less undergraduate teaching to do. In terms of research, however, he felt out of touch with the current RAE climate and with the 'fact that research money and research profile seems to be the centre of everyone's concern'. He has published work in the past and felt that was a time 'when I had something different to say and I said it'. But he now felt unable to produce publications on demand as he feels is required by the RAE. He was interested in research and publishing but not to any particular time scale or level of production. Like Mrs Jeffries, therefore, his current end goal strategy is retirement since he felt the academic environment had changed into a competitive and divisive one. His interests and certainly any strategies to compete in this social field have ceased.

Other members of staff faced with a similar lack of research capital have renewed their interests and strategies towards the accumulation of academic capital and continue to struggle towards an accumulation of research capital.

Mr Booth (Royal County University)

Mr Booth described himself as a teacher rather than a researcher. Most of his efforts were directed at teaching and his publications have been mainly for 'aiding teaching rather than pure research'. So, for example, he had been involved in producing textbooks for students. He argued that although the roles of teacher and researcher are not necessarily in opposition, they are demanding in different ways.

> And it really does depend, at the end of the day, whether you see your primary role as being a teacher and inspirer of the young or whether you see yourself as the producer of, em, books and scholarship. These two things aren't necessarily exclusive but they tend to be in my experience, people tend to be teaching people or going away and doing their own thing sort of people. There is overlap, you can get and there is some truth in the case that, em, there is something to be said and I think it is quite true that some very good researchers are wonderful teachers. It is not as true I think as some people wish because I think the demands of research are so all devouring and encourage you to be intensely selfish. It is very difficult then to just turn off because teaching is exhausting. It may not be exhausting in the way that teaching a primary school is exhausting but it is still exhausting. It is giving of yourself and it is a fairly tiring and selfless activity, I think, with teaching. It requires effort in preparation and effort in delivery and effort in marking and feedback and that does actually take up a lot of time that if people think they are good researchers will resent. It is a circle that is difficult to square.

Mr Booth did not have a PhD and without this, or a substantial research trajectory as part of his career history, Mr Booth felt somewhat at odds with the new demands being made for research productivity of staff within the department.

> I have been trying to work on another article but it is still very much in the early stages and I can't see the end of it, whether it is going to work, whether it is publishable or not. But, of course, I shall keep at it for the simple reason that, em, I now find myself, as we all do in this situation, where I don't have much choice. Y'know that I have to keep trying even

if I am not very successful I am going to try and think in research terms while before, for the twenty-odd years that I have been in the job I have never thought of myself as a researcher at all.

Mr Booth is changing his practices and reorienting himself towards a strategic accumulation of research capital in much the same way that the 'new recruits' of these departments, such as Dr Millen (Royal County University) and Dr Honner (Golden County University), are learning how to 'play the research game'. Strategies for getting publications dominate the research practices of these two individuals. However, this can be a difficult process and it is not easy for beginning researchers to get started especially when, like Dr Honner, one is working in an 'urban' (Becher 1989) research area which is 'contentious and competitive'. As he explained:

Research work can be divided into periods and can be a problem. (There is) encouragement for people to stay within those fields of study. If you are working at the junctures [1820s and 1930s] then it might be difficult to get work published. Not necessarily because of individual prejudice but the fields tend to be self-confirming.

Mr Booth also emphasizes the importance of the *time economy* of research, the need to build up a research profile through years of dedicated work to a particular research area. But this time economy can be split between the process of *production* and the processes of *representation* of research work (Bourdieu 1988). Mr Savery also gives a profile of the new 'professional' English researcher.

Mr Savery: Yes, I guess and in many ways there are pay-off for that but it seems much more professional. People are much more conscious of how you manage your CV, how you organize your life around publications and public profile and so on. There are very positive dimensions to this I think and I ... I think it was more generous, more leisurely in some way, culture within the department. But it may have also been less geared towards the wider audience, you know, talking to colleagues and teaching and so on and not engaging enough in larger events.

Interviewer: So becoming more specialized?

Mr Savery: Now, I think we have become more specialized, em, and more building up around one project leading to another, a more driven rational version of a professional career, I think, has emerged. And I guess I don't find myself, I don't easily identify with it. I am impressed by it but I don't actually incorporate it ...

The struggles of staff within the English departments have much in common with those of staff in the biology and sociology departments, despite the difference in departmental and disciplinary organization. That is, those members of staff who do not possess the necessary forms of research capital and who struggle to reorientate the priority given to certain forms of research work and to attempt to redefine the meaning of academic work and research work being imposed. They tend, however, to fail and ultimately to be excluded from these departments where their dispositions, practices and values in relation to being an English academic are no longer tenable.

Struggles over researcher identity within academic life: academic habitus and principles of differentiation

Professor Rosewall: So of course, em, a research positive climate, a climate which favours research which is willing to put resources into backing research is going to help, that is clear. But there is something mysterious about what makes people want to write or able to write that may be beyond all that.

Interviewer: You say that it is mysterious?

Professor Rosewall: It is mysterious in the way that human beings are mysterious you know. It has to do with what they want out of life, isn't it, their priorities. This is why, I mean watching other people over the years I can see that their, they change, sometimes being productive and writing five books in one year is the most important thing they want to do and then they want to do something else with their life. And there is a kind of assumption in a sense behind the whole research culture philosophy that we will always be equally productive. People always ought to do something but the drivenness that is behind a lot of research, the drivenness comes from elsewhere don't you think?

Where academics struggle to establish their research identity, there is some difficulty with learning the complex and sometimes contradictory 'rules of the game' both within disciplinary and sub-specialist fields, and this is accompanied by the corresponding modes of evaluation of research work within the RAE process. The embeddedness of RAE criteria in the struggles and strategies of individuals as well as at the department level is very explicit and the concern of new members of staff in particular with publication strategies implies a new form of enculturation within university departments, which defines both the production of disciplinary knowledge and the more general meaning and significance of academic work.

Evidence from the interviewees in the departments at Golden County University and Royal County University shows clearly that all 'research active' staff orient their strategies and practices of publication, funding proposals, conference attendance (all forms of investment in symbolic capital) towards their perception of what is demanded by RAE criteria. 'Non-research active' members of staff have a similar orientation to their academic practices, particularly those who are 'new recruits' at the beginning of their careers. Others, predominantly those members of staff with a large investment in academic capital, attempt to subvert the dominant value accorded to research activities by refusing to engage in research activities and arguing instead for the positive recognition of forms of academic capital.

One of the key principles of differentiation of academics within the case study departments, is that of being defined as research active or non-research active. Those members of staff defined as non-research active can be placed into three different groupings. Firstly, there are those members of staff who are just beginning their academic careers and have yet to build up a research profile and publications list. Secondly, there are those individuals who have 'opted out' of research activities, and thirdly, there are the researchers who despite being actively engaged in research are not classified as such. These 'groupings' of staff should not, however, be read as fixed or as ordering the academics interviewed into 'types'. The reality of these positions is much more fluid and dynamic. In order to understand the definition of 'research' and 'research active' within the context of English studies, it is important to analyse the struggles of classification (Bourdieu 1988) over these activities. The values and beliefs of academics are not fixed but involve 'struggles to resolve competing interests and values' (Trowler 1998).

There are cases of academics who were not submitted in the 1996 RAE but were subsequently returned in the 2001 RAE (Dr Casey and Ms Chandler in sociology, Dr Honner in English and Dr Martin in biology), and only Dr Battersy in biology who was submitted in 1996 but not in 2001. Many of the examples of biologists in particular demonstrate how research fortunes along with research funding can go up and down and it is a fluid, changing and temperamental marker of researcher status. Equally, the quotation by Professor Rosewall at the beginning of this section makes the point that the research process and the process of writing may not be so easily managed. It is a 'mysterious process', which depends on a sense of 'drivenness' by the researcher. However, to drop a ball or fail in accumulation of appropriate forms of research capital can result in the loss of researcher status and the loss of value attributed to one's academic work and position.

The struggles of the academics in these biology, sociology and English departments over their academic and research identities is clear, they struggle over the valuing of academic work (teaching and administration) and over the valuing of research work (research areas, publications, the generation of research funding). Each individual represents a position within a myriad of institutional and departmental strategies and principles of differentiation as well as the complex fields of disciplines and sub-specialist areas. To succeed in accumulating appropriate research capital is a complex and uncertain process, the outcome of which can extend or limit the entire formation of an academic career.

8
The Future of the Academic Research Game

I would rather see all the vice-chancellors lined up for a hundred yards dash and just assign (research) money on that basis, because that exercise would take at the most two minutes. Even the weakest vice-chancellor could do a hundred yards in two minutes and then get on with life. It is about as rational as that. At least you could train your vice-chancellor and pick a healthy one. At least you would have a use for a vice-chancellor at long last, you'd be able to select on a rational basis. It might televise well and you might get money from the rights on watching it. And you might get rid of a few each time.

(Dr Martin, biology, Golden County University)

This book began with a sentiment that the UK RAE had transformed universities and university life in a number of negative ways and the opening quotation to this closing chapter once again expresses the disdain with which many UK academics respond to the RAE. The picture painted throughout the book, however, is a complex one and is based on only a small sample of case study departments so does not claim to represent the experiences and perceptions of the wider UK higher education community but only to provide an in-depth look at a number of biologists, sociologist and English academics within these two institutions at a particular time. I want to close by summarizing and reflecting on some of the key themes and issues that have traversed the book and by finally questioning the future direction of funding and evaluating university research and by implication the whole university sector.

Funding and evaluating university research: global convergence?

My rationale for choosing the comparative higher education systems of Hong Kong, Australia and the Netherlands was to explore the differences they demonstrated in their policies for evaluating and funding university research. However, there seems to be a significant move towards greater convergence of such policies despite some continuing differences in emphasis. For many systems the evaluation of research is becoming more closely linked to funding and evaluation is conducted using both qualitative and quantitative measures. As argued in Chapter 2, this is being driven mainly by the imperative of international competition and the demands of the global knowledge economy. The influence of international league tables and particularly those produced by the Shanghai Jian Tong University (Marginson 2005) is clear. There is an expectation for universities to be 'world leaders' by policy makers across the globe and the best way to achieve this is argued to be the increased concentration of research resources in elite, world-class research universities. Intended or not the UK RAE has served to deliver this but with spectacularly negative results for many universities and university departments. Evidence has been provided by the study on the significant move to more corporate managerialist strategies within universities in response to the demands of international competition and particularly in relation to the management of research.

The political context within these institutions is one of intense competition and pressure to increase research ratings. Institutional managers were struggling to ensure a favourable positioning of their university within the 'main game' of research success. It is evident from the experiences presented here that the RAE was a central driver and of significant symbolic value to these institutions in order to secure their reputations in research and their status within the hierarchy of the higher education field.

Looking to the future 2008 RAE, some moderations have been made, particularly in the case of the main panel/sub-panel structure, which may help to address some of the more restrictive aspects in terms of valuing different forms of research, such as applied research and interdisciplinary research. Similarly, the move to a grading profile rather than a single rating may serve to limit the possibilities for positioning universities into hierarchies, although no doubt a way will be found to do this. League tables are probably here to stay. However, the impacts of these changes for the 2008 RAE will be minimal.

The House of Commons Select Committee on Science and Technology report engaged with the possibility of relying more on a metric formula for funding, particularly in science subjects, where such quantitative indicators are more meaningful and for those high-performing departments where, likewise, information on funding and citation counts may be good indicators of quality. They argue that, 'a range of measures could be used to replace the peer review process in some subject areas such as the physical sciences. There are strong reasons to believe that they could be as reliable as the current system while being more cost effective and imposing less of a burden on institutions and panel members' (House of Commons Science and Technology Committee 2004).

The danger of relying too much on metrics, however, has been highlighted by the Australian case. Particularly in relation to citation indices and publication counts, where bias is evident and which is inappropriate in the main for trying to assess the quality of research in the social sciences and humanities. This raises the question of whether all subject areas should be treated in the same way and also whether more fundamental changes need to be made to the RAE process than have been considered so far. The research evidence presented here on the case study departments of biology, sociology and English, would tend to support the view that not all disciplines should necessarily be treated in the same way. Since natural science subjects like biology are so reliant on significant capital investment, then a concentration of resources may be inevitable. However, it seems clear that for some areas within biology and certainly for many areas within sociology and English, capital investment is of less significance. The danger, which has been central to some of the experiences of academics within this study, is that volume of research input becomes the sole determinant of judgements of research quality. Many academics felt that they were under pressure to apply for and receive research funding even where it was not necessary to carry out their research. For many areas of research in the natural sciences, research funding is critical but for other subject areas this is not always the case.

Yes, it seems apparent from the evidence here that the accumulation of material capital is now central to the functioning of university departments and academics working within them. The comments from the HEFCE official at the beginning of Chapter 7 made it clear that a 'traditional' (teaching and research) job was no longer affordable within all universities. Academic time for research as well as the cost of the research now has to be paid for by external funding. In the race to play in the main game of university research and to be successful in the RAE, therefore, the pressure is on to accumulate more and more material capital to support research work within universities.

But do all subject areas have to engage in high-cost, discovery-based research? In the House of Commons report, the question is also raised about the possibilities for expanding the definitions of research and also incorporating evaluations of research environment, management of staff, institutional strategies and innovation, which would expand the definitions for quality of research practice. Similarly, the example from the Hong Kong RAE of using the Carnegie classifications of scholarship serves to emphasize the point that scholarship (discovery, applied, integration and teaching), may be a more fruitful way of conceptualizing research without losing the idea that the production and dissemination of knowledge are ultimately linked. The two most significant areas of struggle for the biologist, sociologist and English academic in this study were the perceived undervaluing of particular areas of research and the imperative to present research as 'international'. Confusions over the definition of the latter had significant implications for inclusion and non-inclusion of staff in the 1996 RAE. It may be more fruitful to engage in debates, which seek to extend the definitions of research and it may also be important to recognize the importance of nationally focused research. On the latter point some changes have been made for the 2008 RAE in some subject areas to ensure that definitions of 'international' refer more to comparable international standards of research work (RAE 2008 criteria, www.hefce.ac.uk/rae).

The proposed changes deal only with some tweaking of the structure and process of the RAE and the opportunity was perhaps missed to engage with more fundamental questions, which recognize that the RAE has never been and never will be simply a means of identifying and rewarding excellent research. The research evidence presented here shows clearly the important role that the RAE plays in dominating the direction of activities within universities and creating competition and divisions between institutions, between departments and between individuals. The chance was perhaps missed to engage with a more radical repositioning of the exercise to encourage better constructive and collaborative support across and within institutions. The opposite appears to be the case, and the intensification of the differentiation both across and within universities seems to be increasing.

Differentiation of universities: divisions between research and teaching

The RAE has served to increase the hierarchy and differentiation between universities, divisions created within university departments, steering and directing research efforts resulting in a homogenizing of research areas towards the mainstream, short-termism and lack of innovation, and also ensuring that research has become the prime motivator and mover within university departments detracting attention, resources and energy away from non-research activities, primarily teaching, and undervaluing applied and interdisciplinary research (Brown 2000; Henkel 2000; Harley 2002; Lucas 2003; McNay 2003). The differential valuing of teaching, administration and research, although perhaps always a feature of university life, has intensified and left many feeling demoralized.

There is the very implicit danger, as research funding becomes more and more concentrated to a smaller number of institutions, that a divide is being created between research and teaching universities. The policy makers may have won the argument that a return to any Humboldtian ideals of all universities being involved in research and teaching in equal measure is impossible and cannot be resourced. But there must be another answer, other than allowing the many to suffer for the sake of the few. Surely, the arguments over the dynamic relationship between research and teaching as a fundamental bedrock to the work of academics has not yet been lost, despite government attempts to deny it (most forcefully in the 2003 Higher Education White Paper). There is also plenty of evidence to investigate this from the perspective of institutions (Fram and Lau 1996; Zamorski 2002; Robertson and Bond 2005), academics (Rowland 2000; Elton 2001; Robertson and Bond 2001, 2003) and students (Neumann 1994; Mullen 2000; Lindsay, Breen et al. 2002). There is much evidence to support it (Jenkins 2005) despite departmental cultures often working against it (Deem and Lucas forthcoming). Perhaps not all academics can be engaged in high-cost discovery-based research but there is certainly scope for a greater valuing of the diversity of research work that exists within universities and envisioning how this can be encouraged and supported such that academic environments and the experiences of academics and students can benefit from the stimulation and challenge of engaging in research.

The research presented in this study has shown the differentiation of the two case study institutions, one 'old' pre-1992 university and one 'new' post-1992 university. Despite the differential possession of symbolic and material capital within each institution, both were engaged intensively in the 'main game' of research and responding to the need to accumulate research capital appropriate for the RAE. The departments at Royal County University were moderately successful in the 2001 RAE compared with the greater success of departments at Golden County University. Where Royal County University did succeed in gaining funds from the RAE in 2001, these were likely to be extremely small compared to those received by Golden County University. The results of the 2001 RAE may effectively have served to limit a lot of the research development of the departments at Royal County University, particularly within biology, although this might not be the case for the English department. Royal County University may continue to thrive but there are certainly many UK universities that have extremely limited capacity for research development and are becoming primarily teaching institutions (as Table 3.1 shows).

What this study has served to highlight is the ways in which the dominance of research as the main game activity within universities has served to influence and often distort management and academic practices. I would argue, based on the evidence from this study, that in relation to research, management and governance within universities the corporate and/or political model is the most appropriate for describing managerial relations. Despite some evidence of collegial forms of decision making and participation at departmental level within institutions, there is very little supporting evidence for the collegial ideal in relation to research planning and management. The experiences of many academics within these institutions points more to a hard-edged corporate model of target setting and monitoring of staff, at least at the institutional level. Clearly there were attempts to manage this in a 'humane' way, as was emphasized in the English department at Golden County University. The evidence presented from this small sample of departments shows significant changes made in relation to management procedures, socio-cultural forms of organization and staff appointments and conditions of service.

There was a clear division in all departments between staff who were engaged in research and those involved in teaching activities, and a substantial perception that staff engaged in teaching and administration were being undervalued. In the larger biology departments, there was more evidence of academic activities being divided with a number of 'research only' or 'teaching only' positions. In the sociology and English departments, there was less evidence, but still significant divisions existing between staff who were perceived as 'research active' or 'research inactive'. All staff were required to be research active unless they had been placed on teaching-only contracts. The definition of being 'research active' could vary across departments, however, depending on the demands of the discipline and the expectations departments had of the RAE rating they were aiming to attain. There might be an expectation of having four publications, of having an international reputation and being invited as a keynote speaker at conferences or of having gained substantial external research funding, or all of the above. There were examples where academics, despite being 'successful' researchers were classified as 'research inactive' because they did not adequately meet the demands for their department's RAE submission. This was a label that had potentially damaging consequences for their academic identity and possibly their future career.

Despite the environment of division and competition, there was evidence that staff within departments and within faculties were collaborating more on research. And particularly, within the biology departments, there was often a clear need to collaborate across institutions in order to share expertise and equipment. Much evidence is presented here in support of earlier arguments I made for the need to envision a more collaborative engagement of university research across and within universities (Lucas 2006).

A competitive or collaborative future for university research

It can be argued that the concentration of research funding to an increasingly smaller number of institutions in the UK has gone far enough and is detrimental to the development of universities and university research work (Universities UK 2003). The point may be accepted that the funding pot is too small to fund research across all universities in the UK but it may be more constructive to search for ways to promote further collaboration across institutions to allow for involvement in research to be spread more widely. This aim was stated in the 2003 White Paper on Higher Education but it is perhaps less clear how this is to be achieved (Department for Education and Skills 2003). This perhaps may be more feasible for non-science subjects and again, therefore, raises the question of whether all subject areas need to be treated in a standard way, subject to the same research funding model. It is possible to examine the devolved systems in the United Kingdom to establish commonalities and difference at the same time as looking for new ideas to question more substantially the core assumptions not just of the process and structure of the RAE but the means by which research in UK universities are not simply evaluated and funded accordingly, but to look for ways to encourage, support and revitalize research activity across the sector.

The different emphases of research policy in both Scotland and Wales have been identified: in these smaller higher education systems there seems to be a much greater degree of change towards increased collaborative efforts across universities. The 2003 White Paper on the Future of Higher Education stated a similar concern in the English context. For example, the White Rose Consortium is given as an illustration of three northern universities, Sheffield, York and Leeds who are working to create a collaborative critical mass of 'research, teaching and enterprise facilities' (Department for Education and Skills 2003). The importance of such developments is recognized in this policy document.

Perhaps we need to re-vision and position the UK research funding system, relying not only on ideas for possible changes to the RAE but the research funding system as a whole and to respond better and be more constructive in achieving different priorities and commitments. Priorities could include possibilities for: encouraging collaboration between and within institutions; seeing research work as important to the identity and successful operation of universities and so supporting and encouraging research activity, where possible, inclusively across the sector; expanding the definition of research to better incorporate excellent applied and interdisciplinary work and the notion of excellence in research practice, strategies etc. as indicated above. Priorities for research funding need to be determined not just by pragmatics (how best to distribute scarce resources, how to evaluate quality research) important though this may be, but they must also be informed by priorities and commitments to a university system that is not hierarchical and exclusive in its outlook but provides a stimulating and exciting learning environment for students and a stimulating working environment for staff across all universities, and reaches out to the potential changes and impacts research can have in the local, national and international arena.

Universities should lead the way in promoting a collaborative, shared venture to create knowledge that can transform the world and provide a challenge to the neo-liberal competitive model of higher education currently being mapped out and by rejecting the potentially hollow 'thrill of victory' within the research 'main game' as the guiding motivation of academic life.

Bibliography

Association of Universities in the Netherlands (VSNU) (2004) *Connections*, VSNU Annual Report, Amsterdam.

Baldridge, V.J. (1971) *Power and Conflict in the University*. New York: John Wiley and Sons Inc.

Bargh, C., Bocock, J., et al. (2000) *University Leadership: The Role of the Chief Executive.* Buckingham: SRHE/Open University Press.

Barnard, C. (2004) One trick pony won't win race. *The Times Higher Education Supplement.*

Bartelse, J. (1999) *Concentrating the Minds: The Institutionalisation of the Graduate School Innovation in Dutch and German Higher Education.* Utrecht: Uitgeverij Lemma BV.

Becher, T. (1989) *Academic Tribes and Territories: Intellectual Enquiry and the Culture of the Disciplines.* Buckingham: SRHE/Open University Press.

Becher, T. and Kogan, M. (1992) *Process and Structure in Higher Education.* London: Routledge.

Becher, T. and Trowler, P. (2001) *Academic Tribes and Territories: Intellectual Inquiry and the Culture of the Disciplines.* Buckingham: SRHE/Open University Press.

Blackmore, J. and Sachs, J. (2001) Women leaders in the restructured university, in A. Brooks and A. MacKinnon, *Gender and the Restructured University: Changing Management and Culture in Higher Education*, Buckingham: SRHE/Open University Press.

Bok, D. (2003) *Universities in the Marketplace: The Commercialization of Higher Education.* Princeton: Princeton University Press.

Bourdieu, P. (1984) *Distinction: A Social Critique of the Judgement of Taste.* London: Routledge.

Bourdieu, P. (1986) The forms of capital, in J.G. Richardson (ed.), *Handbook of Theory and Research for the Sociology of Education.* New York: Greenwood Press.

Bourdieu, P. (1988) *Homo Academicus.* Cambridge: Polity Press.

Bourdieu, P. (1989) For a socio-analysis of intellectuals: on homo academicus. *Berkeley Journal of Sociology* 34: 1–29.

Bourdieu, P. (1990) *The Logic Of Practice.* Translated by R. Nice. Cambridge: Polity Press.

Bourdieu, P. (1993) *Sociology in Question.* Translated by R. Nice. London: Sage.

Bourdieu, P. (1994a) *Academic Discourse: Linguistic Misunderstanding and Professorial Power.* Cambridge: Polity Press.

Bourdieu, P. (1994b) *In Other Words: Essays Towards a Reflexive Sociology.* Translated by M. Adamson: Cambridge: Polity Press.

Bourdieu, P. (1995) Concluding remarks: for a sociogenetic understanding of intellectual works, in C. Calhoun, E. Lipuma and M. Postone (eds) *Bourdieu: Critical Perspectives.* Cambridge: Polity Press.

Bourdieu, P. (1996) *La Noblesse d'Etat: Grandes Ecoles et Esprit de Corps.* Cambridge: Polity Press.

Bourdieu, P. (1998) *Practical Reason: On the Theory of Action.* Cambridge: Polity Press.

Bourdieu, P. and Wacquant, L.J.D. (1992) *An Invitation to Reflexive Sociology.* Cambridge: Polity Press.

Boyer, E.L. (1990) *Scholarship Reconsidered: Priorities of the Professoriate.* Princeton: Carnegie Foundation for the Advancement of Teaching.

Brown, R. (2000) Teaching is the main event, not a sideshow to research. *Research Fortnight,* 12 January.

Bush, T. (1998) Collegial models, in A. Harris, N. Bennett and M. Preedy, *Organizational Effectiveness and Improvements in Education.* Buckingham: Open University Press.

Butler, L. (2003) Explaining Australia's increased share of ISI publications – the effects of a funding formula based on publication counts. *Research Policy* 32: 143–55.

Cai, Y. (2004) Confronting the global and the local – a case study of Chinese Higher Education. *Tertiary Education and Management* 10: 157–69.

Calhoun, C., LiPuma, E., et al. (1993) *Bourdieu: Critical Perspectives.* Cambridge: Polity Press.

Castells, M. (1996) *The Rise of the Network Society.* Oxford: Blackwell.

Clark, B.R. (1998) *Creating Entrepreneurial Universities: Organizational Pathways of Transformation.* Oxford: Pergamon.

Clark, B. (2004) *Sustaining Change in Universities: Continuities in Case Studies and Concepts.* Maidenhead: SRHE/Open University Press.

Clarke, J. and Newman, J. (1997) The Managerial State: Power, Politics and Ideology in the Remaking of Social Welfare. London: Sage.

Clegg, S. and J. McAuley (2005) Conceptualising middle management in higher education: a multifaceted discourse. *Journal of Higher Education Policy and Management* 27(1): 19–34.

Court, S. (1996) The Use of Time by Academic and Related Staff. *Higher Education Quarterly* 50(4): 237–260.

Cutler, T. and Waine, B. (2000) Managerialism reformed? New Labour and public sector management. *Social Policy and Administration* 34(3): 318–32.

CVCP (1985) Report of the steering committee for efficiency studies in universities (the Jarratt Report). London.

Dale, R. (2005) Globalisation, knowledge economy and comparative education. *Comparative Education,* 41(2): 117–49.

Deem, R. (2001) Globalisation, new managerialism, academic capitalism and entrepreneurialism in universities: is the local dimension still important? *Comparative Education* 37(1): 7–20.

Deem, R. (2004) The knowledge worker, the manager-academic and the contemporary UK university: new and old forms of public management. *Financial Accountability and Management* 20(2): 107–28.

Deem, R., Fulton, O., et al. (2001) New managerialism and the management of UK universities: Full Report. ESRC No. R000 237661.

Deem, R. and Lucas, L. (forthcoming) Research and teaching cultures in two contrasting UK policy locations: academic life in education departments in five English and Scottish universities. *Higher Education.*

Deer, C. (2003) Bourdieu on higher education: the meaning of the growing integration of educational systems and self-reflective practice. *British Journal of Sociology of Education* 24(2): 195–207.

Department for Education and Skills (1995) The Development of Higher Education into the 1990s, Green Paper, May.

Department for Education and Skills (2003) *The Future of Higher Education*: London.

Dreyfus, H. and Rabinow, P. (1993) Can there be science of existential structure and social meaning?, in C. Calhoun, E. Lipuma and M. Postone (eds), *Bourdieu: Critical Perspectives.* Cambridge: Polity Press.

Elton, L. (2000) The UK Research Assessment Exercise: unintended consequences. *Higher Education Quarterly* 54(3): 274–83.

Elton, L. (2001) Research and teaching: conditions for a positive link. *Teaching in Higher Education* 6(1): 43–56.

Evans, C. (1993) *English People: the experience of teaching and learning English in British universities.* Buckingham: Open University Press.

Fazacherley, A. (2004) Russell Group rift over anti-RAE Stance. *The Times Higher Education Supplement* (online), 29 October.

Fisher, M. and Marsh, P. (2003) Social work research and the 2001 Research Assessment Exercise: an initial overview. *Social Work Education* 22(1): 71–80.

Fowler, B. (1996) An Introduction to Pierre Bourdieu's Understanding. *Theory, Culture and Society* 13(2): 1–16.

Fram, E.H. and Lau, G. (1996) Research universities versus teaching universities – public perceptions and preferences. *Quality Assurance in Education* 4(3): 27–33.

French, N., Massy, W.F., et al. (2001) Research assessment in Hong Kong. *Higher Education* 42(1): 35–57.

Fuller, S. (2000) *The Governance of Science.* Buckingham: Open University Press.

Gambrill, E. (2002) 'I am Not a Rubber Stamp': my experience as a non-UK RAE Adviser. *Journal of Social Work* 2(2).

Gibbons, M., Limoges, C., et al. (1994) *The New Production of Knowledge: the dynamics of science and research in contemporary societies.* London: Sage.

Gibbs, G., Lucas, L. and Simonite, V. (1996) Class size and student performance: 1984–94. *Studies in Higher Education* 21(3).

Gouldner, A. (1971) *The Coming Crisis of Western Sociology.* London: Heinemann.

Gouldner, A. (1973) *For Sociology: Renewal and Critique in Sociology Today.* London: Allen Lane.

Grenfell, M. and James, D. (1998) *Bourdieu and Education: Acts of Practical Theory.* London: Falmer Press.

Grenfell, M. and James, D. (2003) Change *in* the field – chang*ing* the field: Bourdieu and the methodological practice of educational research. *British Journal of Sociology of Education* 25(4): 508–23.

Group, A. (2005) Researching Quality Framework: assessing the quality and impact of research in Australia. Canberra.

Hallett, T. (2003) Symbolic Power and Organizational Culture, *Sociological Theory,* 21(2): 128–49.

Halsey, A.H. (1995) *Decline of Donnish Dominion: the British Academic Professions in the Twentieth Century.* Oxford: Oxford University Press.

Hare, P.G. (2003) The United Kingdom's Research Assessment Exercise: impact on institutions, departments, individuals. *Higher Education Management and Policy* 15(2): 43–61.

Hargreaves, A. (1981) Contrastive rhetoric and extremist talk: teachers, hegemony and the educationist context, in L. Barton, and S. Walker (eds) *Schools, Teachers and Teaching*. Lewes: Falmer.

Harley, S. (2002) The impact of research selectivity on academic work and identity in UK universities. *Studies in Higher Education* 27(2): 187–205.

Harley, S. and Lee, F.S. (1997) Research selectivity, managerialism, and the academic labour process: the future of nonmainstream economics in UK universities. *Human Relations*, 50(11): 1427–60.

Harley, S. and Lowe, P. (1998) *Academics Divided: The Research Assessment Exercise and the Academic Labour Process*. Leicester: Leicester Business School.

Harman, G. (2005) Australian social scientists and transition to a more commercial environment. *Higher Education Research and Development* 24(1): 79–94.

Harvie, D. (2000) Alienation, class and enclosure in UK universities. *Capital and Class* 71 (Summer): 103–32.

Hearn, J. (2001) Academia, management and men: making the connections, exploring the implications, in A. Brooks and A. MacKinnon, *Gender and the Restructured University: Changing Management and Culture in Higher Education*. Buckingham: SRHE/Open University Press.

HEFCE (2004) Quality profile will provide fuller and fairer assessment of research. HEFCE press release, 11 February.

Henkel, M. (2000) *Academic Identities and Policy Change in Higher Education*. London: Jessica Kingsley.

House of Commons Science and Technology Committee (2004) Research Assessment Exercise: a re-assessment: eleventh report of session 2003–04. London: The Stationery Office Ltd.

Jenkins, A. (1995) The Research Assessment Exercise, funding and teaching quality. *Quality Assurance in Education*, 3(2): 4–12.

Jenkins, A. (2005) *Guide to the Research Evidence on Teaching–Research Relations*. York: The Higher Education Academy.

Johnes, J. and Taylor, J. (1990) *Performance Indicators in Higher Education*. Buckingham: SRHE/Open University Press.

Kenway, J. and McLeod, J. (2004) Bourdieu's reflexive sociology and 'spaces of points of view': whose reflexivity, which perspective? *British Journal of Sociology of Education* 25(4): 525–44.

Kerr, C. (1963) *The Uses of the University*. Cambridge: Harvard University Press.

King, D.A. (2004) The scientific impact of nations. *Nature* 430 (15 July): 311–6.

King, R. (2004) *The University in the Global Age*. Basingstoke: Palgrave Macmillan.

Knight, P.T. and Trowler, P.R. (2001) *Departmental Leadership in Higher Education*. Buckingham: SRHE/Open University Press.

Krull, W. (2005) Exporting the Humboldtian University. *Minerva* 43: 99–102.

Lambert, R. (2003) *Lambert Review of Business University Collaboration*. London: Department of Trade and Industry.

Lewis, J. (2000) Funding Social Science in Academia. *Social Policy and Administration* 34(4): 365–76.

Lindsay, R., Breen, R., et al. (2002) Academic research and teaching quality: the views of undergraduate and postgraduate students. *Studies in Higher Education* 27(3): 309–28.

Liu, N.C. and Cheng, Y. (2005) Academic ranking of world universities – methodologies and problems. *Higher Education in Europe*, 30(2).

Lucas, L. (2003) Reclaiming academic research work from regulation and relegation, in M. Walker and J. Nixon, *Reclaiming Universities From A Runaway World*. Buckingham: SRHE/Open University Press.

Lucas, L. (2006) 'To them that have shall be given but ...': the future of funding and evaluating university research in UK universities, in I. McNay, *Beyond Mass Higher Education: Building on Experience*. Maidenhead: SRHE/Open University Press, 120–33.

MacGregor, S. (2003) 'We did not simply mimic received opinion.' *Journal of Social Work* 3(1).

McKay, S. (2003) Quantifying quality: can quantitative data ('Metrics') explain the 2001 RAE ratings for Social Policy and Administration? *Social Policy and Administration* 37(5): 444–67.

McLeod, D. (2004) This could be the last time. *Guardian Unlimited* (online), 9 November.

McNay, I. (1995) From the collegial academy to corporate enterprise: the changing cultures of universities, in T. Schuller (ed.) *The Changing University?* Buckingham: SRHE/Open University Press.

McNay, I. (1997) The Impact of the 1992 Research Assessment Exercise on Individual and Institutional Behaviour in English Higher Education. Chelmsford: Anglia Polytechnic University.

McNay, I. (2003) Assessing the assessment: an analysis of the UK Research Assessment Exercise, 2001, and its outcomes, with special reference to research in education. *Science and Public Policy* 30(1): 1–8.

Marginson, S. (1999) After globalization: emerging politics of education, *Journal of Education Policy*, 14(1): 19–31.

Marginson, S. (2005) 'There Must be Some Way Out of Here': a paper about the Yin and Yang of university positioning in the Nelson system. Key address to the Tertiary Management Conference, Perth, 27–9 September.

Marginson, S. and Considine, M. (2000) *The Enterprise University: Power, Governance and Reinvention in Australia*. Cambridge: Cambridge University Press.

Merton, R.K. (1970) Social Conflict over Styles of Sociological Work, in L. Reynolds and J. Reynolds (eds), *The Sociology of Sociology*. New York: David McKay Company Inc.

Merton, R.K. (1996) *On Social Structure and Science*. Chicago: University of Chicago Press.

Middlehurst, R. (1993) *Leading Academics*. Buckingham: SRHE/Open University Press.

Middlehurst, R. (2004) Changing internal governance: a discussion of leadership roles and management structures in UK Universities. *Higher Education Quarterly* 58(4): 258–79.

Miller, H. (1995) *The Management of Change in Universities*. Buckingham: SRHE/Open University Press.

Mok, K. (2003) Globalisation and Higher Education Restructuring in Hong Kong, Taiwan and Mainland China. *Higher Education Research and Development* 22(2).

Mok, J.K. and Lee, M.H. (2003) Globalization or Glocalization? Higher Education Reforms in Singapore. *Asia Pacific Journal of Education* 23(1): 15–42.

Moore, P. (1996) University Financing 1979–1986, in M. Shattock, *The Creation of a University System*. Oxford: Blackwell.

Morley, L. (2003) *Quality and Power in Higher Education*. Buckingham: SRHE/Open University Press.

Mouzelis, N. (2000) The Subjectivist-Objectivist Divide: against transcendence. *Sociology* 34(4): 741–62.

Mullen, C.A. (2000) Linking Research and Teaching: a study of graduate student engagement. *Teaching in Higher Education* 5(1): 5–22.

Naidoo, R. (2004) Repositioning Higher Education as a Global Commodity: opportunities and challenges for future sociology of education work. *British Journal of Sociology of Education* 24(2): 249–59.

Neumann, R. (1994) The Teaching-Research Nexus: applying a framework to university students' learning experiences. *European Journal of Education* 29(3): 323.

Newby, H. (2001) *The Research Assessment Exercise 2001.* RAE 2001: Review, Reflection ... Reformulation. University of Greenwich.

Newman, J.H. (1931) *Select Discourses from The Idea of a University.* Cambridge, Cambridge University Press.

Olssen, M. (2004) Neoliberalism, globalisation, democracy: challenges for education. *Globalisation, Societies and Education* 2(2): 231–75.

Parker, M. and Jary, D. (1994) *Academic Subjectivity and the New Managerialism.* Labour Process Conference, University of Aston, 23–5 March.

Prichard, C. (2000) *Making Managers in Universities and Colleges.* Buckingham: SRHE/Open University Press.

Ramsden, P. (1999) *Learning to Teach in Higher Education,* London: Routledge.

Reay, D. (2004) Cultural Capitalists and Academic Habitus: classed and gendered labour in UK higher education. *Women's Studies International Forum* 27: 31–9.

Robbins, D. (1993) The Practical Importance of Bourdieu's Analyses of Higher Education. *Studies in Higher Education* 18(2): 151–63.

Roberts, G. (2003) *Review of Research Assessment,* Bristol, HEFCE, Bristol.

Robertson, J. and Bond, C.H. (2001) Experiences of the relation between teaching and research: what do academics value? *Higher Education Research and Development* 20(1): 5–20.

Robertson, J. and Bond, C. (2003) *The Research/Teaching Relation: Variation in Communities of Enquiry.* Unpublished paper presented to the Society for Research in Higher Education Annual Conference, 'Research, Scholarship and Teaching: changing relationships', 16–18 December, Royal Holloway College, University of London.

Robertson, J. and Bond, C.H. (2005) The research-teaching relation – a view from the edge. *Higher Education* 50(3): 509.

Rowland, S. (2000) *Teaching and Research: A Marriage on the Rocks?* Paper presented at the European Conference on Educational Research, Edinburgh, 20–23 September, http://www.leeds.ac.uk/educol/documents/00001622.htm.

Santos, B. de Sousa (1999) A multicultural conception of human rights, in M. Featherstone and S. Lash, *Spaces of Culture.* London: Sage.

Sayer, A. (1990) *Method in Social Science.* London: Routledge.

Schimank, U. and Winnes, M. (2000) Beyond Humboldt: the relationship between teaching and research in European university systems. *Science and Public Policy* 27(6): 397–408.

Schirato, T. and Webb, J. (2003) Bourdieu's concept of reflexivity as metaliteracy. *Cultural Studies* 17(3/4): 539–52.

Scott, P. (1995) *The Meanings of Mass Higher Education.* Buckingham: SRHE/Open University Press.

Sharp, S. (2004) The Research Assessment Exercises 1992–2001: patterns across time and subjects. *Studies in Higher Education* 29(2).

Sharp, S. (2005) Ratings in the Research Assessment Exercise 2001 – the patterns of university status and panel membership. *Higher Education Quarterly*, 59(2): 153–71.

Shattock, M. (1994) *The UGC and the Management of British Universities*. Buckingham: SRHE/Open University Press.

Sidaway, J.D. (1997) The production of British geography. *Trans Inst British Geography* 22: 488–504.

Slaughter, S. and Leslie, L. (1997) *Academic Capitalism: Politics, Policies and the Entrepreneurial University*. Baltimore: The John Hopkins University Press.

Sweetman, P. (2003) Twenty-first century dis-ease? Habitual reflexivity or the reflexive habitus, *Sociological Review*, 51(4): 528–49.

Tapper, T. and Palfreyman, D. (1998) Continuity and change in the collegial Tradition. *Higher Education Quarterly* 52(2): 142–61.

Thomson, A. (2004) Scrap the RAE, says report. *Times Higher Education Supplement* (online), 10 September.

Tight, M. (2000) Do league tables contribute to the development of a quality culture? Football and Higher Education Compared. *Higher Education Quarterly*, 54(1): 22–42.

Tight, M. (2003) *Researching Higher Education*. Maidenhead: SRHE/Open University Press.

Treasury, H. (2004) *Science and Innovation Investment Framework*. London.

Trowler, P. (1998) *Academics Responding to Change: Higher Education Frameworks and Academic Cultures*. Buckingham: SRHE/Open University Press.

Universities UK (2003) *Funding Research Diversity*. London.

University Grants Committee (2004) Facts and Figures, UGC, Hong Kong.

Urry, J. (1998) Contemporary Transformations of Space and Time, in P. Scott, *The Globalization of Higher Education*. Buckingham: Open University Press.

Vidovich, L. (2004) Global-national-local dynamics in policy processes: a case of 'quality' policy in higher education. *British Journal of Sociology of Education* 25(3).

Wacquant, L. (1993) Bourdieu in America: notes on the transatlantic importation of social theory, in C. Calhoun, E. Lipuma and M. Postone (eds), *Bourdieu: Critical Perspectives*. Cambridge: Polity Press.

Walford, G. (1987) *Restructuring Universities: Politics and Power in the Management of Change*. London: Croom Helm.

Westerheijden, D.F. (1997) A Solid base for decisions: use of the VSNU research evaluations in Dutch universities. *Higher Education* 33: 397–413.

Willmott, H. (2003) Commercialising Higher Education in the UK: the state, industry and peer review. *Studies in Higher Education* 28(2): 129–41.

Winsborough, H.W. (1992) Sociology departments and their research centres: an essential tension? in T. Halliday and M. Janowitz, *Sociology and Its Publics: The Forms and Fates of Disciplinary Organisation*. Chicago: University of Chicago Press.

Ylijoki, O. (2003) Entangled in academic capitalism? A case-study on changing ideals and practices of university research. *Higher Education* 45: 307–35.

Zamorski, B. (2002) Research-led teaching and learning in higher education: a case study. *Teaching in Higher Education* 77(4): 411–27.

Zipin, L. (1999) Simplistic fictions in Australian higher education policy debates: a Bourdieuian analysis of complex power struggles. *Discourse: Studies in the Cultural Politics of Education*, 20(1): 21–39.

Index

academic capital, 2, 61, 71, 106, 137, 164
    accumulation of, 150, 153, 154, 160,
        161,
    management of, 62
academic capitalism, 9, 10, 13, 15, 17,
    106
academic career, 149, 156, 164
    functioning of, 59
    reproduction of, 154
academic habitus, 63, 72, 134, 135, 142,
    163
academic identity, 29, 46, 52, 72, 132,
    133, 148, 170
academic labour, 62
academic life, 1, 2, 3, 72, 85, 142, 154,
    160, 171
academic power, 61, 62
academic staff, 4, 39, 42, 60, 62, 72, 85,
    93, 107, 157
academic values, 15, 17
anomie, 45
applied research, 44, 49, 50, 51, 103,
    106, 166
Australia, 3, 5, 6, 9, 13, 14, 26, 29, 47, 53,
    63, 165
    higher education system, 50
    higher education funding structures,
        10
    research quality, 51
    research quality framework (RQF),
        51, 52

Bargh, C. 17, 18, 19, 20, 73
Becher, T., 17, 24, 68, 69, 102, 103, 115,
    119, 162

Bernstein, B., 69
Blackmore, J., 19
block grant funding, 32, 33, 47
Bok, D., 13
Bond, C.H., 142, 169
Bourdieu, P., 2, 3, 4, 6, 16, 24, 55–65,
    66–71, 75, 76, 96, 103, 105, 107,
    117, 134, 138, 151, 155, 162, 164
    analysis of power, 24
    reflexive sociology, 66
    theoretical framework of thinking
        tools, 54
Bourke, P., 127
Bush, T., 18, 82, 83, 88
Butler, L. 51

Cai, Y. 10
Calhoun, C., 56, 68
capitalism, 15
Castells, M., 8
centrifugal, 120
charities, 33, 104, 106, 118, 129, 141
Cheng, Y., 8
citation, 11, 37, 166, 167
Clark, B., 13,15,20,74
Clarke, C., 7
Clarke, J., 3, 7
class sizes, 2
Clegg, S., 19, 21, 24
collaboration, 43, 50, 108, 130, 153, 170,
    171
collegial, 18, 24, 28, 76, 89, 90, 92, 94,
    113, 114, 169
    collegial ideal, 17, 19, 20, 74
    collegial model, 18, 19, 21, 22, 84

collegial practices and organisation,
    17, 20, 24, 28
collegial spirit, 83
community of scholars, 25
confidentiality, 5, 75
Considine, M., 2, 13, 14, 19, 27
contract researcher, 16
contrastive rhetoric, 90
Court, S., 44
critical mass, 76, 84, 100, 107, 108, 171
critical social science, 4
cultural capital, 16, 59
Cutler, T., 32

Dale, R., 11
Deem, R., 10, 11, 15, 19, 20, 21, 22, 54,
    73, 74, 169
Deer, C., 54, 68
deterritorialization, 8
DevR, 33, 34
disciplinary specialism, 5
dispositions, 53, 58, 59, 61, 69, 71, 96,
    134, 135, 148, 157, 158, 163 *see also*
    habitus
Dreyfus, H., 69

elite universities, 35
Elton, L., 3, 39, 169
enterprise university, 13
ethics, 5
ethnographic, 5, 74
Evans, C., 126

Fazacherley, A., 35
field,
    academic field, 56, 60, 62, 63, 64, 65,
        66, 67, 68, 70
    biology field, 68, 102
    english field, 130
    higher education field, 72, 94, 166
    intellectual field, 53, 66, 68
    scientific field, 56, 65, 66, 67
    social field, 58, 59, 60, 63, 69, 109, 118
    sociology field, 109, 118
    university field, 59, 60, 62, 63, 68
fieldwork in philosophy, 55
Fisher, M., 36, 44, 109
formula funding, 33, 34, 130
Fowler, B., 54, 55, 69
Fram, E.H., 169
French, N., 25, 49, 53, 54, 59, 62
Fuller, S., 25, 26

G8 Nations, 11, 15, 40
Gambrill, E., 36
game playing, 2
Gross Domestic Product (GDP), 13
Gibbons, M., 27, 152
Gibbs, G., 2
global knowledge economy, 166
globalisation, 3, 6, 7, 8, 9, 11, 13, 38, 52
    globalised localism, 8,9
    localised globalism, 8
god professordom, 19
golden age, 1, 16
Gouldner, A., 65, 66
governance (university), 17, 18, 20, 24,
    169
    confederal model, 18
graduates, 9, 154
Grenfell, M., 54, 55, 56, 68, 94, 134

Hallett, T., 19, 71, 93, 96
Halsey, A.H., 44, 147, 154
hard knowledge, 102, 103
Hare, P.G., 40
Harley, S., 39, 40, 43, 45, 46, 85, 93, 113,
    132, 168
Harman, G., 14, 15
Harvie, D., 15, 16, 45, 46
Hearn, J., 19
Higher Education Funding Council for
    England (HEFCE), 5, 33, 36, 37, 38,
    39, 40, 73, 80, 133, 167
Higher Education Funding Council for
    Wales (HEFCW), 33
Henkel, M., 46, 168
Higher Education Research and
    Organisation (HERO), 97, 105, 106,
    109, 116, 118, 121, 128, 129
hogescholen, 47
homo academicus, 54, 59, 67, 68
Hong Kong, 3, 5, 6, 10, 29, 40, 47, 50,
    165,
    Higher Education Review (2002), 50
    Higher Education System, 48
    Hong Kong RAE, 48, 49, 52, 167
House of Commons Science and
    Technology Committee, 36, 37, 38,
    40, 166, 167
Humboldt, 25, 26
hybridization, 10

ideology, 7, 8, 9, 13, 21, 46
illusio, 63, 72

impact factors, 11, 51
intellectual commons, 16
interdisciplinary, 36, 37, 43, 53, 125, 153, 166, 168, 171
international comparison, 3
international competitiveness, 6, 11, 50
international excellence, 36, 116, 127
international reputation, 87, 98, 99, 100, 128, 144, 146, 152, 159
internationalization, 8
Institute for Scientific Information (ISI), 51

James, D., 54, 55, 56, 68, 94, 134
Jarratt Report, 32
Jenkins, A., 44, 169
Johnes, J., 12, 32

Kenway, J., 54, 66, 67
Kerr, C., 25, 27
King, D.A., 11, 12, 14, 40
King, R., 8, 11, 26
knowledge economy, 11, 52
knowledge creating societies, 9
knowledge flows, 8, 9
Koninklijke Nederlandse Akademie van Wetenschappen (KNAW), 48
Krull, W., 25, 26

Lambert Review, 20, 74
Lau, G., 169
leadership, 20, 41, 43, 75, 83, 84, 92, 98, 100, 111
league tables, 7, 27, 29, 32, 166
Leavisite, 126
Lee, F.S., 11, 14, 39, 43, 46, 132
Lehrfreiheit, 25
Leslie, L., 9, 10, 11, 13, 15, 27, 106
Lewis, J., 43, 105
liberal, 13, 26, 64
libido, 58, 63
Lindsay, R., 169
London School of Economics, 71
Lowe, P., 45, 85, 93, 113
Lucas, L., 40, 168, 169, 170
Lui, N.C., 8

MacGregor, S., 36
management, 3, 20, 48, 50, 114, 121, 125
  bureaucratic management, 21
  central management (teams), 87, 92
  hard management, 21

humane management, 91, 122
industrial management, 21
manager–academic, 73
management-administration, 73
management of RAE process, 42, 52
management of staff, 167
management station, 24
managerial surveillance, 85, 93, 113
performance management, 32
research management, 36, 40, 41, 42, 47, 72, 74, 84, 85, 87, 94, 166
soft management, 81
Marginson, S., 2, 8, 13, 14, 19, 27, 51, 166
market-driven, 9
marketization, 3, 6, 7, 10, 13, 14, 17, 21, 32, 38
Marsh, P., 36, 44, 109
Marxist, 15, 46, 54
mass higher education, 2, 27
McAuley, J., 19, 21, 24
McKay, S., 38
McLeod, D., 35, 54, 66, 67
McNay, I., 17, 22, 36, 40, 41, 42, 43, 44, 45, 75, 78, 83, 94, 109, 168
mentoring, 92, 93, 123, 125, 131
metrics, 38, 166
Middlehurst, R., 20, 74
Miller, H., 20
mode 2 knowledge production, 27
Mok, K.H., 10, 11, 13, 14
monitoring, 90, 92, 169
  of academic work, 85, 93
  of research activities, 41, 84, 86, 89, 92, 93, 101, 102, 123, 124
  of universities, 32
Moore, P., 31
Morley, L., 19, 21
motivation, 66, 69, 70, 171
Mouzelis, N., 64, 70, 71, 72, 96
Mullen, C.A., 169
multiversity, 27

Naidoo, R., 54, 68, 69, 71, 72
Napoleon, 25
national excellence, 34
Nederlandse Organisatie voor Wetenschappelijk Onderzoek (NOW), 48
negotiated order, 19, 71, 93, 96
neo-liberal, 3, 7, 8, 9, 11, 13, 40, 46, 171
Netherlands, 3, 5, 6, 29, 47, 48, 52, 165

higher education system, 47
performance agreements, 48
networked society, 8
New Labour, 31, 32
new managerialism, 7, 19, 21, 28
Newby, H., 39
Newman, J.H., 3, 25, 26
non-formula funding, 34
non-mainstream (research), 43

Olssen, M., 9
Orwell, G., 1, 2
Oxford model, 26

Palfreyman, D., 18
parity of esteem, 50
pedagogical research, 36
peer review, 32, 33, 37, 39, 48, 166
performance indicators, 20, 22, 32, 41,
    76
perspectivally enriched realism, 55, 69
phenomenology, 56
political model, 22, 75, 169
politics of authorship, 142
postmodernist, 54
practical sense, 56, 57, 63, 134, 135, 147,
    148
Prichard, C., 20, 21, 24
private sector, 9, 32
privatisation, 9, 10
publications,
    high ranking publications, 16, 113,
        116
    importance of publications, 138
    in refereed journals, 150
    international publications, 116
    multi-authored publications, 141
    publications database, 41
    publications game, 105
pump priming, 86, 100

Quality Research Funding (QR), 30, 32,
    33, 81, 83, 86, 156

Research and Development (R&D), 13,
    14, 15
Rabinow, P., 69
RAE,
    criteria, 36, 96, 97, 115, 117, 127, 141,
        145, 150
    department strategies, 95, 129, 131,
        156

grade inflation, 40
grading, 40, 97, 98
    impact on academics, 45
    impact on disciplines, 42, 43
    impact on institutions, 29, 38, 39
    impact on teaching, 44, 45
    individual strategies, 156
    panel, 37, 96, 100, 103, 132
    questionnaire, 92
    strategy, 2, 76, 77, 110, 159
    staff return, 78, 98, 103, 125, 143, 144,
    submission, 76, 77, 85, 95, 97, 98, 99,
        100, 103, 104, 110, 111, 115, 128,
        138, 170
RAE-value, 45
Ramsden, P., 51
rational action theory, 56
realism, 54, 55
Reay, D., 16, 83
reflexivity, 4, 53, 66, 67
research active staff (RAS), 33, 40, 80,
    81, 83, 86, 91, 97, 113, 125
research and teaching (links between),
    25, 26, 96, 157, 159, 168, 170
research capital, 2, 16, 71, 72, 80, 137,
    143, 145, 146, 148, 151, 152, 155,
    157, 161
    accumulation of, 117, 134, 137, 140,
        141, 142, 149, 153, 158, 159, 162,
        164, 169
    forms of, 96, 100, 114, 133, 134, 143,
        155, 156
    importance of, 156
research capitalist, 16
research centre, 47, 53, 114, 119, 120,
    123, 125, 157, 159
research culture, 15, 125, 131, 163
research evaluation, 3, 38, 47
research funding, 6, 14, 38, 46, 47, 78,
    117, 118, 128, 129, 130, 149, 152,
    153, 155, 164, 168, 170, 171
    applying for, 114, 143, 145
    Australia, 50, 51
    commercial, 13, 14, 27
    Hong Kong, 52
    internal distribution, 82, 83, 86, 101,
        106, 107
    Netherlands, 48
    significance of, 30, 132, 167
research game, 2, 29, 39, 135, 147, 162
research group, 47, 107, 108, 111, 112,
    119, 120, 129, 137, 141, 143

research impact, 51
research input, 167
research intensity, 29, 84
research management, 3, 74, 84, 169
research mission, 4, 39, 50
research output, 45, 51, 107, 116, 118, 124, 128
research power, 2, 16, 27, 32, 61
research proposals, 137
research quality, 2, 51, 167
research quantum, 51 *see also* Australia
Research Schools, 47
research strategy, 36, 78, 81, 84, 86, 89, 110, 156
research worker, 16, 76
resource dependency theory, 9
Robbins, D., 68
Roberts Report, 36, 37, 51
Robertson, J., 148, 149, 153, 154, 157, 169
Rowland, S., 169

Sachs, J., 19
Santos, B. de Sousa, 8
Sartrean phenomenology, 56
Sayer,, A., 54
Shattock, M., 18, 32
Schimank, U., 26, 27
Schirato, T., 66
scholarship, 44, 49, 50, 110, 111, 114, 115, 117, 119, 123, 146, 151, 161, 167
    UK RAE definition, 49
science budget, 13
scientific authority, 66
scientific field, 56, 65, 66, 67
scientific power, 61, 107
scientific prestige, 61
Scott,, P., 32, 147
self socio-analysis, 66
semi-structured interviews, 4
Shanghai Jaio Tong University, 7, 27, 166
Sharp, S., 37, 97, 130
Scottish Higher Education Funding Council (SHEFC), 33
Sidaway, J.D., 1, 43
Slaughter, S., 9, 10, 11, 13, 15, 27, 106
social capital, 59, 61, 84, 120, 142, 149, 152, 153
    accumulation of, 108, 156
    forms of, 129

importance of, 132
social science, 40, 43, 55, 65, 89, 109, 115, 118, 167
sociology of higher education, 54
soft knowledge, 102, 103, 104
soft money, 137
Standard Evaluation Protocol, 48
state of hostilities, 24
strategy, 64, 67, 160
    rational strategying, 70, 71, 96
    syntagmatic strategying, 71
    (un)conscious strategying, 72, 94, 96
Strategy for Higher Education into the 1990s, 31
structural functionalist, 54
structuralism, 56
structure/agency, 55, 56
supranational, 11
Sweetman, P., 70, 72
symbolic capital, 2, 24, 27, 56, 59, 60, 62, 66, 69, 70, 76, 78, 84, 133, 138, 153, 155, 163
    accumulation of, 59, 62, 72, 105, 138, 152
    forms of, 55, 58, 60, 66

Tapper, T., 18
Taylor, J., 12, 32, 148, 149, 155, 157
Taylorism, 21
teaching mission, 4
technological innovation, 9
Thatcher, M., 31
theory of practice, 56, 63
Thomson, A., 35
Tight, M., 2, 20, 29, 53
time economy, 162
Times Higher Education Supplement (THES), 35
transdisciplinary, 27
transfer market (of researchers), 42
transnational, 8
Trowler, P., 20, 68, 69, 164

Universities Funding Council (UFC), 32, 33
Universities Grants Committee (UGC), 31, 32, 33, 49, 50
university organisation, 17, 18, 22, 23, 24
university status, 31, 48, 72
university system, 9, 21, 23, 26, 32, 54, 59, 62, 171

Unit of Assessment (UOA), 5, 33, 34, 38,
    99, 121, 128
Urry, J., 8

vocational, 64
VSNU, 47, 48

Waine, B., 32
Walford, G., 23
wealth creation, 7, 9
Webb, J., 66
Westerheidjen, D.F., 48

White Paper, 7, 168, 170, 171
White Rose Consortium, 171
Willmott, H., 15, 29
Winnes, M., 26, 27
Winsborough, H.W., 120
world class universities, 7, 27, 28, 29, 52,
    166

Ylijoki, O., 15

Zamorski, B., 169
Zipin, L., 64, 68

HIGHER EDUCATION PEDAGOGIES

Melanie Walker

- What does higher education learning and teaching enable students to do and to become?
- Which human capabilities are valued in higher education, and how do we identify them?
- How might the human capability approach lead to improved student learning, as well as to accomplished and ethical university teaching?

This book sets out to generate new ways of reflecting ethically about the purposes and values of contemporary higher education in relation to agency, learning, public values and democratic life, and the pedagogies which support these. It offers an alternative to human capital theory and emphasises the intrinsic as well as the economic value of higher learning. Based upon the human capability approach, developed by economist Amartya Sen and philosopher Martha Nussbaum, the book shows the importance of justice as a value in higher education. It places freedom, human flourishing, and students' educational development at its centre. Furthermore, it takes up the value Sen attributes to education in the capability approach, and demonstrates its relevance for higher education.

Higher Education Pedagogies offers illustrative narratives of capability, learning and pedagogy, drawing on student and lecturer voices to demonstrate how this multi-dimensional approach can be developed and applied in higher education. It suggests an ethical approach to higher education practice, and to teaching and learning policy development and evaluation. As such, the book is essential reading for students and scholars of higher education, as well as university lecturers, managers and policy-makers concerned with teaching and learning.

Contents: Acknowledgements - **Part one: Context** - The context of higher education - **Part two: The capability approach and higher education** - Core ideas from the capability approach - What are we distributing? - **Part three: Pedagogies and capabilities** - Learning and capabilities - Widening participation capabilities - Selecting capabilities - **Part four: Change in higher education** - Pedagogy, capabilities and a criterion of justice - Bibliography - Index.

176pp   0 335 21321 9 Paperback   0 335 21322 7 Hardback

THE ENQUIRING UNIVERSITY

Compliance and Contestation in Higher Education

Stephen Rowland

- What is the purpose of higher education?
- How do teaching and research relate?
- Are the intellectual purposes of higher education in need of restoration?

The Enquiring University explores the ways in which teaching, research and learning are related to each other and to a wider social context, one in which ideas about the nature of the university and knowledge are changing. The book is readily accessible, drawing upon insights that emerge from a wide range of disciplines.

Throughout the book, Stephen Rowland develops a conception of enquiry which can play a central role in how we are to understand academic work. It is a concept which values the academic tradition of a love for the subject, while at the same time encouraging exploration across disciplinary and other cultural boundaries. While such a notion of enquiry may seem to be under threat from many of the recent developments in higher education, this book indicates ways in which the appropriate spaces can be opened up to enhance a spirit of enquiry amongst academic staff and their students.

The Enquiring University is key reading for university lecturers, those studying for higher degrees in higher education and policy makers.

Contents: Acknowledgements - Have we lost the plot or changed the story? - Compliance and contestation - Teaching for democracy - The skills agenda - Fragmentation in academic life - Academic development - Interdisciplinarity - Enquiry and the reintegration of teaching and research - Conclusions - References - Index.

152pp   0 335 21602 1 Paperback   0 335 21603 X Hardback

RESHAPING THE UNIVERSITY

New Relationships between Research, Scholarship and Teaching

Ronald Barnett

What is the emerging shape of the University? Are there spaces for present activities to be practised anew or even for new activities? If these questions have force, they show that the metaphors of shapes and spaces can be helpful in understanding the contemporary university.

Research, teaching and scholarship remain the dominant activities in universities and so it is their relationships that form the main concerns of this volume. Are these activities pulling apart from each other? Or might these activities be brought more together in illuminating ways? Is there space to redesign these activities so that they shed light on each other? Is there room for yet other purposes?

In this volume, a distinguished set of scholars engage with these pertinent but challenging issues. Ideas are offered, and evidence is marshalled, of practices that suggest a re-shaping of the University may be possible.

Reshaping the University appeals to those who are interested in the future of universities, including students, researchers, managers and policy makers. It also addresses global issues and it will, therefore, interest the higher education community worldwide.

Contributors: Ronald Barnett, David Dill, Carol Bond, Lewis Elton, Mick Healey, Mark Hughes, Rajani Naidoo, Mark Olssen, Bruce Macfarlane, Kathleen Nolan, Jan Parker, Michael Peters, Alison Phipps, Jane Robertson, Peter Scott, Stephen Rowland.

Contents: Introduction - **Part 1: Myths and distortions** - Overview - The mythology of research and teaching relationships in universities - Universities in the marketplace: The distortion of the teaching and research nexus - 'Useful knowledge': Redefining research and teaching in the learning economy - **Part 2: Reconceiving of spaces** - Overview - Divergence or convergence? The links between teaching and research in mass higher education - Linking research and teaching: Exploring disciplinary spaces and the role of inquiry-based learning - Being in the university - Intellectual love and the link between teaching and research - **Part 3: Possibilities for spaces** - Overview - Scholarship and the research and teaching nexus - Publish or cherish? - Performing a dissertation in/between research spaces - Making academics: Work in progress - A mis-en-scene for the theatrical university - Placing service in academic life - The degradation of the academic ethic: Teaching, research and the renewal of professional self-regulation - Concluding note - Bibliography - Contributors - Index.

240pp   0 335 21701 X Paperback   0 335 21702 8 Hardback